EVERYTHING

YOU NEED TO KNOW ABOUT...

Toddlers

LINDA SONNA, Ph.D.

David & Charles

A DAVID & CHARLES BOOK
David & Charles is a subsidiary of F+W (UK) Ltd.,
an F+W Publications Inc. company

First published in the UK in 2004
First published in the USA as The Everything® Toddler Book,
by Adams Media Corporation in 2002

Project Manager Ian Kearey
Cover Design Ali Myer

A catalogue record for this book is available from the British Library.

ISBN 0 7153 2059 9

Printed in Great Britain by CPI Bath
for David & Charles
Brunel House   Newton Abbot   Devon

Visit our website at www.davidandcharles.co.uk

David & Charles books are available from all good bookshops;
alternatively you can contact our Orderline on (0)1626 334555 or
write to us at FREEPOST EX2110, David & Charles Direct,
Newton Abbot, TQ12 4ZZ (no stamp required UK mainland).

Acknowledgments

Thanks to the many who helped with this project, especially
Brandy Corry, Lois Mark, Irene Duncan, Akemi Rush, Susan Malone,
Jessica Quintana, Colleen Finley, Mary Gugino, Michele Potter,
Lauren Bjorkman, Kimber McDonald, Claire Brandenburg,
Jean Westland, Kathleen Knoth, Mauna Richardson, Dan Ritchey,
Elena Aguirre, Mark Sonna, Kobe Bellis, Michael Majors and my
agent, Peter Rubie.

Special thanks to foster children Zion, Michele, Timmy, Shea,
Ruben and Christina for reminding me of what it's like to be little
in a big people's world.

Contents

Introduction

If many parents find the toddler years the most challenging, they also agree that nothing is quite as gratifying as being present through this special stage. Even though an hour spent coping with a fretful toddler can seem like a year, the opposite is also true: those 24 months from ages one to three pass in the blink of an eye.

While each stage of childhood contains special joys, the intensity of the toddler years offers more emotional highs than any other stage, if parents can open their hearts to the blessings of the many precious moments. Toddlers' enthusiasm as they discover the world is infectious, and through it parents can re-experience the miracle of life in all its fascinating manifestations.

These are the years to relive the thrill of leaves blowing in the wind; to marvel at fingers and toes turning to prunes in a bathtub; to revisit the wondrous lands of Intsy Wintsy spiders, 'London Bridge' and Winnie the Pooh; to delight again in the mystery and beauty of butterflies, wiggly worms and dandelions.

These two short years offer parents the chance to revel in their child's long string of victories: building a block tower and sending it crashing to the floor; getting a bite of egg from plate to mouth with a fork; sleeping in a big bed; doing up a zip and using a potty. This time offers parents the chance to experience the warmth of a spontaneous kiss, the comfort of a consoling hug, and the reassurance of knowing they are special, important and oh so needed.

This book contains tips for every aspect of guiding youngsters through these critical years of rapid intellectual, physical, emotional and moral development. It summarizes the best available information on everything from diet to safety, from discipline to fun and games.

My best advice to parents shepherding a young one through this special stage of life can be summed up in a nutshell: relax; smile – and enjoy!

CHAPTER 1

One Giant Leap for Baby

There are so many 'firsts' in a baby's life, and each one is a miracle – part and parcel of that gradual unfolding into humanness through which a helpless infant becomes an independent person. But of all the 'firsts', none is as momentous as when a baby lets go of a protective hand or solid piece of furniture and puts one small foot in front of the other.

An Infant Reborn

On taking that first independent step, the expression that crosses a toddler's face is one of amazement. If the youngster appears as startled as if he were entering the world for the first time, it may be because, in one sense, that is exactly what he is doing.

Just as baby kangaroos finish developing in their mother's pouch, human babies aren't ready to be born until they can walk, according to some scientists. Infants' oversized heads dictate that they leave the womb long before they could possibly survive on their own; in that sense, all babies are born prematurely. It's not until little ones can walk that they become fully fledged members of the human race!

Although it is impossible to know exactly what is happening inside their minds as they take those first tentative steps, there are indications that toddlers realize they have undergone a remarkable transformation. For the most part, their faces reflect ecstatic joy and wonder, and they immediately set about perfecting their new skill. Some youngsters, however, are frightened by the dramatic change in perspective, and quickly retreat to the safe, familiar world near the furniture or floor. It takes them a few days or weeks to risk more unassisted steps, as if they need more time to prepare to enter this new stage.

Free at Last

Walking is a life-altering accomplishment. Just as an upwardly mobile youngster's expanded reach frees her body, walking frees her mind. Given their rudimentary verbal skills, babies are limited in their ability to make sense of the world via indirect learning, which occurs from asking questions and listening to explanations. Therefore they need to experience the world directly, by using their senses to unravel the thousands of mysteries that surround them.

To comprehend objects and understand the relationships between them, toddlers need to touch, taste and smell those objects. Crawling enabled them to begin unravelling some of the world's mysteries; walking opens the way to discovering areas far from their mother's side.

Once toddlers get the hang of walking, they'll probably want to practise all day and may protest loudly at bedtime. Although they do need to go to bed whether or not they want to, try to indulge their desire for exercise during the day – they need to keep practising!

WALKING STATISTICS	
SKILL(S)	**AGE OF MASTERY FOR 90% OF TODDLERS**
Walks holding on	12.7 months
Stands alone briefly	13.0 months
Stands alone well	13.9 months
Walks well	14.3 months
Begins to run	18.0 months
Walks up steps	22.0 months
Runs with ease, stands on tiptoe, steps back	24.0 months
Jumps, kicks a ball forwards, balances on one foot, climbs a low ladder, leans forwards without losing balance, pedals a tricycle	30.0 months
Jumps 38cm (15in), hops, uses alternating feet when walking up and down stairs	36.0 months

The First Classroom

Education experts have long insisted 'a child's play is his work'. Now accumulated research proves that if a child's job is to learn, the experts are definitely correct! That said, it can be hard for parents to understand that their toddler is having an important educational experience when their child stumbles into the living room, retrieves a toy ball from under the sofa and licks the plastic, or spends 15 minutes drumming on pots and pans with a wooden spoon.

Parents may think toddlers are merely making useless mischief. But by getting to know the unique texture of plastic or the sound a spoon makes hitting a pot, toddlers are actually gathering data, developing hypotheses, conducting experiments, analyzing the results and drawing conclusions. Imagine! Every time the spoon hits the pot, Mum yells! A spoon's ability to make noise come from the pot and Mum's mouth is amazing to a toddler.

Although you often have to curtail your toddler's explorations because they are too dangerous or messy, try to accommodate his or her urge to explore. It's important to accept the fact that your house won't be as tidy as it was before your tot became mobile.

Prodding, poking, tasting and smelling are crucial for children's long-range intellectual development. Researchers have long known that toddlers with fewer opportunities to use their senses end up less intelligent than their peers who are given freer reign.

More recently, scientists have used imaging equipment to study toddlers' brains to find out exactly what happens when they engage in various kinds of play activities. The results are nothing short of amazing. Different areas of the brain respond when children engage in different kinds of exploration. When toddlers manipulate objects, brain cells and those all-important connections between them can be seen in the act of being born. They appear, grow and proliferate. When a child is deeply engrossed in a toy, the growth of this rootlike structure speeds up, and a complex web of long thin cells emerges. As children continue to play, those cells deepen until they make permanent creases in the grey matter of the brain.

Ballerinas, They're Not!

Toddlers aren't particularly graceful when they're learning to walk. In fact, they are very awkward until they figure out how to coordinate so many body parts at once. Few youngsters master the smooth heel-to-toe motion until the age of two. Until then, don't be surprised if you see your child:

- Lifting her knees so high that she appears to be goose-stepping. She may put a lot more energy into stepping about than needed until she realizes that walking doesn't have to be such a big deal.
- Pointing his knees and toes out instead of forwards. This wider base provides him with a better sense of balance.
- Walking on tiptoes. As she gains confidence and her balance improves, she should settle to the ground. However, tiptoe walking can also stem from the heel cords being too short or tight. To check, see if your youngster can keep her feet flat on the floor when she's squatting. If she can't, consult your doctor.

Pigeon Toes

Walking with the toes pointed in, or pigeon-toed, helps toddlers balance by compensating for their flat feet. If the angle doesn't interfere with your toddler's ability to walk, and if the movements of the foot are smooth rather than rigid, there's no need for corrective action. Alert your doctor if the angle of the feet is severe enough to hamper walking, if the feet aren't straight when at rest or if they don't straighten out before the age of three. Encourage toddlers to sit cross-legged or with their feet stuck straight out in front. Some experts believe that sitting with their feet tucked underneath their bodies or turned out in a **W** shape can cause the legs to curve. Most children outgrow being pigeon-toed, but some never do – an estimated eight or nine per cent of adults walk with their toes pointed in.

Baby Walker

If you are considering using a baby walker to help a late walker develop the skills needed to walk alone, don't bother! Doctors say walkers do not help children learn faster. Crawling teaches more about balance and coordination than gliding through the house in a walker. If you are using a baby walker for its entertainment value, you need to be aware of how dangerous they are. Hundreds of children each year have an accident in rolling walkers serious enough to send them to hospital. If you decide the risks are worth it, it's important to supervise your child every moment and to walker-proof your house:

- Level all bumps in the floor. Children moving fast can be ejected if they hit a bump; this is how many of the more serious accidents happen.
- Protect floor lamps that could be knocked over, hitting the toddler on the head or breaking and starting a fire.
- Stabilize wobbly stoves and tables so they can withstand a hard bump without spilling hot food or liquid onto a child's head.
- Be aware of hot oven doors that can burn the palm of a tender hand, and of cooker knobs that are within reach.
- Make sure the refrigerator door handle is too high for a toddler to open, or that glass jars and heavy containers can't be pulled off the shelves.
- Make sure that the safety gate at the top of the stairs is sturdy enough to survive a crash. Spring-action gates will not withstand the force of a walker in motion; wall-mounted gates are best.
- Don't use a walker with springs or coils within reach of little fingers – they can pinch.

Since an upright child's reach is much longer than a crawler's, objects on end tables, bookshelves, window sills and sofas become a threat. That includes the dog lying down on the sofa and the cat curled up in the rocking chair. Pets have been known to bite the little hands pulling their fur and yanking on their tails.

What is tibial torsion?
Tibial torsion is a condition that can cause pigeon toes. The leg bone is turned from having been squeezed inside the uterus. The angle of the feet should straighten out as the shinbones become properly aligned (usually by the age of 18 months).

Little Athletes and Einsteins?

The truth is that there is no relationship between walking and athletic ability and intelligence. In fact, early walking does have its drawbacks: it complicates emotional development, because younger ones more often wander from Mum or Dad's side and then become terrified at finding themselves alone in another room.

> Did you know that the brains of children who don't play much are 20 to 30 per cent smaller than normal? And that what toddlers learn as they poke and prod and lick and chew and sniff actually becomes part of the brain itself?

Larger youngsters may have more trouble with balance, and coordination can be a problem if their joints are highly extensible (that is, when the knee bends more than 180 degrees). Until these toddlers develop more muscles to support their unsteady joints, walking will be difficult and can be delayed for up to six months.

Whether your child is up and running or taking his time, there are things you can do to make things a little easier for him and reduce some risks. Open up space in the rooms of your house so toddlers don't have to navigate an obstacle course as they waddle about. Be careful to carry out the following safety routines:

· Remove furniture from high-traffic areas.
· Keep toys picked up.
· Pad hard edges of furniture to guard against head injuries.

Don't trip them up – make sure that toddlers' shoes fit properly; their feet should be measured every six weeks. Allow toddlers to go barefoot inside whenever possible.

Stairs

Stairs are as dangerous as they are intriguing for toddlers. Until toddlers can negotiate them safely on their own, place a safety gate at the top and bottom of the stairs. Remember: what goes up can also fall down. To prevent stair-related injuries, follow the suggestions overleaf.

- Keep steps and landings free of clutter.
- Secure the edges of carpeting.
- Place skid-proof mats on slippery hardwood and linoleum.
- Keep the stairs well illuminated.
- Place guards on railings, windows and patios above the first floor.

Finally, when your youngster is old enough to begin practising climbing up and down (at around two), move the bottom gate up to give her an opportunity to practise on the first few stairs.

Bathroom Safety

Between the cramped space, slippery floors that invite falls and the unforgiving porcelain fixtures that hurt so much in a crash, bathrooms need special attention to protect wobbly toddlers.

Use skid-proof flooring and mats on your bathroom floors, and make sure you place a skid-proof mat or transfers on the bottom of the bath and shower. Stick non-slip transfers on the rim of the bath and shower walls; if there is a slip, that bit of friction may help break a fall. If your youngster can climb out of his cot and doesn't have a bed yet, put night-lights in the bedroom and bathroom to create a well-lit trail.

Mother Nature constructed toddlers to withstand some pretty heavy-duty spills. Their layer of baby fat functions like a built-in cushion, while their still-soft skeletons absorb the kinds of shock that would cause the brittle bones of older folks to fracture and break.

Concentration Counts!

Balancing a head and torso on two tiny moving feet is no small task, so walking requires a beginner's undivided attention. Tots are too busy figuring out how to coordinate their movements to think about – much less avoid – an obstacle looming ahead, so it's important to smooth out the bumps in the rugs and clear some paths.

Don't assume that your child is defiant because she doesn't slow down when you warn her that she's about to crash, or doesn't return when you call her. She may not have heard a word you said. If she did, she probably didn't understand what you meant.

When freedom and independence become overwhelming, toddlers may retreat to the more predictable world of babyhood. If your toddler is too heavy to carry, offer to hold his hand; perhaps that additional security will be enough. After outings, offer some extra TLC and temporarily scale back some of your demands for more mature behaviour at home. And next time, take the buggy!

Shoes and Socks

Toddlers don't need to wear shoes except for warmth and protection. Non-skid socks provide traction as well as warmth. Prewalkers have sturdier fabric or soft-leather soles, so they provide protection for walks outdoors. They should fit snugly enough that they don't slip, but the fit is larger than a proper shoe.

When buying these proper shoes, however, the fit is very important. Shoes must fit correctly at the outset because soft baby feet can't break them in. It's normal for your child's feet to be slightly different in size. Your child needs a pair that fits the *larger* foot; a shoe that is too small can inhibit the foot's development. The fit on proper shoes must be checked frequently since toddlers grow so fast. With a good fit:

· The heel shouldn't slip. Your little finger should fit between the back of the shoe and the child's heel.
· There should be enough room for the toes to wiggle, which requires about 1.2cm ($^{1}/_{2}$in) from the longest toe to the tip of the shoe.
· The height should be adequate, so there is room to wiggle the toes up and down. To test, press down on the top of the shoe over the big toe. You should feel space between the shoe and the toe.

- When you pinch the side of the shoe at the widest point, you should get a little bit of shoe. If you can't pinch any leather, the shoes are too narrow; if you can hold a good-sized piece, they're too wide.
- After your child walks (or is walked) in the shoes for a few minutes, make sure they haven't left any red marks on your child's feet.

Baby feet can be so sensitive that even the seam of a sock can cause them pain. Stretch socks are the easiest to fit and last the longest. Socks that are too big will wrinkle and bunch up, which can cause blisters; if they're too small, they'll leave red marks and can cause cramp.

Stepping Into Tomorrow

With the increased independence that comes with walking, toddlers experience a surging desire for autonomy. Combine this desire with the changes that walking introduces into their lives, and it is typical for their behaviour to deteriorate a bit. Expect more crying, defiance and trouble getting your child to go to sleep.

CHAPTER 2

Communication Coups

The toddler years are a time of astounding language development. At the age of 12 months, 50 per cent of youngsters can say six or more words. When the toddler years end, speaking vocabulary has shot up to 1,000 words; three-year-olds can combine them to express thousands of ideas. At this age it's the ability to comprehend speech that influences how adept children will be at language skills later in life.

The Language Ladder

It doesn't work to apply the averages to individual toddlers, of course, because the age at which a child begins talking is governed by physical growth. Typically, however, the language progression is:

- Cooing
- Gurgling
- Babbling
- Gibberish
- Individual words
- Two-word sentences
- Complex sentences

The most common progression is for children to begin with one word, gradually add others, and then combine them into two-word sentences before creating more complex sentences. This is not the only pattern, however.

When it comes to saying those first dozen words, researchers say that simply practising doesn't make speaking perfect. Toddlers will be able to get the words out when the speech centres of the brain mature. But vocabulary comprehension grows quickly. Don't judge your toddler's progress with language by her ability to speak, because the amount youngsters *understand* is a much better prediction of later language ability. Just keep talking to your toddler, even if you don't receive a reply.

Some youngsters mouth rapid streams of gibberish. Their voices rise and fall as if they were expounding on the state of the universe. Their facial expressions are as serious and their gestures as dramatic as Shakespearean actors, yet they don't utter a single recognizable word. This apparent delay can be worrying for parents, but when toddlers finally start saying words people can understand, they usually begin with short sentences rather than individual words, and continue to progress rapidly. Einstein didn't begin to talk until he was almost three.

On average, girls start talking at an earlier age than boys do, if only by a few months. Some children speak later than others because there is simply no need for them to talk – their parents and older siblings are all too adept at figuring out the meanings of their grunts and whimpers. They fulfil their toddler's requests without letting them know that there are other, better, ways to communicate.

The best way to encourage youngsters to use words rather than gestures to communicate is to demonstrate the correct way to ask for an item. For instance, when your toddler points at a glass of water and grunts, you can respond, 'Water? Can you say "water"?' After a brief pause to let the question sink in, hand over the water, whether or not he attempts to say the word. Your child may be unable to speak because his brain is not sufficiently mature. Trying to force him will only make him feel bad. Pushing toddlers is a definite no-no. There will be plenty of times when you find yourself using the 'just tell me what you want' line when you really don't know what your toddler is trying to communicate. But there's no point in creating a scene when you do understand the gesture.

Children who have delays in several areas, as premature babies often do, may have language delays, too. Parents can expect toddlers with slower overall development to begin talking later rather than sooner. There's no need to be concerned about *exactly* when children start talking as long as the child is younger than two, or the following signs are present:

·   Gibberish and babbling continue
·   Attempts to imitate sounds continue
·   Comprehension continues to improve
·   The child responds to your hearing tests (see page 25). Still, if you can't shake the feeling that something's wrong, talk to your doctor.

Cooing seems to be innate. Even deaf infants coo. But if babies cannot hear their parents' responses and feedback, instead of progressing to gurgles, babbles and gibberish, the coos will gradually disappear. If you are worried, consult your doctor or health visitor.

From the Mouths of Babes

It's never too soon to begin conducting language lessons – within the context of daily interactions, that is. By understanding the fine points of human communication, parents can provide a rich learning environment and better verbal stimulation. Acquiring speech is a two-step process that involves (1) listening to language being spoken, and (2) practising talking. You can engage your youngster in her first conversation by placing your face close to hers and alternate between talking to her and mimicking the noises she makes. This is the time to giggle, tickle, tease, snort, crow like a rooster, quack like a duck, moo like a cow and make every kind of funny noise you can think of.

The give-and-take of sounds encourages your youngster to mimic you, thereby engaging in the work that is essential for good language development: listening carefully to sounds and trying to reproduce them. When she's had enough, she'll signal her desire to stop by turning her head away. When she wants to continue, she'll again make sustained eye contact. Be sensitive to your child's readiness to play language games, as well as to her wish to stop. Failing to at least back off for a while leads to overstimulation and toddler stress.

Talking Hands

To speed communication, many parents now teach some basic sign language to their toddlers. Baby sign language started as an experiment at Ohio State University's laboratory school in the USA. It was so successful that children as young as nine months old were able to communicate some of their basic needs by signing, thereby eliminating a lot of crying on the part of the little ones because the staff could more readily determine their needs. Some older toddlers could sign up to 30 words.

You don't need to do any kind of special drills to teach sign language. Simply make the sign for 'more', 'down', 'potty', 'stop' and so on, while saying the word (don't forget to keep talking). In time, your child will mimic your motions. There's no need to know sign language, and it's OK to invent signs rather than using the standard gestures, as long as you are consistent.

However, a definite advantage to using the standard signs is that toddlers can then readily communicate with people other than their parents. It is becoming increasingly common for toddlers and the adults who work with them to know some sign language. If caregivers don't know sign language, you can facilitate communication by providing them with a photocopied page of the signs your toddler knows, along with the list of emergency numbers and other important information.

FIGURE 2-1: **All gone**
Right hand, palm down, sweeps across
top of left hand.

FIGURE 2-2: **Down**
Point index finger down.

FIGURE 2-3: **Drink**
Shape right hand as if holding a glass,
bring to mouth.

FIGURE 2-4: **Eat**
Pinch right hand fingers together, bring
to mouth.

FIGURE 2-5: **Go**
Hold hands at chest, with index fingers pointing up. Rotate hands forwards, so index fingers point out.

FIGURE 2-6: **More**
Pinch fingers of both hands, then bring hands together.

FIGURE 2-7: **No**
Hold right hand with thumb out and index and middle fingers straight up. Bring fingers to thumb in pinching motion.

FIGURE 2-8: **Now**
Keeping hands palm up and bent at fingers, lower hands slightly.

FIGURE 2-9: **Please**
Move hand over heart in circular motion.

FIGURE 2-10: **Share**
Hold left hand palm open and thumb up. Sweep right hand, also palm open, along side of index finger of left hand.

FIGURE 2-11: **Sit**
Tap index/middle fingers of right hand on index/middle fingers of left hand.

FIGURE 2-12: **Stop**
Right hand comes down on palm of left hand in 'cut' motion.

FIGURE 2-13: **Thank you**
Open-palmed right hand starts with fingertips at mouth, then moves forwards.

FIGURE 2-14: **Tired/bed**
Right hand, flat palmed, is alongside tilted head.

FIGURE 2-15: **Toilet**
Make a fist with right hand, thumb between index and middle fingers, and shake right to left.

FIGURE 2-16: **Yes**
Make a fist with right hand, thumb across fingers. Bend up and down at wrist.

Fine-Tuning Listening

Seize opportunities to encourage your toddler to tune in to the world of sound. For example, when you're in the car, point out the shriek of a police siren, the blare of a horn or the whistle of a train. When you go for a walk around the neighbourhood, help your toddler notice the tweet of a bird, the rustle of leaves or the whoosh of the wind. In the house, listen together to the crackle of a fire, the hiss of a kettle or the ring of a kitchen timer. Use your voice as well: hum, whistle and sing to your little one – she won't care if you can't stay in tune. And, by all means, play music.

Careful listening helps toddlers to reproduce the sounds needed for speech today, to recognize the subtle differences in sound needed for speaking tomorrow, and to sound out the words when they're learning to read in the years to come.

Words, Words, Words

In addition to normal hearing and listening in general, children need to hear words spoken in context. I hope you've been uttering streams of them since Day 1, so by the age of 12 months your toddler has had continuous exposure to millions of words. If not, start now to make up for those lost months.

Unfortunately, the TV won't provide the kind of exposure to words that toddlers need. Child experts warn that TV dialogue drifts by in a blur. The crucial ingredient is missing: the association of the sounds of language with the objects to which those sounds refer. In fact, the TV shouldn't even be playing in the background, since the noise can keep toddlers from hearing language that is being spoken.

Speaking Parentese

Highly educated parents often pride themselves on not using baby talk with their little ones, believing that they can speed language development by using normal adult speech. However, baby talk can in fact be helpful. The high-pitched sing-song voice adults typically use when addressing babies is sometimes called 'parentese'. It involves subtly emphasizing important syllables, lengthening the vowels, and often simplifying or eliminating pronouns, such as saying 'he' or 'she' or the child's name instead of 'you', even when speaking directly to the youngster.

Baby talk makes language more comprehensible to youngsters. To get a feel for this kind of speech, imagine a relative picking up a baby and speaking directly to it while saying things like, 'Oh, look at this precious little cutie pie! Oh, he's sooo tired. Does Edward want to go sleepy-bye now? I think he does!'

Adults all over the world naturally use parentese when addressing babies. Research shows that little ones respond by listening longer and more intently to baby talk than to normal adult speech – even if parentese is spoken in a language the baby isn't familiar with! However, language experts say that there's one aspect of parentese that does not help toddlers: parents referring to themselves as 'Mummy' or 'Daddy' instead of as 'I' or 'me', and to their child by saying his or her name instead of saying 'you'. Toddlers have a hard enough time with personal pronouns. Don't complicate it by saying things, such as 'Mummy is going now' and 'Does Susie want some milk?' Say, 'I am going now' and 'Do you want some milk?'

Although speaking parentese to young toddlers can facilitate learning, it's probably a good idea to use correct sentence structure, especially correct pronouns, with increasing frequency as your child's comprehension improves.

First Sounds

The first discernible sounds embedded in English-speaking youngsters' gibberish are *b*, *p*, *m*, *t*, *d*, *n*, *h*, *k* and *g*. Although parents celebrate the arrival of the word they've been longing to hear – 'Mama' or 'Dada' – they usually first occur by accident, as random sounds tucked in among the youngster's babbling. It may take several more months for toddlers to use the words consciously and attach meanings to them.

During the gibberish phase, some parents have been known to exclaim, 'He's speaking a different language!' There is an element of truth to this. Babies are born with the capability to learn any language and emit sounds from every language in the world. As they imitate adults and receive praise for repeating certain sounds while other sounds are ignored, the variety of the sounds they make diminishes. They gradually lose their ability to make the sounds needed to speak other languages. That is why learning to speak a foreign language like a native becomes harder after the age of six, and impossible for most after 12–15 years. Certainly the remarkable ability of young humans to go from completely non-verbal to fluent is the envy of any adult who has tried to learn a foreign language.

Don't be surprised if a bilingual baby is somewhat behind in speech development – her brain has more to process. The 'window of opportunity' for foreign language fluency is up to six years old. Studies suggest that it's best to expose babies to the second language *before* they begin speaking. Starting the day they are born is best of all.

Life Lessons

Although maturation dictates when children will be able to talk, parents are crucial partners in helping to develop language skills. The amount of exposure to language that toddlers receive is key, and it is associated with intelligence as measured by IQ tests at the age of three.

To spur your child's language development, verbalize your thoughts whenever your toddler is around, not just when you have something specific to say, like 'Let's get your coat. We're going out now.' Instead, try this: 'It's about time to do the errands. Let's see, I need to pick up some food for dinner, but where did I put my keys? Oh, here they are. And I need to stop at the bank on the way to the supermarket to get some cash.

Well, maybe I'll just use the debit card instead. OK, let's get your coat. We're going now.'

When parents speak their thoughts aloud in an ongoing, running narrative, youngsters hear words in context and in grammatically correct sentences. They are also exposed to a host of other important information. By hearing a parent think out loud as he gets ready to go to the gym, for example, the child learns how to prepare for this kind of outing, which actually involves quite a bit of planning and organizing: 'Where is my gym bag? Oh, it must be in the cupboard. Oops – I forgot to wash these socks. No wonder this bag smells!' To teach children to think ahead, you need to show them, again and again, task after task, the kinds of things to think about.

Teaching Meanings

As you go through your day, dedicate yourself to helping your child grasp the meaning of individual words. Saying, 'Do you want milk or juice?' while holding up a carton of milk and a bottle of juice is a way to teach children that different objects have different names. If your child points to the juice, only to get upset after taking a drink and frantically pointing to the milk, this isn't necessarily a sign he's being negative. He simply may not have learned to associate the word milk with the carton. By hearing their parent say a word and having the chance to experience the object, children learn what things are called.

First Conversations

Some parents have a hard time remembering how very important it is to continue talking to their child when they don't get a verbal response. Parents need to speak directly to toddlers about daily affairs, leaving pauses to teach them about the normal give-and-take of verbal exchanges – no matter that the infants are still too inexperienced with language to hold up their end of the conversation. For example, you might say, 'I was thinking I'd make tuna pasta for lunch. What do you think about that?... No, it looks as though I'm out of tuna. Perhaps we'll have sandwiches. Would you like sandwiches for lunch?'

A child's inability to respond with words doesn't mean that nothing is going on. It is quite the contrary. When the parent pauses, youngsters formulate responses in their minds long before they can demonstrate their knowledge by speaking.

Parents can focus their toddler's attention by getting down to their eye level and speaking directly to them. For instance, you might say, 'We're going to visit Grandma. Do you want to show her your new hat? (Pause) Come on, let's find your hat.' Even if your tot doesn't know what a 'hat' is at the beginning of the conversation, by the time you've said, 'Here's your hat. Let's put it on you. It's cold outside. Your hat will keep you warm' (to teach about the purpose of a hat), and later, 'Grandma, how do you like Jonathan's new hat? Jonathan, show Grandma your hat,' he should associate the word with the object.

Explaining the World

As you go through your days, concentrate on telling your child about the world. 'See the brown car?' 'That's called a traffic light. When it's red, all the cars stop.' 'This is the aisle where they keep all the cereal.' 'The lady who rings up our shopping is called a cashier.' 'This yellow flower is a dandelion. See how it tickles your nose?'

And don't forget to repeat yourself... again and again and yet again. Toddlers love repetition. It makes them feel more secure because the world feels more predictable; when they hear about things they already know, it gives them a sense of mastery.

First Words

By the time toddlers can say 25 words, they can understand about 170. At that point, their spoken vocabulary is apt to consist of a few names of family members, foods, body parts and animals; a smattering of actions like [pick me] *up* and *open*; some adjectives, such as *soft* and *pretty*; the adverbs *where* and *there*.

When beginning speakers point at an object while saying its name, they usually mean 'I want it'. After youngsters are able to say about 50 words, somewhere between 16 and 22 months, they realize that every single thing has a name. Then the pointing changes from a demand to a question. They don't want the item; they want to know what it is called. Suddenly their vocabulary explodes as they flit from object to object, asking to know the name of everything they see. Parents' responsiveness pays off in a big way. Toddlers going through this stage can master several new words each day.

First Sentences

After accumulating a store of individual words, the next developmental step is to combine them into sentences. At first toddlers use two words to create short sentences, such as 'Want juice!' for 'I want some juice' and 'What dat?' for 'What is that?'

What does telegraphic speech mean?
Using two words to create short sentences, such as 'What dat?' for 'What is that?' is called 'telegraphic speech'. The term dates back to when people used the telegraph for long-distance communication. They had to pay by the word, so they were very creative about using just a few words to convey an entire message.

Expanding Language Skills

When your toddler is able to signal her desire for a drink by saying 'water', you can encourage her to take the next step to more elaborate sentences by saying, 'Can you say "Water, please"?' Or you can respond with a full sentence ('You want some water') or with a grammatically correct question ('Do you want some water?') to help move her towards the toddler version of a complete sentence, 'Want water'. Again, you should hand over the cup even if the only reply is a nod, which means, after all, that she has heard and understood the question.

Similarly, if a toddler sees a cat and starts a conversation by pointing to it and saying 'Cat', a caregiver can engage in conversation by expanding on the subject he brought up. To do this, the adult might say, 'Yes. It's a cat', or 'Yes, it's a big, white cat. And look at its long tail!' By giving a verbal response as opposed to simply nodding when toddlers speak, adults encourage them to say more.

After all, if toddlers don't receive a response when they initiate a conversation, there is no reason for them to talk. By responding with longer, more complex, sentences, adults help build toddlers' vocabularies.

Pronunciation Errors

New speakers make many 'errors of articulation'; that is, they mispronounce words in predictable ways. Although articulation problems may stem from hearing problems, cerebral palsy, cleft palate or dental problems, all toddlers make many errors. The vast majority improve with a little time and a lot of practice.

By the time your child is three, strangers ought to be able to understand his speech. If they cannot, it's time to talk to your doctor or health visitor about a referral for a speech and language assessment. By eight, children should correctly produce all the sounds of the English language.

Common errors include (1) omitting sounds, saying 'at' for 'hat' or 'muhk' for 'milk'; and (2) substituting easier sounds for more difficult ones, saying 'danks' for 'thanks', 'medsur' for 'measure', 'wabbit' for 'rabbit'. The letters s, r and l are especially difficult for toddlers to pronounce, and many children take several years to get them right. It is not unusual to hear pupils say 'wunning' for 'running' in the early years of school. The same goes for lisping – substituting the 'th' sound for the 's' so that 'sand' becomes 'thand'.

Do You Hear What I Hear?

Since children must be able to hear accurately to learn to speak correctly, even mild hearing losses can take a toll on speech. If people's words sound muffled to the toddler, his speech will take on a similarly muffled or slurred quality. You should regularly screen your toddler's hearing at home. To do this, be sure that:

She turns her head towards sounds. Youngsters should signal an awareness of sounds by turning towards the front door when someone knocks or the doorbell rings, towards the sky when a helicopter or aeroplane flies overhead, towards the phone when it rings, towards the dog when it suddenly begins to bark.

He hears sounds coming from behind or the side. Even little ones can learn to do some lip-reading, so it can be easy to miss the fact that a youngster has a hearing problem if he converses comfortably with people standing in front of him. A tell-tale complaint from parents of children who are hard of hearing is, 'She ignores me unless I'm in her face. Otherwise, I have to yell at her to get her to notice.'

She hears correctly. Strange responses to questions may indicate hearing loss. An example would be if you ask a simple question like, 'Do you want strawberry or vanilla ice cream?' and you receive a bizarre answer, such as 'Yes, play outside.'"

Chronic ear infections, allergies and upper respiratory infections interfere with hearing. They are the most common culprits behind delayed speech and poor pronunciation.

Correcting Errors

Children's mispronunciations are often so cute that it can be tempting to adopt their errors as part of the regular household vocabulary. Soon you are routinely saying things such as 'Carolina want wa-wa with din-din?' This is not the way to teach toddlers to speak so that others will be able to understand them.

You must continually demonstrate the proper way to speak so your child has a good model to copy. At the other extreme, continually correcting toddlers can produce self-consciousness and frustration that increases shyness and reticence about speaking. After all, if a child says, 'Wa-wa' and points, it's probably because he still lacks the physical ability to coordinate tongue, breath and lips to produce all the sounds in the word water. So instead of saying, 'It's not "wa-wa"; it's "water",' which can discourage a beginning speaker, emphasize correct pronunciation and grammar by responding, 'Do you want some water? Here you go – one cup of water coming up.' Producing the water lets your toddler know that he is successfully communicating, which encourages him to continue to speak to get his needs met. Repeating the correct word several times in grammatically correct sentences encourages toddlers to pay attention to correct pronunciation and usage.

Teach vocabulary by saying an object's name while moving it, and toddlers learn the words faster, experts say. Somehow it helps to roll the toy car when you say 'car', bounce the ball when you say its name, or make Barbie dance as you say 'doll'.

Most toddlers, just like adults, are sensitive about having their speech corrected. Hearing language spoken correctly and having opportunities to practise speaking is what improves verbal skills. After all, people receive more benefit from feedback telling them they have done something right, because then they know exactly what to do. Receiving feedback that they have done something wrong doesn't clue them in as to exactly what they should do. Being told, 'It's not "wa-wa"; it's "water"!' doesn't tell a toddler how to make all the complicated mouth movements needed to say the word. But when he finally says 'wah-tuh', point it out and encourage him to practise while the memory is fresh by exclaiming, 'You did it! You said "water"! Can you say it again? Wow! My baby's growing up!'

Naming Parts of the Body

Besides talking directly to your toddler, voicing your thoughts when your toddler is within hearing range and responding when she initiates conversations, set aside some time for helping her learn specific vocabulary. A good place to start is naming the parts of the body. This is basic vocabulary that toddlers need to know, the words are easy to teach, and the lessons provide an opportunity for fun parent/toddler interaction.

Simply say, 'This is Mummy's nose' while touching your nose. Then say 'This is your nose' while touching your child's nose. Then ask 'Where is Mummy's nose? Here it is!' and place your child's hand on your nose. With repetition, children learn not only the word 'nose' but also those important phrases: *this is*, *where is* and *here it is*.

Once the nose has been mastered, begin adding other parts of the body, such as ear, mouth, hair, eye, hand and foot. Once toddlers can talk, they can take turns asking their parents to point to different parts of the body. Keep it fun by incorporating these suggestions:

· Squeeze your nostrils when you say, 'This is my nose', to make your voice sound nasally.
· Smack your lips when you say, 'This is my mouth'.
· Bat your eyelashes wildly when you say, 'These are my eyes'.
· After you ask, 'Where is your tummy?' quickly answer your own question by saying 'Here it is!' and giving your toddler a quick tummy tickle.

Parents as Teachers

As any school head teacher can tell you, the best teachers spend as much time entertaining as they do teaching. Developing a positive attitude towards language and learning and being receptive when a parent steps into the role of teacher is more important than any individual lesson. Learning (and teaching) requires a clear head, so if your child can't attend to the task at hand or you're feeling frustrated, don't push it. Also, avoid drilling at all costs: lessons should be enjoyable enough to make you both smile and short enough that you'll both look forward to playing again. If your toddler isn't finding it fun, forget it.

Here are some simple ways to boost your toddler's verbal skills:

· Let her talk to relatives on the telephone.
· Ask him to tell you about his favourite activity at nursery.

- Write down the details of a trip or outing and read them back to her.
- Tell him a bedtime story instead of reading him one (and if the main character has the same name as your child, so much the better).
- Turn off the TV at meal times, and talk.
- Turn off the radio in the car and recite nursery rhymes.

Teach vocabulary by asking your youngster to hand you clothing when you're dressing him ('Please pass me your sock'), kitchen items while you set the table ('Please get a cup'), things you need to go out ('Where is your changing bag?'). Remember, it's never too early to teach manners, so include 'please' and 'thank you'.

The 'Where Is It?' Game

Another way to give vocabulary lessons is to play the 'Where is it?' game with your child:

1. Place three familiar objects – such as a cup, a teddy bear and a sock – on a table.
2. Point to each object while naming it. For example, 'See? This is the cup.'
3. Then ask your child, 'Where is the cup? Please show me (or give me) the cup.'
4. Provide prompts by pointing to or placing your child's hand on the correct object.
5. If she responds correctly, nod immediately and say, 'Yes, that's the cup', to provide feedback and to reinforce correct answers. For wrong answers, say, 'No, that's the sock. This is the cup. Can you say "cup"?' Pause briefly after asking him to repeat a word, but then move on.

The goal of the 'Can you say?' questions should be to call the child's attention to an object and to build the association between the object and the sound of its name. Don't try to get a toddler to actually say the names of the objects. Remember that vocabulary comprehension is more important than speaking ability for long-term development. Physical maturation will determine when children are able to speak.

Taking Turns

If your child is able to say the names of some household objects, vary the game by giving her a turn to call out a name and then respond by pointing to the object or handing it to her while saying its name. For instance, say, 'Now it's your turn. Ask Mummy for the cup. Can you say "cup"?' When she says 'cup', point to it or hand it to her and say 'Here is the cup.' Then get her to ask you for the sock. Continue providing prompts until she can call out the names of objects by herself. When she's successful with the first three objects, stop the game. Use different objects on another day.

Toddlers are really just babies in disguise, and it can be hard for them to grasp that this game doesn't involve banging the cup on the table, cuddling the teddy bear or eating the sock. If your child lacks the maturity or ability to concentrate on the practice session, so be it. Let a month elapse before trying again. In the meantime, place a few of his toys around the room and ask him to bring each one back to you.

Bundles of Books

Books are excellent vehicles for teaching vocabulary. By pointing to pictures and saying the names, children learn to associate the sound with the visual image. Librarians and bookshop assistants can steer you towards books that are best for your child's developmental level. See Chapter 13 for tips on reading to youngsters.

Most adults feel rejected when the person they're talking to turns his or her back. The same goes for toddlers. Be a good listener and engage your child. Get down to her level, maintain eye contact and ask questions to show that you're interested.

Grappling with Grammar

Many routine grammar errors may actually show that toddlers correctly comprehend very complex grammar rules of the English language. For instance, the past tense in English is usually formed by adding *-ed* to the present tense of the verb, as in *reach/reached*; *seat/seated*; *hope/hoped*; *jump/jumped*. When toddlers say 'She teached me', they demonstrate their grasp of this basic rule. The best way to teach the correct forms of irregular verbs is to correct the errors each time they occur by restating the sentence correctly.

Unlike trying to get toddlers to pronounce words properly, which may be impossible until they mature physically, correcting grammar is important to keep bad speech habits from developing. So, if your child says 'It's bended', respond by saying 'Yes, it's bent'. You should respond to 'I done it' with 'Yes, you did it'.

Stuttering

To talk li-li-like this is a normal hesitation for young speakers. To-to-to talk like like like this is normal, too. Wh-wh-when th-th-ey t-t-talk li-li-like th-th-is, it's considered stuttering.

Most toddlers stutter because their thoughts are moving faster than their tongues, mouths and cheeks. The great river of words rushes from their brains and crashes into those giant dams, their tongues, so only a slow trickle emerges from their mouths. When they become adept at coordinating the two, the stuttering will go away. In the meantime, their struggle to get the words out can be observed in the tension in their facial muscles.

The key to curing stuttering is to eliminate the child's need to get the words out fast. To this end, you must be patient in order to help your child relax. Yelling at a child to 'slow down' certainly doesn't promote relaxation. Instead, it increases the rush of thoughts in the child's mind because, in addition to the words he wants to say, he now must think about slowing down.

Discussing how the child is speaking while the child is trying to speak also makes the stuttering worse. Children naturally mimic their parents and copy their speech patterns, so an effective way to get them to slow down is to slow your own rate of speech to a snail's pace. If toddlers have a hard time getting a word in edgeways in a family of talkative extroverts, they may feel pressured to talk faster, so it's important to dedicate more time to uninterrupted listening.

The majority of sufferers – 60 per cent – eventually overcome stuttering without help from professional speech therapists. To help the process along, keep these tips in mind:

- Don't draw attention to stuttering.
- Don't interrupt, even to help finish a sentence.
- Don't allow siblings to interrupt, tease, mimic, or comment about the stuttering.
- Serve as a model by slowing down your own speech.
- Spend some undivided time each day talking a little and listening a lot.
- If your child is frustrated or upset about stuttering, provide reassurance: 'I can understand you, and that's all that matters.'
- Don't criticize *what* your child says or *how* it is said. Fear of being criticized increases anxiety, which increases stuttering.

If the stuttering persists more than a few months or other speech problems develop, consult your doctor or health visitor.

It is common for toddlers to talk to themselves when they are playing, falling asleep, or lying awake in bed in the morning. Don't discourage them; they are practising their language skills! Once they've got all the mouth movements down pat and have matured, they'll be able to *think* their words without saying them out loud.

Language Disabilities and Speech Defects

The cause of most language disabilities is unknown, but here are some terms to be familiar with:

Developmental aphasia. A problem in developing language that can result in poor pronunciation, limited speech and grammar problems.

Expressive language disorder. A limited ability to speak (comprehension may be normal).

Receptive language disorder. A limited ability to understand the spoken word (speech may be normal).

Elective mutism. The use of language only in certain situations, due to emotional blocks.

Echolalia. A limiting of speech to repeating what others have said.

Autistic speech. An abnormal inflection and intonation that gives the voice a robot-like quality.

Psychotic or disorganized language. Language content is bizarre and lacks context.

Even if a child has a severe speech defect that makes it almost impossible for others to understand her, parents should still try to teach the basics of conversation by doing the following:

· Continuing to talk.
· Leaving pauses so the toddler can respond.
· Listening to the tone of voice, and watching facial expressions and gestures for clues as to what is being said.
· Listening respectfully.
· Providing neutral responses that encourage talking, such as 'Oh', 'Really?' and 'Tell me more'.

Remember that even if you can't understand what your toddler is saying, she may well understand what you are saying. As long as you keep talking, she'll keep learning!

The Association of Speech and Language Therapists in Independent Practice (ASLTIP) will help you to find an independent therapist. Its members are registered members of the Royal College of Speech and Language Therapists. The website, *www.asltip.co.uk*, offers FAQs, a searchable database of independent therapists, case studies and links to other helpful sites.

The British Stammering Association (BSA) is a UK charity whose website *www.stammering.org* has helpful information for different age groups including pre-school children.

The Royal College of Speech and Language Therapists has an online leaflet called 'Delayed language', via *www.rcslt.org*. It explains the problems associated with delayed language, and provides some advice for parents on helping children with speech development.

CHAPTER 3
Growing Bodies

Physical development follows a path, beginning at the centre of the body and leading out to the fingers and toes. Babies control their backs and necks to sit up before they can deliberately grasp objects. Development also proceeds from head to foot. As infants, they lift their heads; as babies, they use their hands; and as toddlers, they develop enough control of their feet to walk.

Developing Physical Skills

Toddlers grow taller and their shapes change dramatically as they turn from babies at 12 months into little people at the lofty age of three. Nevertheless, physical growth has less to do with gains in height and weight, which slows down after the first 12 months, and much more to do with the maturing of the central nervous system, which consists of the brain and spinal cord. As the central nervous system develops, toddlers gain increased control of their muscles, both large and small, and of some internal organs, like the bowel and bladder. This enables them to handle increasingly complicated physical tasks – everything from walking up stairs to buttoning buttons to potty training.

Unless there is a physical problem requiring special therapy, parents can support physical development in their children by letting nature take its course. Allow children to follow their natural inclination to move freely about the house during virtually every waking moment, provide an opportunity for vigorous outdoor play, and clear an area inside for vigorous play during inclement weather. Trips to the park will be good for both of you, too, both physically and socially.

The Home Gym

The accent should be on having fun when helping toddlers with physical skills. In designing activities, it is important to provide a wide range of physical outlets to stimulate different areas of the brain, which develops rapidly from one to three years. Lots of repetition is also important so they can master important skills.

Beginning walkers need to work on *balance*. Parents can help by encouraging them to do the following:

- Stoop to retrieve a toy from the floor.
- Walk carrying an object in each hand.
- Walk while pulling a pull-along toy.
- Chase a balloon or bubbles.

- Walk on a strip of paper 1.5m (5ft) long by 15cm (6in) wide that has been placed on the floor as if it were a tightrope
- Lie tummy down, feet touching the ground, on an oversized ball and roll. (Supervise this activity carefully. Toddlers are top-heavy and can easily land on their heads.)

To help with *flexibility*, try the following:
- Play 'This Big'. (Ask, 'How big is baby?' and then sweep the toddler's arms up over his head and encourage him to respond, 'This big!')
- Make a maze by cutting 'doors' in several outsize cardboard boxes; push the boxes together and let toddlers crawl through them.
- Teach toddlers to dance the twist.
- Put a blanket over a table to make a tent to crawl around in.

To develop *agility*, it's helpful for toddlers to do the following:
- Walk in a large sandpit or on a sandy beach.
- Run on grass.
- Jump over puddles.
- Jump into and out of a hoop lying on the grass.
- Practise somersaults and roly poly games.
- Jump on a beanbag chair (on carpet or a pad to cushion falls).

Toddlers can be helped to develop *strength* by doing the following:
- Climb the steps of a slide. (Be sure to stand behind your child so you can catch her if she falls.)
- Pedal a tricycle.
- Pull a trolley.
- Hold on for a merry-go-round ride.
- Ride a bouncing toy or seesaw at the park.
- Fill and carry small buckets of sand.

Locomotion Skills

Locomotion skills use large muscle groups – including the arms, legs, torso and head – to move in space. Not all children master locomotion skills in the same order, but the typical progression is:

Crawling. Not all babies crawl. However, the world looks different from the floor, and the worm's-eye view from this vantage point is thought to enhance visual–spatial organization. Therefore, crawling should be encouraged.

Pulling himself up. A toddler should be able to pull himself up to a standing position using furniture, a leg or whatever sturdy object is handy. From a kneeling position, place your child's hand on a coffee table for balance and help him position one foot on the floor and then the other.

Lowering herself to the ground. Adults know they can reach that toy at their feet without collapsing into a heap, but a toddler may not know how to manage without falling. Show her how to hold onto the edge of the end table for support (cover sharp corners and hard edges), and then help her bend first one knee and then the other to lower herself slowly.

Climbing. By 12 months, most babies can climb at least 30cm (12in) at a time. Steps are a great place to practise. With a safety gate at the third step, put your baby into a crawling position at the bottom landing, put an enticing toy on the top step, and show him how to extend his hands and slide his knees forwards to climb up to it.

Alternating feet. To help a youngster master this skill needed for walking, get her to straddle a scooter. Show her how to push her feet to make it move forwards.

Cruising. Children make their way around the room using furniture to steady themselves. To encourage cruising, put an enticing toy on a coffee table a few centimetres beyond the reach of the child when he is standing up, holding onto the table.

Walking. Timid souls may be reluctant to let go of steadying objects, so they walk a bit later. While a toddler is standing up holding onto a piece of furniture, sit just out of reach and call her to you. Catch her before she falls and exclaim, 'Wow! My baby's walking!' When she's confident enough to let go for half a step, expand the distance a little.

Running. Clear an area in the house where the toddler can practise this important skill. Your decor may suffer if you must push furniture against the wall of a small living room to make space, but your child's development and safety are definitely more important! Eliminate the lumps from the carpeting and use non-slip rugs to soften hardwood and tile floors.

Jumping. You may need to demonstrate and help your toddler until he figures out what, for him, is a complex movement. After demonstrating, grasp the child under the arms, lift him up a few centimetres, lower him until his feet touch the ground and then quickly lift him back up. Repeat several times.

If a sedentary toddler shuns physical activity, he may need some incentives to get proper exercise. Parents can enroll themselves and their toddler in a baby gym class. Check the newspaper, local magazines, private gyms and spas, and early childhood education programmes for leads. Friends with toddlers are good sources of information, too.

Galloping. This is a more advanced skill for toddlers closer to the age of three. Do it in slow motion first. The trick to galloping is to make sure that one foot always lands flat on the ground while the other foot remains bent so the child lands on the ball of his foot, without pressing down on the heel. Show him how to step forward, place his whole foot on the ground, then move the other foot forwards and step down on the ball of the foot before moving the first foot forwards again.

Skipping. Skipping involves combining walking and hopping, so the motion is step-hop-step. This is unusual in a toddler, but it can occur.

Stationary Gross Motor Skills

These skills include stretching, bending, turning and twisting. If not every day, at least once a week:

Play follow-the-leader. Encourage your toddler to copy you as you reach for the sky, touch your toes, move your arms like windmills or turn to look behind you.

Put on a children's exercise video or encourage your toddler to dance with the kids on *Tweenies* or copy *Teletubbies*.

Turn on some music and dance. Do it freestyle. Do the twist. Do it fast and slow and every which way to any music your child likes.

Manipulation Gross Motor Skills

A variety of activities help children improve their ability to coordinate their legs, feet, arms and hands:

Kicking. Spare the furniture and his toys. Tie some rags together with string to make a large ball, and let the fun begin!

Striking. Besides children's tool kits and workbenches, try attaching empty cotton reels to a board with large nails. Instead of pounding the nails all the way in, provide a toy hammer so she can spend the next five years finishing the job herself. Alternatively, provide a plastic hammer she can use for pounding plastic golf tees into expanded polystyrene.

Throwing. Roll up a pair of socks to throw and set up a paper plate to use as a target. Or use a clothes basket, shoebox or bucket for beanbag tossing. When you weary of socks and beanbags, toss lids from cottage cheese cartons into a pot. For a very young toddler, put the target on the floor at their feet. Continue to move it a few centimetres further away as their skill improves.

Catching. Show your child how to extend and steady his arms while you toss a large soft ball into them from a distance of 30–60cm (1–2 ft).

Rolling. Sit on the floor facing each other, and roll a foam rubber ball back and forth.

When toddlers receive information via the senses, the spinal cord carries it to the brain. The brain interprets the information, decides how to react, and sends commands back down the spinal cord telling the muscles or internal organs exactly what to do. If an adult sees a toy on the floor, experience tells him the toy is an obstacle. A toddler doesn't have the benefit of such experience. He will need to trip over a few things before his brain can correctly interpret these kinds of threats.

Misunderstandings and Misbehaviour

If toddlers avoid crashing into the chair but lose their balance and hit the floor, it may take a few seconds for their brains to interpret the pain signals, which are arriving from a different part of the body than they had expected. It will take another few seconds for their brain to communicate with their throat and eyes so they can let out a large wail and begin to cry. Don't conclude your child isn't hurt because he didn't start crying at once. If the child isn't injured, provide comfort by helping him up and telling him he's OK. Let him think through what just happened rather than admonishing him to 'be more careful'. To avoid collisions, clear an area of your home where your toddler can run safely or provide an opportunity each day to play outside.

Perhaps an example will help you understand just how a toddler's mind and body interacts. If a toddler is reaching for a freshly iced cake sitting on the table and hears his mother yelling, 'Don't touch!', his natural response is to turn his face towards the sound. Then, when he sees that Mother is addressing him, he must figure out what she's trying to tell him. Once he comprehends that her words refer to his hand reaching for the cake and realizes that she wants him to stop, he must work out which muscles to contract and which to relax to get that little hand to drop to his lap. By then, the hand may well be covered with icing.

If a child is approaching serious danger, such as heading towards the top of the stairs, grab her! She won't be able to comprehend a verbal warning in enough time to avoid the danger.

It's understandable that a parent who doesn't have a grasp of toddler development gets very upset in this situation. After all, she said, 'Don't touch', and her toddler looked straight at her and stuck his hand in the cake. It's tough enough to have the problem of a ruined cake and an icing-covered toddler. The anger that comes from believing the toddler has deliberately misbehaved can cause the mother to punish her child, which leaves the toddler feeling upset without even understanding what he did wrong. So instead of attributing evil intentions to toddler misbehaviour, be considerate of their inability to process information quickly, and above all, be patient.

Clumsy Kids

Difficulty coordinating large and small muscle groups and/or a lack of clarity about physical boundaries cause clumsiness – and both causes are basic characteristics of toddlers. The usual solution is years of practice. The school of hard knocks will teach them exactly where their body leaves off and the rest of the world begins.

However, some toddlers have a high threshold for pain, so the usual bumps and bruises don't teach them to stop before colliding with the chair, the end table or the ground – or even with themselves. They step on their own feet and their own hand thumps them in the jaw. They may cry each time it happens, but they are so readily distracted that they forget to watch what they're doing and the same or similar accidents keep recurring. 'Careful!' 'Look out!' 'Don't hurt yourself!' 'Next time, watch where you're going', their hapless parents repeat as these seeming daredevils continue to knock and scrape and batter themselves in their heedlessly rough-and-tumble play.

But children aren't daredevils if they don't comprehend the risk. Warnings work only if youngsters know what to do to prevent another injury. They learn from their mistakes only if their intellect enables them to remember what went wrong last time, to work out what to do differently when the same situation arises, and to concentrate to avoid a repetition of the same problem.

If warnings and frequent bumps don't slow your youngster down, provide comfort after she's been injured, and then encourage her to repeat the same movement, but this time without hurting herself. Praise her for being successful. Multiplied over many situations, this kind of concentrated teaching can help toddlers tune into the position of their bodies and be more aware of the proximity of their limbs, head and torso to other objects. Meanwhile, encourage better body awareness by combining song and movement, such as 'The Hokey Cokey'.

Some experts say swimming lessons before the age of four don't help children learn faster because of the limitations of their central nervous systems and muscle development. Still, water babies' classes can be lots of fun and encourage them to stretch their little muscles.

The Pincer Grasp

Fine motor coordination involves the muscles of the finger, hand, mouth, face and throat. The pincer grasp – the ability to pick up small objects with the thumb and forefinger – is what separates humans from other animals. It enables children to do everything from button a shirt to manipulate a pencil.

Young toddlers begin developing their pincer grasp by picking up and manipulating toys and household objects in the course of normal play. Toddler toys are large not only to prevent youngsters from swallowing them, but also because poor coordination makes it difficult for them to pick up very small objects.

Provide toys in a variety of interesting colours, shapes and textures to encourage your child to practise this important skill. By 18 months, tots should be ready for more concentrated practice. The following toys and activities can help:

Play dough. Even 12-month-olds will enjoy making designs in a play dough pancake by poking at it with straws and plastic spoons, so you may want to make a batch (see the recipe in Chapter 11).

Drawing. Toddlers' early artistic productions don't look like much. But they enjoy manipulating pencils, markers and crayons and practising fine motor coordination in the process. Don't praise their work. The point isn't what they did – it's the doing of it!

Tongs. Give your toddler a pair of kitchen tongs and show her how to pick up small toys and place them in a tin or box.

Cheerios. Have your child feed herself dry breakfast cereal from a bag. Break off a small piece of cereal or cracker and hold it on your palm. To take it from you, she will have to use her thumb and forefinger.

Peas. Let your toddler eat his peas without help. Whether he picks them up and puts them directly into his mouth or uses a spoon, peas offer lots of concentrated practice to develop the pincer grasp.

Don't put any money on whether you're raising a little left-hander until the age of three. Even then you may lose, because many children don't settle on a hand preference for another few years. About 20 per cent never do, and remain ambidextrous.

Work Those Facial Muscles

Toddlers develop strength and coordination by chewing, vocalizing and talking. If children are not yet talking, encourage them to babble. Take turns making funny sounds. Making funny faces also encourages tots to use their facial muscles. This is a good time for lots of clowning.

Because the muscles in the face, mouth and throat are poorly developed, even soft food can cause toddlers to choke if they stuff their mouths – and it's inevitable that sooner or later they will do just that.

Taking a first-aid course that teaches abdominal thrusts could be one of the best decisions of your life – doing them wrong can cause injury.

The soft spot in the front of a child's skull shouldn't be noticeable after 18 months. The skull plates continue to grow as the brain increases in size. They don't fuse until brain growth slows at about two.

Brand-New Teeth

Most children have some teeth when they enter the toddler years, and by age three, many have a full set (FIGURE 3-1). Beginning around six months, the two lower middle teeth appear. Next, the two upper middle teeth (the incisors) come in. Then the teeth on either side of the two front teeth appear (more incisors), followed by more bottom teeth. By the age of two, most children have 16 teeth. However, both the timing and pattern can vary dramatically. Eventually they should end up with ten on top and ten on the bottom.

These baby teeth, also called milk teeth or primary teeth, will gradually be replaced by a set of permanent ones beginning after the age of five. The health of the baby teeth affects the permanent teeth, so they need to be well cared for.

Toddlers will need parents to brush their teeth for them until they are coordinated enough to make the proper motions. (At the first dental checkup, typically at three years, the dentist may give them a lesson.) To teach proper brushing techniques, parents can simply place their hand over their toddler's and guide them through the process. Expect toddlers to chew and otherwise mangle the toothbrush bristles. Overleaf are some tips to make brushing teeth easier for you and your child.

FIGURE 3-1:

A: Central incisors
(6–10 months)

B: Lateral incisors
(10–13 months)

C: Canine
(17–23 months)

D: First baby molar
(14–18 months)

E: Second baby
molar
(23–31 months)

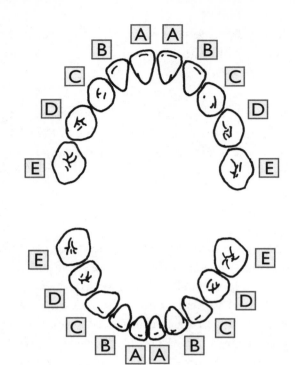

- Use a soft-bristled child-size brush. If you buy several, you can let the toddler choose which to use at each brushing.
- Brush a doll or teddy's teeth first to give your toddler a chance to witness what is going on and become comfortable with the idea.
- Use your child's natural urge to mimic by brushing your teeth while she brushes hers.
- Provide a pea-size spot of toothpaste (choose a brand formulated for children; adult toothpaste is too strong), and try to keep her from swallowing it.
- After she's finished, give her a once-over lightly to make sure the job is done properly, especially at bedtime.
- Schedule a trip to the dentist, then cloak yourself in the voice of authority: remind your child that the dentist said she must brush her teeth every day to keep them healthy.

'Where Do I Come From?'

One day, precocious 33-month-old Jamie asked the question many parents dread: 'Mum, where do I come from?' Jamie's parents had promised each other that when The Question arose, instead of resorting to the stork story, they would give an accurate recounting. And since Jamie was a boy, they decided his father would be in charge of teaching him the facts of life. With a red face and occasional stammer, Dad began fumbling through the tale of Daddy's seed and Mummy's egg, praying Jamie wouldn't ask exactly how Daddy puts the seed there. Mum listened for a bit, then interrupted. 'Jamie, you come from Battersea', she said. Jamie nodded and returned his attention to his toy piano.

There are three morals to this story:

1. Find out exactly what information your toddler is requesting before trying to answer his question.
2. In general, less information is better. Let toddlers ask if they want to know more.
3. Don't overwhelm either of you by serving up more information than your toddler is ready to hear.

Gender Issues

A few differences between the sexes seem to be innate. For instance, toddler boys tend to be more active and fussier than girls. Although boys don't actually cry more, their sleep tends to be more disturbed. As a group, girls' language skills develop faster than boys'. Girls also develop bladder and bowel control a few months earlier.

Of course, these are tendencies and group averages. The differences vanish when individual children are considered. There are lots of calm, moderate-energy boys who sleep soundly and are potty trained at an early age. Lots of active, fussy little female insomniacs reach their fourth or fifth birthday before they make it through the night without wetting the bed. Most differences are due to how boys and girls are brought up. When 12-month-old boys build towers out of blocks and zoom toy cars across the floor, for example, research has shown that parents nod, smile and praise them more than when little girls do the same thing. The older boys get, the more support they receive for playing with 'boy' toys, and the more they are subtly or actively discouraged from playing with Cinderella. Parents are less upset and react less intensely when girls cross the gender line in their choice of play activities.

Adults typically talk to boys and girls very differently. They subtly encourage boys' independence, offering more support when they head off to explore, and providing the kind of guidance that helps them solve problems themselves. In contrast, adults typically provide girls with fewer problem-solving tools by ignoring them more or by solving problems for them. Studies show that adults are more likely to use baby talk with girls than with boys, employing diminutive forms like 'doggy' or 'dolly' nearly twice as often.

Guys and Dolls: Teaching the Stereotypes

It is not possible to predict what sexual orientation a toddler will ultimately adopt. It is normal for toddlers of both sexes to imitate the behaviour of both parents. Sensitive boys with tastes that run more to the artistic than the athletic will have a harder time developing comfort with their masculinity if their parents cannot accept these traits, and instead try to push them into more macho roles.

When children of either sex play with baby dolls, they are doing what they see parents, childminders and nursery staff do: take care of babies. Baby dolls can be helpful to boys as well as girls in several ways. They provide practice nurturing and taking care of a baby, enhance feelings of closeness to parents, and prepare toddlers for coping with uncomfortable situations. Dolls can also help older toddlers resolve their feelings about trying situations and traumas. After imagination has developed and before children can talk effectively about their problems, re-enacting upsetting events through play helps children work through anxieties and come to terms with troubling emotions. Playing with dolls doesn't turn boys into homosexuals any more than it turns girls into lesbians.

Core gender identity is formed during the toddler years. Children may go through phases of being a Mummy's boy or Daddy's girl and regularly mimic the behaviour of both men and women, but by two years old they should have a conception of themselves as being male or female. Three-year-olds usually identify with the same-sex parent, which is often reflected in their stance, the way they walk, their gestures and some of their speech patterns. Toddlers typically identify people's sex by their peripheral characteristics, such as clothing, hairstyle or use of make-up; they don't have a real conception of what it means to be male or female. To increase identification, the same-sex parent should:

· Spend more time engaging in activities the child enjoys, since this can strengthen the parent–child bond.
· Be more accepting and less critical, since children emulate people they feel close to.
· Be kinder towards a spouse. (Children are protective of both parents, and commonly align themselves with the one they feel is being picked on or unfairly attacked.)

Sugar and Spice

Most modern parents want to avoid raising their children in accordance with old gender stereotypes. They want their daughters to have a positive self-image, be comfortable asserting themselves and have wider career aspirations. They want their sons to be able to express a range of emotions, nurture others and cooperate as well as compete. However, researchers say it is almost inevitable that parents will pass on the sexism they've absorbed from the culture at large because so much of it is unconscious. Other research has demonstrated the following:

· Parents react differently to videotapes of toddlers engaged in routine play. For instance, subjects describe a child's response to a jack-in-the-box as 'fearful' if they're told the little one is a girl, but 'angry' if they're told the child is a boy.

- Most parents are now OK with little gun-toting girls, and are far more comfortable than in decades past when little females oversee Duplo, Lego, Brio and building-block construction sites. But many still squirm when a boy expresses more than passing interest in a doll or dresses up in a girl's clothes.
- Parents display more pleasure and spend more time interacting when their little boy tosses a foam rubber ball in the house than when their little girl does the very same thing.
- Girls receive more encouragement for holding tea parties and playing house.
- When the daily dose of words and hugs is tallied, nursery-school teachers respond far more often to boys than to girls.
- Gender stereotyping on TV remains intense; it doesn't take kids long to work out who is supposed to want My Little Ponies and Hot Wheels.
- In disputes over toys, adults commonly urge little girls to 'share', and reprimand them for taking a boy's toy. Adults help little boys 'protect their patch' by helping them fend off interlopers who try to take their toys.

That's So Cute!

The differences in the way adults respond to cutely dressed kids shows how subtle but powerful sexist stereotypes are transmitted. When one little miss entered a nursery school dressed to the nines, the staff clucked, 'Aren't you sweet!' 'You're so cute!' 'Isn't she lovely!' The belle of the toddler crowd smiled and wiggled with delight. A moment later a little boy entered the same school. He, too, was all dressed in a coordinated outfit. The same staff members clucked, 'What a lovely little sweater!' 'Such cute trousers.' 'Look at those sweet elephants!' The little boy leaned over to study the embroidered elephants trudging across the front of his sweater. The messages unwittingly conveyed to these children were clear: when she dresses up, she is cute; her clothes merge with her and together form her identity. When he dresses up, his clothes are cute, but the clothes remain separate from him and he continues being who he is.

Parents as Role Models

It's not just the differential treatment from adults that instils sexism at such a tender age, researchers say. All toddlers need to do is observe the daily household routine to see that most mothers devote more time to food, clothing, cleanliness and children's feelings, while fathers are chiefs when it comes to maintaining gardens, cars and rules. (If spouses argue about who doesn't do enough of what around the house, watching who-does-what when their child starts playing house can settle it.)

Given that most youngsters are exposed to adult sexuality via TV shows, music videos and advertisements, it isn't surprising that curiosity runs high, or that many try to mimic the behaviour they see. This is yet another reason to monitor – and limit – children's TV viewing.

Even when 'Mr Mum' is responsible for the household and the mother is the breadwinner, men relate to children differently than women do. For example, women tend to carry infants facing in, towards their chest, while men more often carry them facing out so they can see the world.

It should come as no surprise that by 24 months toddlers are adhering to their sugar-and-spice versus puppy-dog-tail roles. If they're not, she's probably being labelled a 'tough nut', rather than a self-possessed little girl, while adults are probably running out of patience with his tendency to wear his heart on his sleeve, and are searching for ways to help him develop a thicker skin.

Toddlers Are Sexual Beings

Taboos around childhood sexuality remain strong. The past practice of admonishing toddlers that touching 'down there' would land them an eternity in hell has largely disappeared, to be replaced by the myth that only youngsters who have been sexually abused engage in sexual exploration or activities, or display a keen interest in sexual matters. Thus, instead of considering toddler's sexuality to be immoral, many view it as an indication of 'sickness', or a symptom of post-traumatic stress.

In truth, toddlers are sexual beings, though not in the adult sense. Their genitals are very sensitive, so they readily discover that the physical sensations produced by touching and rubbing are pleasant. Fondling the genitals for comfort is also common. Some youngsters may also hold themselves in hopes of stopping themselves from urinating. It also is common for little boys to have erections. When little girls see naked boys, many express concerns about their own lack of a penis. To reassure them, parents can simply explain that little girls have a clitoris and vagina instead. Girls grow into women, and only women can have babies. Babies grow inside the mother's body and pass through the vagina when they're ready to be born.

Answer your toddler's questions in a straightforward manner:

Q: 'Why is Daddy's penis so big and mine so small?'

A: 'Daddy is bigger everywhere. When you grow up, your feet, hands and penis will be big, too.'

Q: 'Why don't I have a penis like Daddy?'

A: 'Girls have a vagina. Boys have a penis.'

Q: 'Where do babies come from?'

A: 'They grow inside a mother's uterus until they're big enough to be born.'

Parents will have to handle sexual issues in accordance with their personal beliefs. The best approach seems to be to teach youngsters the social rules: masturbation is something to be done in private. Telling toddlers that they should only touch themselves when they are in the bathroom or bedroom and must refrain when around other people can be as straightforward as telling them that it's not nice to belch at the dinner table. If parents can be calm and matter-of-fact in discussing sexual issues, children will feel freer to turn to them with future questions.

Let Me Be Naked!

Lots of toddlers decide clothes are something they'd rather do without. Every time parents turn around, they find their little one has managed to wriggle out of her clothes again. The dislike of clothing isn't surprising. If children are warm enough, they will feel much more comfortable with the freedom of movement that comes from being in bare skin. It may not be a problem if toddlers want to run around the house in their birthday suits, although this can get pretty messy if they're not toilet-trained. (That's an incentive some parents have successfully used with determined strippers: if you use the toilet, birthday suits are allowed at home.)

Regardless of what policies are in force at home, parents should insist that toddlers observe the social niceties of keeping their clothes on outside the house. Even if you don't care, other parents will be offended. Dressing toddlers in blouses that button up the back and trousers with belts, and double-knotting shoelaces can slow down little strippers so parents can catch them before they completely disrobe.

However, there's no need to be upset or to shame them about it. Since they're too young to comprehend adult views on the subject, instilling guilt might make them feel that their body is bad or dirty. It should be enough to firmly state 'Undressing outside the house is a no-no' and to put their clothes back on again and again until they get the message. Don't comfort them if they howl; there are times when staying dressed is non-negotiable. Also, avoid attempting to make re-dressing fun. Otherwise, they may conclude that removing their clothes is a way to initiate a great game.

Potty Mouth

Children only use words they have heard someone else say. If the naughty words have come from outside the household, the best strategy is simply to ignore them, which makes it likely that they'll go away. Otherwise, you'll spark your toddler's curiosity about the magic of a word to make you laugh or get angry, increasing the likelihood that he'll use it more often. Even if naughty words don't bother you, they can upset teachers, other parents and children enough to dampen your youngster's social life.

If the offensive words don't disappear on their own, or if she's using words she's heard at home, eliminate these no-no's from the family vocabulary before they become a habit. Tell your child that saying that word is a no-no and provide a brief time-out. To help yourself and other family members clean up their vocabularies, say 'Oops, somebody just said a no-no', and put your child in charge of walking the offender to his or her bedroom for a brief time-out.

Parental Nudity

There's nothing to indicate that young toddlers are in any way harmed by exposure to parental nudity. However, they will undoubtedly have questions and may want to touch, too, so be prepared.

As children approach the age of three, many become uncomfortable about witnessing the nudity of the opposite-sexed parent. Whether this is because they are experiencing conflict about their emerging sexual feelings towards that parent, as some psychologists believe, or because the societal taboos they have absorbed conflict with what is happening at home, it is important to respect their wish for boundaries. Eliminate joint father/daughter and mother/son baths, and close the bathroom door and oust little ones of the opposite sex from the room before changing.

Sexual Abuse

The definition of sexual abuse accepted by most child welfare professionals includes acts of exposing children to sexual stimuli that are developmentally inappropriate. Parents place themselves at risk of being accused if they allow toddlers to witness parents having sex, touch parents' genitals, watch adult films or view other pornographic materials. Symptoms commonly displayed by sexually abused children include:

· Mimicking adult sexual behaviour.
· Possessing sexual knowledge and vocabulary beyond what is normal for the child's age.

- Engaging in persistent sexual play (commonly with dolls, other children, pets or themselves).
- Having abrasions, pain, bleeding or swelling of the mouth, genitals or anus.
- Having an obsession with touching or poking objects into the genitals or anus.
- Incurring unexplained urinary tract or vaginal infections.
- Suffering from a sexually transmitted disease.
- Making direct or indirect comments about having been molested.
- Displaying a sudden, exaggerated upset over being touched when having a nappy changed, being bathed or helped to the potty, or during physical examinations.
- Suddenly manifesting phobias or exaggerated fearfulness around particular people or in specific locations.
- Experiencing frequent nightmares.

If a parent suspects sexual abuse and there is no physical evidence, discovering the truth can be difficult. Given children's propensity for saying what they think parents want to hear, and the ease with which false memories are implanted, it's best to consult a professional with expertise in interviewing children, and let him or her ask the questions.

Youngsters need not be physically injured during molestation to suffer severe psychological repercussions. The aura of secrecy can be upsetting. Threats of retaliation against the child or a loved one for revealing what has transpired can produce significant trauma. If you suspect sexual abuse, consult a professional immediately.

Protection Against Sexual Predators

It is so easy for adults to manipulate and physically overpower toddlers that trying to teach them about bad people who hurt children won't enable little ones to protect themselves – and it can terrify them. In 90 per cent of sexual molestation cases, the abuser is well known to the child.

The concept of keeping secrets is hard enough for toddlers to grasp. Don't complicate it by urging them to keep secrets about birthday surprises or anything else. It will be impossible for them to differentiate secrets that are OK from secrets that are not OK. When youngsters are old enough to understand, they can be taught that some secrets are OK and others are not, and that they must inform you immediately if someone tries to get them to keep a secret from you. In the meantime:

· Keep track of your child's whereabouts at every moment and leave him or her with trustworthy caregivers.
· Instruct your older toddler to be sure to tell you if anyone touches him or her in a way he or she doesn't like.
· Teach your children the correct names of all body parts, including 'penis' and 'vagina', so that if something untoward does occur, they will have the words they need to communicate.

Societies Differ

Exactly what constitutes abuse? In societies where families sleep in the same room, youngsters routinely witness parents' sexual intimacies without ill effect. However, children are born imitators, and their playground re-enactment of bedroom scenes may be a problem in countries with more conservative sexual norms.

In Western societies, any unnecessary touching of genitals is regarded as abuse. When youngsters reach adolescence and reflect on what transpired, they realize that a sacred parent–child trust was broken. Many spend their lives trying to heal from the devastation.

CHAPTER 4

Brain Power

In this school of life, the most important learning takes place in the principal classroom: the home. The textbooks are the objects around toddlers and the events that transpire as they make their way through each day. Parents and caregivers are the principal teachers. The majority of lessons occur via independent study. As toddlers look, listen, prod, poke, wave, clang, roll, tear, bang, pat, sniff and mimic others, they learn. Field trips, including everything from walking down the road to accompanying parents on errands, enrich the curriculum by giving them glimpses of the greater world.

Absorbent Minds

Toddlers' ability to soak up vast quantities of information is legendary. Maria Montessori, the founder of the famous developmentally based Montessori schools, calls the early childhood years the time of the 'Absorbent Mind'. More brain growth occurs during these 24 months than during any other period. The combination of brain development and daily learning accounts for their dramatic gains in understanding, remembering, thinking, reasoning and solving problems. In two short years, the foundation is laid for all future learning.

Daily Living Skills

Between 12 and 36 months, the educational curriculum for toddlers is focused on learning important daily living skills. These skills include washing their hands, eating, putting on their clothes, picking up their toys, brushing their teeth and using the toilet.

But these important units of instruction constitute only a fraction of the daily living skills little ones work on. When toddlers wipe the end table with a small rag while an adult dusts, or follow a parent around the lawn with a toy lawnmower while gardening is being done, they are exposed to some of the general methods and specific skills they will need to care for an entire house one day.

Toddlers' dedication to learning is so intense that they are veritable super-students. Many are so enthusiastic they don't want to pause to eat, sleep or even go to the toilet.

Parents: The Roles

Just as toddlers are born students who are genetically programmed to learn, parents are programmed to teach. Without even stopping to consider what they are doing, parents automatically begin imparting the knowledge needed to master a host of important daily living skills.

Just look more closely at exactly what you do to teach a skill like handwashing, and you will realize that you can teach toddlers almost everything they need to know:

1. You explain exactly what needs to be done. ('Let's wash your hands before you eat.')
2. You give instructions. ('Put your hands all the way under the water.' 'Let's get some soap on the backs of your hands, too.')
3. You set limits to reinforce the idea that people must continue caring for themselves, whether they feel like it at a given moment or not. ('I know you don't want your hands washed just now, but they're sticky.')
4. You provide feedback. ('That looks good.' 'Oops, your hands still have some spots of chocolate. We need to get those off, too.')
5. You help when your child is having a hard time. ('Try rubbing your hands together.' 'Let's put on a little more soap.')

As toddlers progress, parents do less for them and spend more time monitoring and giving feedback to help them improve. Parents still need to participate actively in helping three-year-olds with basic self-care skills, but youngsters aged from one to three can make great progress in handling many self-care tasks.

Parents: The Responsibility

It's obvious that you will often feel less than enthusiastic about your endless teaching duties. Sometimes you will be as discouraged as a classroom teacher on a Friday afternoon in June. Even pedagogues voted Teacher of the Year are sometimes overwhelmed by their students' apparent failure to grasp what they are trying to teach.

Doubts about having entered the child-rearing business may surface when a parent walks into the bathroom and discovers water all over the floor and dripping down the walls while a proud toddler stands in the middle of a puddle, drying her freshly washed hands. Or when the tot has decided to change clothes and is now clad in an inside-out shirt, mismatched socks, shoes that are on the wrong feet, and no trousers.

At such moments it is easy to be so impressed by the extra work that the toddler has caused that her accomplishment is forgotten or, even worse, belittled. But it is important to acknowledge the toddler's initiative in tackling these kinds of self-assigned homework tasks, even if you don't feel inclined to award extra marks for a project so poorly done.

Getting an A Grade

Daily living skills are like maths problems. Although there may be several routes to solving a problem and there may be more than one correct answer, there are definitely right and wrong ways to do things. The end result can be very good, satisfactory, mediocre or very far off the mark.

Often students approach a maths problem correctly and still get the answer wrong. With daily living skills, toddlers can go through all the right motions with soap and water, make a giant mess, and still not get their hands clean. Mistakes often occur because the task was simply too advanced for the toddler to handle alone, or perhaps he misunderstood the directions or needed more instruction and more practice. You must remember that no toddler wants to fail or get a poor mark. In fact, every child wants to do things correctly, to get an A in his own, as well as in his parents', eyes. When things go wrong, you need to affirm the toddler's efforts, decide what the toddler needs to learn to improve and dedicate yourself to giving remedial instruction.

And of course, you will have to clean up many toddler messes. But since cleaning up is yet another daily living skill, be sure to enlist your toddler's assistance so he can begin learning how.

Problem-Solving Skills

Since there are right and wrong ways to wash hands, brush teeth, get dressed, pick up toys and so on, parents must actively teach and constantly give feedback to help toddlers progress in mastering daily living skills. However, when it comes to mastering other intellectual tasks, it is important to let them do the work by themselves, instead of giving them the answers.

When children manipulate blocks, they learn about size and shape, weight and mass. They solve a series of visual–spatial relationship problems and develop hand-to-eye coordination in the process. If an adult jumps in and manoeuvres the toddler's hand to help stack his blocks, he is distracted from the important preliminary lessons he was working on. He may not yet be ready to tackle the more advanced problem of using mass to counter the effects of gravity to create a stack.

Hands-on help with toys may seem to speed learning, but it actually deprives toddlers of the opportunity to develop the intellect that comes from figuring out how to solve problems; the self-confidence that comes from solving problems without help; and the educational benefit that comes from learning how to learn.

When a child is engrossed in a toy, try not to interrupt. What looks like 'just playing' is actually a toddler working at his own pace on important work. However, if a child is sitting down with a toy and becoming restless or bored with it, this is a good time to provide a demonstration. Show the toddler how to operate the toy while she watches, but don't grasp your child's hand to help her manipulate the toy. Give multiple demonstrations if you wish, but don't try to get your toddler to imitate you. This way the child doesn't feel pressured to perform. She can continue to use the toy in her own way and work at her own pace. She is free to attempt to imitate your way when she is ready, but she will have used her own mind to figure out the solution to a problem when she eventually copies your demonstration.

Maths Skills

Important maths skills for toddlers are much more complex than learning to say 'One, two, three'. To most toddlers, counting aloud is no more than a series of nonsense syllables that mean about as much to them as 'Zog, jib, oomp'. The keys to maths include understanding spatial relationships, understanding cause/effect logic and learning to solve problems with physical objects. When children can point to objects as they count them, they've accomplished a major feat!

To help toddlers learn the real meaning of counting, read them *Kipper's Book of Counting* by Mick Inkpen (Hodder Children's Books). Long before they're ready for the number concepts, they'll love this book.

Different play activities emphasize different intellectual skills. Children practise convergent thinking skills when they work on tasks that have one right answer, such as fitting a piece into a puzzle, sorting blocks by colour or organizing nesting toys so they fit inside one another. Children practise divergent thinking skills when they work on tasks with many solutions, such as building things with blocks or engaging in creative games, such as playing house. Be sure your child has lots of opportunity to practise both.

Building Self-Esteem

When a parent physically moves a toddler's hand to provide assistance with a toy and then gushes 'You did it', the parent is reinforcing the idea that this is what the toddler is to do. When the toddler attempts to repeat the action on her own, she may fail. If so, that will undermine her self-esteem. Toddlers often show that they are feeling overwhelmed by suddenly abandoning the toy the parent has been trying to help them with.

Consider what would happen if a teacher placed a nursery-school pupil in a Year Three numeracy class and gave her the correct answers to ensure she passed the first test. It wouldn't take the student long to realize that she can't do long-division problems on her own. At that point, she might want to give up on maths altogether. Similarly, after a well-meaning parent tries to ensure that a toddler solves a problem he hasn't yet even fathomed, the tot is likely to become discouraged if he discovers he can't do it himself.

On the other hand, if a Year Three pupil is trying to learn long division and is stuck, she certainly deserves more intensive assistance.

Provide hands-on help if your child is trying to achieve a particular goal and is becoming frustrated, or signals a need for help.

The Art of Teaching

Successful teaching is as much art as science. It requires watching the child's struggles and reactions carefully to make better decisions about when to present new material, and when and how to intervene. Parents who are too quick to extricate the toddler's ball from under the sofa deprive her of figuring it out for herself. On the other hand, parents who hang back too long may find that the youngster gets upset, gives up and moves on to a less challenging activity, thereby learning to handle difficult problems by avoiding them together.

Sorting out a child's needs is not easy. Some toddlers become more easily frustrated than others. They may need a lot of verbal encouragement and require more hands-on help than calmer, more easy-going youngsters. Some toddlers are more independent. They may find verbal encouragement more of a distraction than a learning aid, and may become frustrated when parents try to provide hands-on help.

Never wrestle toys away from a toddler or say 'Just a minute' while the youngster begs for his toy so you can do a demonstration. This kind of bullying isn't helpful to young children.

Toddlers will react according to their moods, too, so the child who tends to become frustrated easily may continue to work independently when feeling especially mellow. Independent youngsters may collapse into balls of helplessness if they're having a difficult day. Watch your interventions and your toddler's reactions carefully to determine when to step in and when to back off. If you find yourself saying things such as 'You've been just playing all day. It's time to do x, y or z now', you're not grasping the mental effort that goes into toddler 'play'.

Educational Toys

Ah, it would be so easy to move your toddler's arm or hand or finger to show her exactly what motions to make to operate a toy. But every toy is educational, so don't take the education out of the fun. Unless your child has a physical disability or is so frustrated that it looks as if she's about to give up, confine yourself to picking up the toy yourself and demonstrating. Then let your child tackle the problem again in hopes she can use her own mind to figure out how it works; for example:

· How much pressure must be used to push the button so the buzzer will sound.
· How far to pull the string to make the doll talk.
· How high to lift the beater to make the xylophone notes play.
· How to turn and position the puzzle piece to fit it into the slot.
· How to turn the handle to make the jack-in-the-box pop up.
· How to steady and balance the blocks to make a stack.
· How to create enough friction to make a toy car zoom across the floor.

When it comes to playing with toys, avoid saying 'Do it this way', followed by praise for doing it 'correctly'. Save those phrases for daily living skills.

Crafts: Not for Toddlers

Craft *materials* are great for toddlers to play with. So pull out the paste, sparkles, markers, paper, cotton balls, pipe cleaners, play dough, lolly sticks, paper plates and paints. As they manipulate the textures and colours and sizes and shapes, they'll learn a lot. Just don't try to get your toddler to use them to create a craft *project* of your (or anyone else's) imagining. The finished product may mean a lot to you, but it probably won't mean much to him. Toddlers are oriented towards the 'doing', not the 'having done'. Let them learn by interacting with the materials in their own way. Don't try to direct or control them.

'All Gone!'

It is hard for toddlers to grasp the concept of 'all gone'. For example, to a toddler, a peanut butter *jar* is the same thing as *peanut butter*. She can't comprehend that the empty jar means she can't have a peanut butter sandwich. To help her learn the difference:

· Let her explore the empty peanut butter jar.
· Try adopting her mindset and help her solve the problem by walking her through the steps: hand her the peanut butter jar and a non-sharp knife, and let her work on it.
· Make sure to also provide an emotional outlet by helping the toddler to express her frustrations. This can help her loosen her mental grip on the concept 'Mummy's mean and won't give me a peanut butter sandwich' so she can learn 'I'm angry because the peanut butter is all gone.'
· Remain on your toddler's side when discussing this mini-disaster, and say, 'Where's the peanut butter? You mean it's all gone? No more peanut butter! But my baby wants some! Wait! I know where it is. It's at the shop. We need to go to the shop to get peanut butter for you. But what are we going to do now? My baby wants peanut butter now! She could have some crackers. No? You only want peanut butter? It's all gone. We have to buy more peanut butter at the shop.'

If you react to your toddler's upsets by becoming upset and angry, you may only confirm her belief that you are purposely withholding the goodies. You need to be patient while explaining (again and again) 'It's all gone'. The combination of being allowed to look to see for herself and hearing a calm explanation will eventually help her realize that the problem isn't the parent's stubborn insistence on depriving her of what she wants.

The Concept of Categories

A lot of the intellectual work toddlers engage in involves learning to put objects and events into categories. For instance:

· Dogs, cats, birds and fish belong to the category of animals.
· Dogs, neighbours and classmates belong to the category of friends.
· Dogs, cats, mice and horses belong to the category of four-legged animals.

Parents automatically teach categories all the time without even thinking about it. 'What kind of vegetable should I cook for dinner?' they wonder aloud, 'I think I'll cook some peas'. This communicates that peas are vegetables, a category of food that is served at dinner. As toddlers learn the many different ways particular objects and actions can be categorized, they learn more about them. Understanding different ways that objects and events can be categorized forms the basis of abstract reasoning. Some experts consider abstract reasoning to be the highest form of intelligence.

When people look at one object and can imagine other uses for it, they engage in the kind of creative thought that leads to innovations. Innovations have brought human beings from campfires to microwaves, from horses to jet planes. To help youngsters develop intellectually, parents should target their teaching efforts to helping them learn different ways to categorize objects.

For instance, when toddlers learn that shoes are worn on feet and hats cover heads, they learn specific facts about two concrete objects: shoes and hats. Once youngsters comprehend the basic way in which two objects are *similar* – they both belong to a category called 'clothes' – they have learned an abstract concept. 'Clothes' doesn't refer to any one thing, but to a group of objects that are alike in one important respect: they protect or adorn the body.

Once children grasp an abstract concept such as 'clothes', it suddenly becomes possible for them to engage in creative thought. They can imagine ways to transform other objects into clothes and can place an upside-down pan on their head to turn it into a hat. A small blanket tossed over the shoulders can become a cape.

At first, little ones may categorize all four-legged creatures as 'dogs'. When parents show them pictures of dogs, point out dogs on the street and point out pictures of other four-legged animals and teach the names, toddlers are soon able to tell the difference between dogs and other animals. In fact, they will become so adept at categorizing that if they see pictures of different dogs that bear little resemblance to one another, they will still recognize that they are all dogs.

Any object can belong to many different categories. With help, toddlers eventually learn:

·   That a dog and a cow both belong in the category of animals.
·   That a dog, a cat and a budgie are all pets.
·   That a dog can be a friend, a protector, a danger or a nuisance, depending on the circumstances.

Learning about higher-level categories that require finer differentiation and more specific knowledge will take place in school. The information that dogs, whales and humans are all mammals usually isn't taught until infant school, though many toddlers would be capable of learning this if someone took the time to teach them.

By the age of three, toddlers should be familiar with many objects and a few concepts belonging to the following categories:

·   Parts of the body
·   Family members
·   Clothes
·   Rooms of the house
·   Foods
·   Toys
·   Animals
·   Colours
·   Shapes

- Emotions (happy, sad, angry, scared)
- Physical states (tired, hungry, thirsty, sore throat, tummy ache)
- Occupations (doctor, teacher, bus driver, firefighter, police officer)
- Comparisons (different, the same, good, better, worse, more, less)
- Locations (up, down, under, over, inside, next to, near, far)
- Size (big, small)
- Quantity (many, a few, none)
- Time relationships (now, later, first, then, before, after)
- Temperature (hot, cold, warm, cool)

Learning From Books

One of the reasons that picture books are so important for toddlers' intellectual development is that they give parents a convenient way to teach children about a wider variety of categories. By 12 months, children are ready for books that have information about a particular topic, such as animals, nature or transport. For example, a book on transport may have a picture of aeroplanes, cars, boats, helicopters, space ships and so on, to help children understand that these different objects are alike in an important respect: they are machines that move people and objects from one place to another. By the age of two, children are usually ready for books that have simple stories. A book about a trip on an aeroplane will teach children about related objects and activities, from pilots to seat belts and from take-offs to landings.

Category Errors

Toddlers make some predictable errors in categorization. For instance, many youngsters put every grown man they see into the category of 'daddy'. To help them understand that 'daddies' and 'men' belong to two different categories, follow these tips:

1. Correct their error.
2. Seize opportunities to point out various men over the next few days, and explain that the daddies are men with children.

3. Look at pictures in books and point out that bucks and fawns, tomcats and kittens, bulls and calves all belong to the categories of animal 'daddies' or 'children'.

4. While looking at pictures in books, help them grasp the many other ways men can be categorized: as tall, medium and short (when categorized by height); as fat, average, thin or skinny (when categorized by weight); as grandfathers, husbands, fathers or sons (depending on their relationship to others); as old men, young men and teenagers (depending on their ages).

Teaching Colours

Parents should teach toddlers the names of basic colours. Even adults may not be able to agree about whether the sofa is grey or blue, or blue or green. Muddy and mixed colours can also confuse toddlers, so parents should stick to the basic colours, such as red, yellow, blue and green. Variations like chartreuse and magenta may be better left for the nursery and infant school crowd. Here are tips for teaching colours:

· Use the names for colours in everyday conversation. ('See the white cat?' 'Pass me your red shirt.' 'Those yellow dandelions are so pretty.')
· Get children to help sort washing into white and coloured piles.
· Provide your child with crayons and markers for colouring.
· Show them how to sort their toys into different colour piles.
· When toddlers are finger-painting or colouring Easter eggs, demonstrate how some colours can be mixed to create others.
· Play the 'find the colour' game in the car. See how many red things the two of you can find, then how many green things and so on. Prepare for this game by having some cards with different colours on them, so the child can be sure about which colour he is to look for.
· Read *Spot's Favourite Colours* by Eric Hill (Frederick Warne), a board book for young toddlers. Another toddler favourite is *Elmer's Colours* by David McKee (Andersen Press).

If a child can't learn some colours, parents should consider the possibility of blue-green colour blindness. If he can't learn any, he may be completely colourblind. If you are worried , consult a doctor.

Shapes

Toddlers need to learn to recognize basic shapes, including squares, circles, triangles, hearts, diamonds and rectangles. (Once a child masters two shapes, you can add more.) Here are some tips for teaching shapes:

· Cut the basic shapes out of construction paper, draw them on blank note cards, or cut them out of biscuit dough and bake them. They should be about 5cm (2in) in diameter.
· Focus on two shapes at a time.
· Explain, 'This one is a square. Here's another square. But this one is a circle.' Holding a toddler's index finger while tracing the shapes can aid comprehension and help some youngsters remember them.
· Ask the toddler to point to the square, hand you the card with the square on it, or hand you the biscuit shaped like a square. If the child can talk, hold up a card or biscuit and ask the child to say the name of the shape.
· As you go through the day, point out other objects shaped like circles and squares, such as doorknobs, wheels, boxes, windows, tabletops etc.
· Get older toddlers to try to draw shapes. Don't expect much success.

Locations

Learning words like *up*, *above*, *down*, *under*, *over*, *inside*, *next to*, *near*, *far* and so on, is very hard for toddlers. Use them in your everyday expressions. Take some time for concentrated teaching, too:

Comment about locations regularly. ('The milk is *in* the refrigerator.' 'The milk is *on top of* the worktop.' 'The milk is *all over* the floor!')

Present two concepts. Pick up an object (such as a book) and a container (such as a box). 'The book is *in* the box. The apple is *on top of* the box.'

Then ask, 'Where is the book?' If the child responds by going over to retrieve the book, simply say, 'Yes, the book was *in* the box. Can you put it *on top of* the box?' Keep these games fun, and stop when your toddler loses interest.

Point out location relationships in picture books. ('The dog is *in* the house.' 'The dog is *on top of* his house.' 'The dog is *next to* the boy.')

Focus your child's attention on location relationships. When reading books, maintain a chatty narrative. (Where is the dog? Is he *in* the house? Yes, he's *inside* the house.' 'Where is the boy? There he is. Is he *on top of* the house? No, he's *inside* the house.')

Read *The Foot Book* by Dr Seuss. (Random House).

Toddlers cannot comprehend that some quantities are the same even though they look different. For instance, an adult can pour liquid from a tall narrow glass into a short fat one to show that both glasses hold the same quantity. Still, toddlers will still say that the tall narrow glass holds more than the short fat one.

Organizing

Organizing household possessions teaches children to categorize, so getting them to help with many routine household chores gives them a lot of practice. As soon as they are old enough, ask them to help you with tasks such as matching socks, putting toys into the correct containers before putting them into the toy box, putting clean cutlery into the correct compartment in the drawer, sorting cans and bottles and putting them into the correct recycling bin, and putting vegetables into the refrigerator when you return from grocery shopping.

Memory Bank Deposits

Being able to store and retrieve information keeps people from having to constantly relearn everything by enabling them to build on previous knowledge. Therefore memory is related to intelligence. Remembering is a skill that toddlers develop with maturity and practice. Remembering is a two-step process: storing information in the brain, then plucking it back out of storage.

There are two types of memory: short term and long term. Most everyday information goes into the short-term memory bank, where it remains briefly before disappearing. If information is repeated often enough, it gets moved from short-term memory into long-term memory, although a very intense experience sometimes creates an enduring memory.

The average adult can store about seven bits of information in short-term memory at a time – the length of a phone number. Because they have spent years encountering the same information again and again, adults have transferred massive amounts of data from short-term memory into their long-term memory. Therefore, they can readily recall amazing amounts of information, such as which drawer holds the socks or that the plates are kept in a particular cupboard.

Toddlers can have trouble retaining more than two bits of data. All of the thousands of bits of information that toddlers encounter each day are still very new to them. Until any given piece of information is repeated often enough to be transferred to long-term memory, toddlers will continue to forget many things that parents consider very basic. Because they will find some objects and experiences particularly impressive, they will also remember small details that may surprise parents.

Fragile Memories

Although toddlers are able to remember more with each passing month, their memories remain fragile. 'But you must remember Joshua. You played with him just last week,' a parent tells her daughter. But no, she doesn't seem to remember. And when she sees Joshua again, she is as shy as if she were meeting him for the first time. Yet this same child remembers seeing the big green lorry in the supermarket car park for ten seconds two weeks ago. Moreover, the ghouls and monsters that flitted across the TV screen when she was two suddenly come back to haunt her at three, even though she didn't seem to be affected by them at the time and hasn't seen them for months.

By 12 months old, an area of the brain called the hippocampus enables toddlers to remember events that occurred a few hours or a day before. Between 12 and 18 months, children can engage in deferred imitation; that is, repeating someone's behaviour hours, days or weeks later.

False Memories

Memories not only slip away from toddlers with amazing ease, but it is easy to implant false ones in their highly impressionable minds, according to research reported in the journal of *Consciousness and Cognition* (1994) and the *American Journal of Psychology* (1998). For instance, when researchers told three- and four-year-olds that an alligator had been eating an apple on an aeroplane, and later asked the children if they'd ever seen such a thing, they not only insisted that they had, they filled in the details: 'He was under my bed and he was a pet and then when we was on the aeroplane he licked me right here [gesturing to a spot on his thigh].'

What are false memories?
Toddlers have a hard time separating fantasy from reality. Children's inner imaginings mix with things they have heard or seen in the real world to create 'false memories', or remembrances that bear little or no resemblance to anything that actually transpired.

Toddlers are easily manipulated. If parents falsely accuse their youngster of having done something wrong, the toddler may believe she in fact is guilty and end up apologizing. In conducting interrogations, ask your toddler a question once and live with whatever answers you get. If you ask a second time, you may get the answer you expect, but it's not likely to be more reliable.

Familiar Comforts

Since toddlers' poor memories make even things they've been exposed to many times seem new and different, their love of rituals and predictable routines is understandable, as is the tenacity with which they cling to familiar blankets, toys and soothers. Just as adult travellers long for the comfort of familiar food after spending a few days surrounded by the heady stimulation of strange environments, recognized objects and routines offer toddlers a welcome respite by serving as comforting anchors.

Further, repetition helps toddlers move information into long-term memory. Hearing the same story night after night can be very trying for parents, but the continued exposure to the same words, phrases and ideas increases the toddler's ability to remember them.

Rhyme and Reason

Research shows that toddlers who hear the same nursery rhymes so often that they memorize them do better in school later on. The repetition is believed to help them to develop better memories – not just for the familiar rhymes, but also for remembering things in general. Break out the *Mother Goose* book and start reading, as nursery rhymes are invaluable teaching devices for several reasons:

- Rhythms appeal to toddlers.
- Hearing the same short poems over and over helps youngsters focus on individual words so they can eventually sort out their meanings.
- The rhymes help them notice how small changes in sound create completely different meanings (such as between 'hot' and 'pot' in 'Pease Porridge Hot').
- Children who can recite nursery rhymes by heart do better in reading at school than toddlers with less exposure.

Nursery rhymes that involve pairing movements and words, such as in 'This Little Piggy' and 'Intsy Wintsy Spider' are called 'finger play'. The movements help children decipher the meanings of the words while teaching them concepts, such as *up* and *down* (as when children move their fingers to show the spider going up the waterspout before swooping their arms down to show what happens when rain washes the spider out).

Here are a couple of classic finger-play poems your child will love:

♪ **This Little Piggy**

This little piggy went to market (wiggle your child's big toe)
This little piggy stayed home (wiggle the second toe)
This little piggy ate roast beef (wiggle the third toe)
This little piggy ate none (wiggle the fourth toe)
This little piggy cried 'Wee, wee, wee' all the way home! (wiggle the little
    toe, then tickle up your child's leg) ♫

♪ **Pat-a-Cake**

Pat-a-cake, pat-a-cake, baker's man (holding your child on your lap, clap
    her hands together in the rhythm of the verse)
Bake me a cake as fast as you can
Pat it, and roll it... (roll her arms)
And mark it with a B (hold her hand and use it like a pen to draw
    a B on her tummy)
And put it in the oven for Baby and me! (throw your arms open) ♫

When you need someone else to take over, put on a children's CD or
tape that has everything from 'One, Two, Buckle My Shoe' to 'The Wheels
on the Bus'.

Memory Gaps

A toddler walks into the nursery school he attends two days a week, takes
one look at the teacher he's known for a year, and begins screaming as if
he's never seen this stranger before. He hugs his blanket for comfort, then
settles down as soon as he is handed a toy he recognizes or begins a
familiar activity.

Because toddlers attending nursery part-time don't experience the
people and routines frequently enough to be able to retain many
memories from week to week, they may find each new encounter almost
as overwhelming as the first. Attending nursery for a half day four times a
week can be easier for them than attending for two full days.

The fragility of toddler memories has its benefits, too. If a child spits
out a new food today, try it again in a week or two. There's a good chance
she won't remember she didn't like it.

Early Education, founded in 1923, is the British Association for Early Childhood Education. It is a national voluntary organization for early-years practitioners and parents, and promotes the right of all children to education of the highest quality. It provides support, advice and information on best practice for everyone concerned with the education and care of young children from birth to eight years. Its website is at *www.early-education.org.uk.*

CHAPTER 5

The Road to Independence

The toddler years are a time of great emotional intensity. At no other age are the smiles quite so pure, the sadness so heartfelt, the rage so total or the delight so genuine. Each small incident of disappointment, fear and frustration can produce tears of sadness or anger; then in the twinkling of an eye those frowns can turn to smiles once again.

The Roller-Coaster Years

After experiencing the ready smiles and relatively easy-going attitudes of baby days, many parents are shocked when behaviour markedly deteriorates as tots begin to walk. It is common for them suddenly to resist their parents' requests and directives at every turn. It's not just the new-found freedom that drives the sudden bouts of stubbornness. It's that walking turns the toddlers' world upside down – or vertical, as the case may be. Change, even change for the better, taxes the emotional reserves of human beings of all ages and is therefore stressful.

Shortly after learning to walk, toddlers are likely to:

· Repeatedly dissolve into tears over small frustrations.
· Strike out when they are angry.
· Be stubborn and uncooperative.
· Have a hard time falling asleep.
· Wake up crying during the night.
· Show other signs of stress, such as more frequent infections.

Don't worry that you've created a monster. You can expect the sunnier personality to reappear when the novelty of walking wears off and toddlers have adjusted to the many changes that mobility has introduced into their life. Then during the 'terrible twos' (or 'terrific twos', depending on your point of view), conflict heats up in earnest as struggles over autonomy take centre stage.

But when the terrible twos are successfully negotiated, toddlers trust themselves as well as their parents. At that point, youngsters will still dislike many of their parents' limits and rules. They may make a fuss and try to get them to change their minds. But even if they're at a loss to understand the reasons for many of their parents' more disappointing decisions, they comply more often than not.

Experience as Teacher

Between the ages of one and three, toddlers make great strides in mastering their careening emotions. In this case, 'familiarity breeds content', so toddlers encounter fewer new things that inspire fear. They know what to expect and how to behave in many situations, and they have learned to follow most of the family routines and rules. Still, even older toddlers may become upset when confronting events they find especially distressing – for instance, when Mum and Dad leave them with a sitter and walk out of the door. If the toddlers have been raised in a secure and stable environment, experience will have taught them that they are not being abandoned. Although youngsters nearing their third birthday still break lots of household rules and resist routines at times, they bump into fewer unexpected no-no's while toddling through the house each day. That alone makes parenting far easier.

Growing Bodies

The increased maturity of the frontal lobes of the brain plays a role in children's ever-improving emotional control, too. These physical changes render older toddlers less impulsive and more able to plan ahead, tolerate frustration and delay gratification. Further, as youngsters develop physically, their skin becomes somewhat less sensitive, their digestive system works better and their sleep patterns stabilize. Perhaps hunger pangs don't strike with such intensity at three as at one, so a minute spent waiting seems less like a year... and more like only half a year.

Emotional development during the toddler years means that as they approach the age of three, they shouldn't routinely dissolve into tears while having to wait to have their needs and desires satisfied. Although waiting is still hard, they react less intensely to small stresses but still frequently become overwhelmed and remain overemotional by adult standards.

A Growing Trust

Being able to trust caregivers enough to accept their comfort, help, rules and guidance is critical for toddlers' overall emotional well-being. This foundation of trust should have been established during infancy through the unwavering love and nurturing devotion of parents and other caregivers. Toddlers' growing trust in themselves complicates their trust in parents, which wanes as toddlers put more trust in their own feelings, thoughts and ideas. Emotional swings intensify as youngsters try to balance their trust in themselves and in their parents.

The primary caregiver who rules the household tumbles from grace as toddlers realize that the biscuit they wanted still exists and the parent with the power to produce it is refusing to hand it over on cue. Because toddlers can't tell the difference between their wants and their needs, they become frustrated when they want a biscuit and their path is blocked by a parent's determination that they don't need one. Further, the 'biscuit god' is the same adult who deprives them in lots of other horrid ways – forbidding them to eat the newspaper, write on the walls, stop up the sink and turn on the bath taps at any time – all of which experiences bring so much joy to toddlers.

In order to maintain a strong relationship when trust wanes during the toddler years:

· Be true to your word.
· Invite toddlers to participate in decisions that affect them by giving them choices.
· Soothe upsets by cuddling, kissing and speaking kindly.
· Communicate your understanding that some rules and limits are going to be upsetting.
· Let your child's upset be her own. Don't let the situation escalate by becoming upset yourself.
· Let your child know you love him even if you dislike some of the things he does (criticize the behaviour, not the child).
· Show with your actions that your love and respect for her continue even when you are angry with her.
· Apologize if you become harsh and critical – this will help your child learn it is OK to make mistakes and to apologize for them.
· Understand that if you are the recipient of your child's worst scenes, it is because you are the person she trusts most.

The Parenting Challenge

Toddlers need to flex their psychic muscles in order to become more autonomous or more able to direct their own behaviour. Nevertheless, the toddler power surges that occur after learning to walk, and again during the third year of life, definitely complicate parenting. Virtually overnight, they can transform child-rearing from a joy to a highly demanding endeavour.

Adults who have trouble with self-assertion, feel overwhelmed by conflict or look to their youngster to affirm their sense of self-worth may find parenting a toddler a special burden. It is draining to tangle with a power-tripping youngster several times a day – not to mention every hour. It's hard for parents not to take the struggles personally when they are the targets of toddler wrath. It's important for parents to remember that the stage of development is driving the behaviour – children are not 'choosing' to create problems – and that their toddler is not railing against them, but against the injustices of life itself.

Just when a youngster is feeling oh so powerful, he finds he can't do a simple task such as putting his shoes on by himself. He can't float his toy car in the toilet without a big person appearing at the door to stop him. Life keeps reminding him he's not powerful at all.

 Developmental psychologists agree that a nurturing parent-child relationship is critical for toddlers. This single relationship influences youngsters' relationships with other authority figures from today's teachers to tomorrow's bosses. It also affects how they get along with siblings, peers, friends and future partners.

A parent may feel her youngster doesn't trust her to know what's best, given that the tot works hard to reverse so many of her decisions. In a sense, that's true. Toddlers often trust their own knowledge about what is in their best interest more than their parents'. Realizing they are still dependent on others to make decisions and handle even the most basic aspects of their care delivers continual blows to a budding ego. At the same time, the fear that 'If I can do it myself, Mummy might stop taking care of me' looms large. Thus, failure highlights their inabilities, while success threatens their relationship with their parents. Accepting the disappointing reality that their new-found power to walk hasn't transformed them into an all-knowing god, and that being able to do more for themselves doesn't mean they will lose their parents' love, takes time.

Bonding

Some parents worry that lots of arguing and defiance from their toddlers reflects weak emotional attachment or insufficient bonding. In most cases, the truth lies elsewhere. It is their abiding *trust* in parents that enables toddlers to pit their will against their parents' one minute and relax in their arms the next.

When children can make a parent a target of their bad moods, then turn to that same parent for comfort, it usually means that they trust the parent not to retaliate. In the past, parenting experts were adamant that caregivers should avoid being too solicitous or indulgent. With the recognition of the importance of trust, the advice has changed. Rather than spoiling infants and toddlers by giving them too much time and attention, it is now believed that lots of attention makes children more emotionally secure, enabling them to tolerate more independence sooner. Experts also believe that toddlers more readily cope with rules, disappointments and frustrations from a trusted caregiver who is loving and kind when enforcing limits.

Parents as Safe Havens

Psychologist Harry Harlow (1906–81) conducted groundbreaking research that demonstrated how critical a nurturing parent is for children's emotional development. His studies on young monkeys have important implications for child rearing. Harlow separated newborn monkeys from their parents and raised them in cages that were barren except for a wire mesh structure. When the little orphans nursed from a baby bottle, they would cling to the wire mesh as if it were a mother.

Despite adequate nutrition, it soon became evident that the emotional development of the little ones was seriously distorted. When Harlow placed something frightening in a cage, such as a noisy wind-up toy, each orphan would flee to a corner, hide its face and tremble in terror, unable to summon the courage to approach the object for a closer look. Later, when other baby monkeys were placed in the cage of a little orphan, it didn't know how to play or interact with them. When the deprived orphans grew up, their emotional development was so stunted they couldn't even work out how to mate.

Young monkeys raised with their mothers were much more able to cope with the wind-up toy trauma. They fled to their mothers for comfort when the frightening toy first appeared, but soon became brave enough to approach it. Each time they lost courage, they ran back to their mothers for support and to regroup. Within moments they were happily playing with the new toy.

The parent-child dynamics of these monkeys, Harlow realized, mirrors what happens in the human world. A caregiver to whom the toddler is attached serves as the child's island of safety when a stranger comes into the house, or when she feels frightened for any reason. Once a frightened child has spent a few moments with her human security blanket, she ventures forth with renewed courage.

Stranger Anxiety

Shy, fearful behaviour around strangers (meaning anyone other than the immediate family and trusted caregivers) intensifies around 12 months of age. It gradually lessens and disappears by the age of three, except in the shyest youngsters. Negative reactions during this period tend to be more pronounced towards men than women, and least pronounced towards other children.

When a child is distressed about a 'stranger' (who can actually be a relative or neighbour the child has met many times before), hold her on your lap to help her feel safe, and don't pressure her to interact. Once out of the limelight and given time to observe, most toddlers grow bolder about approaching household guests. Tell Aunt Emily and Uncle Bob not to take the rejection personally.

Support your child's desire not to be touched by saying, 'He doesn't want to be touched just now. He'll let you know when he's ready.' Give your child the words to hold others at bay by instructing him, 'Can you say, "I don't like that. Please stop." Can you say "Stop"?'

This is not the time to teach toddlers about 'dangerous' strangers, or 'good' versus 'bad' touching. They're too young to understand these concepts, and emphasizing the issue may make them more afraid of people than they already are. Instead, begin teaching limits by helping children ward off *any* intrusive actions, including hugs and kisses from 'strangers' such as Aunt Tanya and Great-Grandad David, and either kisses or blows from a toddler friend.

Contact Comfort

Harlow's studies on young monkeys yielded another important finding: little orphans deprived of the warmth of a live mother monkey were less healthy than their peers. Researchers have found that this, too, has parallels in the world of humans. Youngsters in orphanages often have poor weight gain. Some sicken and die if they are not held and cuddled regularly, even if they are otherwise cared for. This medical condition is called 'failure to thrive'.

Experts now agree that loving human touch, 'contact comfort', is a basic need, as important as food and water for physical and emotional development. Contact comfort has important health benefits for people of all ages. By learning to reach out for a hug, toddlers learn a skill that will help them stay healthy.

Soothing Touches

When young toddlers are upset, words alone aren't enough to comfort them because of their limited comprehension of speech. They need:

- A shoulder to cry on when they are sad.
- A lap to bury their faces in when they are afraid.
- Arms to hug them and provide comfort and reassurance.
- Back rubs to soothe them when they are ill.
- Tickles to cheer them up.

Hugging, kissing, rocking, rubbing and cuddling have relaxing and soothing physical effects. A toddler's pulse rate slows and respiration becomes more even. Endorphins released into the bloodstream provide a sense of well-being. Soothing touches are also important for building trust and strengthening the child's emotional attachment to the primary caregiver. Studies show that youngsters in intensive care recover more rapidly if they are regularly massaged, stroked, held or otherwise able to reap the benefits of human touch.

Holding It Together

The last thing enraged toddlers may want is to be held and comforted, especially if they are furious with the person who is trying to do the comforting. Even if out-of-control youngsters attempt to pull away, it can help them to be physically held. They are relieved that someone can contain the anger that feels so huge and overwhelming to them. It is as frightening to a toddler to be out of control as it is to an adult.

To help your toddler feel better about the wildness within her, read *Where the Wild Things Are* by Maurice Sendak (Picture Lion). It can comfort her to know she's not alone. She may also enjoy hearing *Alexander and the Terrible, Horrible, No Good, Very Bad Day* by Judith Viorst (Aladdin Paperbacks).

Since human touch is critical for both physical health and emotional development, parents should try to help standoffish toddlers overcome their resistance to being cuddled. Even if youngsters resist loving hugs and affectionate cuddles, they may respond enthusiastically to playing tickling games, having their back rubbed, having their hair tousled or having their shoulders patted. As they become more comfortable with these less emotionally intense kinds of physical contact that give them a greater sense of control, they may be open to more direct and prolonged affectionate contact.

Caregivers must be sensitive and responsive to toddlers' moods. Besides noting when they are calmer and more relaxed, which may mean they are more receptive to being touched, parents should back off when the toddler expresses an inclination to retreat. Hugging by force is a no-no. Like infants, toddlers signal their desire for emotional distance by looking away. For instance, when being bounced on a hip, toddlers break eye contact when they want the bouncing to end. Next, they try to escape. They may go limp (since the dead weight makes them harder to carry), then try to slide to the ground. And if that doesn't work, they whimper, cry, scream, stiffen and arch their backs in an effort to free themselves from the adult.

These kinds of physical struggles make toddlers more wary of being held, as well they should. Imagine if someone five times your size, even if it were someone you loved, had you locked in an embrace against your will and wouldn't let go, no matter how much you begged or pleaded! It's not surprising that toddlers with overbearing parents or relatives become increasingly standoffish.

On the other hand, physically containing an out-of-control toddler by holding her firmly can reassure her immensely. It helps to know that a big person can safely contain those scary emotions that have taken her over.

Comfort Objects

Harlow also found that if an orphan monkey was raised with two wire structures in the cage, a plain one and one that was wrapped in a soft blanket, the baby monkey chose to cling to the soft one when nursing.

Then, when a frightening toy or a group of baby monkeys was placed in the cage, the orphan again went to the soft 'surrogate mother' for comfort. The blanket didn't make up for a live mum, but these little monkeys weren't nearly so impaired as those raised with only a plain wire structure. The comfort they were able to derive from the soft blanket made the difference.

In the human world, it's common for toddlers to become so attached to a particular object that they can't bear to be separated from it. The object doesn't have to be something soft, like a blanket. Some youngsters develop affection for a toy lorry or a torch. What matters is the bond the child has formed with it. These special objects help toddlers cope with situations that require a separation from their parent, such as going to daycare or to bed.

What is a comfort object?

A comfort or transitional object is the popular term for a blanket, piece of clothing, toy or other object that serves as a child's 'surrogate mother'. If your child derives comfort from one, make sure you respect this important relationship.

Parents may be frustrated if their toddler insists on having the same toy at his side every moment of the day and sleeps with it at night. As the months go by and their child's grip on Mr Teddy or his 'blankie' remains as tight as ever, they begin to picture their toddler walking up to the podium at university graduation clutching the bedraggled toy under his arm.

Fortunately, no such incident has ever been recorded, and there's no reason to believe your darling will be the first. The social pressures of nursery school can be counted on to bring a quick end to the love affair with an inanimate object – at least in public. Lots of teenagers still cuddle their teddy at night, so don't worry about your child's need for a comfort object, and don't push your child to relinquish it. If your child seems too attached to a comfort object for your liking, try to give more hugs and spend more time cuddling.

Feelings

Much of the improvement in emotional control that takes place during the toddler years is due to youngsters' enhanced ability to communicate. As toddlers become more adept at labelling their feelings and communicating their needs, they react less impulsively. Youngsters who cannot talk out their feelings can only act them out. As they become more able to express their feelings in words, they don't have to rely on crying to signal their hunger, thirst, need for a nappy change, desire to be held, or wish to play with a particular toy. Toddlers are not able to identify their feelings with much accuracy. They simply experience a physical or psychological discomfort, and they react.

Parents and other caregivers need to teach toddlers to recognize their emotional and physical states and to use the vocabulary of feelings to express discomfort. What is obvious to an adult is not at all obvious to a little person. Parents need to make it a habit to tell toddlers what they are feeling before attempting to help with whatever is upsetting them:

- 'You're sad that I'm leaving.' ('But I'll be back soon.')
- 'You're frustrated with that puzzle.' ('Do you want some help?')
- 'You're happy that Daddy is home.' ('Stay inside. He'll come inside in a minute.')
- 'You're afraid of that clown.' ('But he's just a man with make-up and paint on his face.')
- 'You're angry because I won't let you play in the sandpit.' ('We need to think of some other fun thing for you to do.')

Unhappy Feelings

Unhappy feelings serve a useful purpose. They let human beings know that something is wrong or that something needs to be changed. These feelings help people determine the source of their distress with greater precision. Once they know exactly what is wrong, they are in a better position to figure out how to get their needs met and desires fulfilled.

Unhappy feelings indicate that something is wrong, but toddlers may not know what that something is. They may be bored, but think they are hungry. They may be tired, but think they are angry at a toy. They may be feeling ill and think they are sad because a parent is talking on the telephone.

Parents must constantly provide corrections:

· 'I don't think your brother's upsetting you. I think you're tired.'
· 'Instead of a snack, I bet a nappy change will help you feel better.'
· 'Your new tooth is coming. That's why so many things are bothering you today.'

Once they are able to correctly identify their feelings, toddlers will be more able to work out what to do to feel better.

Words of Comfort

As toddlers' language skills improve, words alone are often enough to help them feel better. Whether words are combined with hugs or not, parents should apply regular doses of soothing words when calming upset children. Children eventually learn to comfort themselves by being soothed and comforted by parents. With time and repetition the comforting words parents say become so much a part of their toddler, he will use them to comfort himself.

Tapes of crib monologues made after toddlers have been put in bed for the night show that, to comfort themselves, they repeat the words they've heard from parents, such as 'It's OK' and 'Go night-night now'. Other soothing phrases parents can say to their child include the following:

· 'We're going home soon.'
· 'You'll feel better after you eat something.'
· 'You'll see her again tomorrow.'
· 'You're more scared than hurt just now.'
· 'It may taste bad, but this medicine will help make you well.'

Trusting others to provide verbal comfort will enable children to reach out to daycare teachers, childminders and other caregivers for help and solace. During their teenage years, a phone call to share troubles with a friend or a talk with an understanding teacher will provide emotional support. By sharing feelings with trusted family members and friends, adults have access to a lifelong source of important moral support. People never outgrow their need to be nurtured.

Words That Hurt

Normal children will try to fend off criticism to maintain a sense of dignity and self-worth. The problems are likely to escalate if parents shame them for being upset. If a parent routinely heaps criticism on an upset toddler to try to settle her down, the harsh words will eventually begin to echo in the child's mind in an effort to ward off unhappy feelings whenever she is upset.

Always respect your child's feelings – even the unpleasant ones. Since the words you say will echo in your child's mind for the rest of her life, be kind so your child can learn to be kind to herself!

Needless to say, that doesn't work very well. Toddlers' turmoil increases as they battle the belief that they are bad for feeling unhappy in the first place. Harsh comments made in an attempt to contain upset youngsters too often have the effect of compounding their distress. Critical comments may teach children not to verbalize their unhappiness, but that doesn't make the distress go away. The unhappiness lingers. Derogatory statements erode self-esteem. Statements that deny the reality of children's distress increase their confusion about what they are actually feeling. Instead of learning to use their feelings as a guide to getting their needs met, they end up feeling worse and don't know what to do to make things better.

Developing Initiative

Young toddlers may experience innate urges to explore and grow and master their environment, but some youngsters become so discouraged by the difficulties they encounter they begin to back away from hard tasks. When the many things toddlers do that anger their parents are added to all the things that frustrate toddlers because they can't do them well, failure can begin to seem like the inevitable outcome of anything they try. Some youngsters become so overwhelmed by their own inadequacies that, instead of continuing to try to please their parents and develop their skills and abilities, they give up.

How toddlers view themselves – their self-concept and self-esteem – depends in large part on what their caregivers tell them about themselves. Toddlers need help to understand that most of their inadequacies stem from their age and lack of maturity and practice. If toddlers believe their incompetence stems from a basic deficiency or defect, they will lose confidence and give up readily when things are difficult for them, backing away from challenges instead of trying to overcome them.

Psychologists consider the need to develop initiative the central emotional task of the toddler years. 'Failure' at this task means that shame and guilt swamp initiative. Children who feel ashamed and guilty respond to difficult tasks by raging, becoming destructive, crying, quickly giving up and blaming others for their failings.

To help toddlers take initiative, parents need to be supportive of little ones' efforts to do things by themselves. Parents should focus on teaching, refrain from criticizing, and respond with kindness and compassion to their child's frustrations. TABLE 5-1 overleaf shows some example actions, negative (and positive) responses, and how the negative response makes the child feel about himself.

TABLE 5-1

Child's action: tries to insert a straw into a carton of juice

Responses that develop shame and guilt: 'Here, let me do it. It's too hard for you. Now look at the mess you've made. Why do you always have to be so stubborn?'
Child's view of self: 'I'm no good at this. I keep trying to do things because I'm stubborn.'

Responses that develop initiative: 'When you're older, your hands will be stronger and it will be easier for you.
Do you want some help? We need to clean this mess up.'
Child's view of self: 'Someday I'll be strong enough to do it by myself. Now I can ask for help if it's too hard.
When I make a mess we clean it up.'

Child's action: hits his sister because she has a toy he wants

Responses that develop shame and guilt: 'She had it first! Stop being such a bully.'
Child's view of self 'She has all the fun. I'm a bully.'

Responses that develop initiative: 'I know you're angry because you want to play with that, but you aren't allowed to hit. Take time out until you're ready to apologize to your sister.'
Child's view of self: 'I feel angry when I don't get my way. If I hit I have to go to time-out and apologize.'

Child's action: grabs the toy from her sister

Responses that develop shame and guilt: 'I told you she had it first! You never listen! Now go to your room.'
Child's view of self: 'I never listen. Mum takes her side and sends me away.'

Responses that develop initiative: 'You mustn't hit or grab. *Ask* if you can play with her toy. Say, "May I please play with that?"
[Child says, "Play dat?"] Very good. But it looks as if her answer is "no", so you need to find something else to play with or wait in your room. I'll let you know when she's finished with it.'
Child's view of self: 'I'm getting good at asking for what I want. I don't always get it, though. Then I have to play with something else or go to my room.'

Child's action: tries to help mother make the bed

Responses that develop shame and guilt: 'You're not helping, and you're in my way. Go and find something else to do.'
Child's view of self: 'When I try to help, I'm just in the way.'

Responses that develop initiative: 'You got part of the pillow in the case! If I just push it in farther and plump it up, it will be perfect. You're Mummy's little helper!'
Child's view of self: 'I'm learning to make beds. I'm a good helper!'

Child's action: has been told to pick up his toys

Responses that develop shame and guilt: 'I told you to pick those up! Why can't you just cooperate for once? If you don't do it by the time I count to ten, you're in trouble!'
Child's view of self: 'I'm uncooperative. I'm always in trouble.'

Responses that develop initiative: 'Let's have a race. Can you pick up your toys before I count to ten? Ready... steady... go! (The parent drops one toy in the basket and begins counting while the child laughs and scurries to win the race.)
Child's view of self: 'I can pick up toys faster than my mum can count to ten!'

Delaying Gratification

It isn't easy for toddlers to put off until tomorrow what they want right this minute! From 12 to 36 months, toddlers should get much better at managing the tension born of wanting something *now* and not being able to have it. Being able to delay gratification at the end of the toddler years means:

· Not grabbing a biscuit from the surface when Mum steps out of the kitchen even though the chocolate calls to her insistently.
· Protesting but not falling apart when a parent says he can't have a ride on the mechanical pony outside the supermarket.
· Confining herself to some whining and foot-dragging when her father says it's time to leave the park.
· Handling his anger over being forbidden to play with a toy by pleading and pouting.

Being able to delay gratification means that toddlers may whimper a little, whine a bit, shed a few tears, argue and drag their feet before forging ahead. It does not mean that they continue whining until parents want to smack them, wail to the point that they have to be carried kicking and screaming from the shop, argue until parents give up and give in, or fall to the floor in a tantrum. (At least, children close to three should not be doing these things *often*.)

The Lesson of the Marshmallow

In a series of studies that shook parents and teachers in the 1960s (as reported in Daniel Goleman's *Emotional Intelligence*), researcher Walter Michael ushered a group of four-year-olds into his office one at a time, placed a marshmallow on the table, and then announced he had to leave for a minute. He told each child not to eat the marshmallow until he got back, and said that he would bring a second marshmallow. If the first marshmallow was still on the table when he returned, the child could have both. If the marshmallow was gone when he returned, the child wouldn't get a second one.

Video cameras captured the children's reactions, which ranged from gobbling the marshmallow the instant the door closed, to trying to resist the sugary temptation. Some caved in, despite commanding themselves aloud not to touch it, covering their eyes or turning around so as not to see it, hopping on one leg or reciting nursery rhymes in an effort to distract themselves. Clearly, this was a big challenge for them.

Most children were able to control themselves. They got the kind of reward that so often comes to those who can wait: something even better. The eventual conclusion from these studies was that being able to handle emotions constitutes 'emotional intelligence'. On evaluating this research, some psychologists concluded that the ability to manage emotions is even more important than IQ for success in school and in life. The idea that children's grip on their emotions could be more important than their ability to handle intellectual tasks came as a shock, and many heated debates ensued.

There is some evidence that emotional intelligence is a critical ingredient in long-term success and happiness. Studies show that when it comes to delaying gratification and controlling impulses, children who wait their turn are more popular with peers; students who refrain from talking and getting out of their seats without permission do better in school; and young adults who go to work although they'd rather not are better able to keep jobs.

Learning to Wait

How do you teach a toddler to keep it all together and wait? Here are some tips:

Be calm, not angry. Parental anger triggers more emotional upset in tots, making difficult situations all the more taxing for them. Remember that there is nothing wrong with a child *wanting* something. When guilt and shame are added to toddlers' frustration over not having their desires fulfilled, their stress increases, which makes it more difficult to wait.

Don't anticipate trouble. When parents anticipate a scene and react to what they *think* will happen next, they become tense and may then overreact to a simple request. They may precipitate the very scene they want to avoid.

Be a role model. Let your child know when *you* are frustrated because you want something and don't want to wait. Let your toddler see how you handle yourself: 'Oh, doesn't that cake look good! I'd really love a piece right now. But no, that will spoil my appetite. I need to wait until after supper. Oh well.' Soon your toddler will be able to discharge some of the tension of having to wait by talking, too.

Give reasons. Explain why your toddler must wait. It is all too easy for toddlers to conclude that their parent is withholding things and privileges capriciously. That compounds their frustration.

Furthermore, reasonable explanations enable toddlers to apply what they learn in one situation to another. Tots in church may not understand when a parent says, 'You must be quiet now. People are talking to God with their hearts and you're disturbing them. You can talk later.' But as their language skills improve and they continue to hear explanations, they will eventually understand. Then they can use their knowledge to work out how to act in other situations where people are concentrating, such as at a live performance, instead of needing an adult to tell them what to do at every moment.

Sometimes parents can't give explanations because they aren't clear about the reasons for certain rules themselves. They only know they must be observed. If you can't supply a reason at the moment, think about it later. When you come up with a reason, share it with your toddler: 'Remember yesterday when I said you couldn't watch TV until later? That's because too much TV isn't good for kids. Kids need to play to exercise their bodies and minds.' There is sometimes a benefit to sharing reasons later rather than during a contentious moment. Children are more able to listen and consider the parents' words more objectively.

Here are some other things to consider:

- If after thinking about a conflict, you can't come up with a reason why your toddler needed to wait, it's time to hold the mirror up to yourself and consider whether you actually needed to deny your child's request.
- Keep bullying to a minimum. Every parent will have to use the 'No, because I said so' line from time to time. Still, it is a power play. Children who are regularly bullied learn to bully others – including their parents when they get big enough. No one likes a bully. Toddlers who bully others at three are at greater risk for a lifetime of home, school, social and work problems.
- When you promise your toddler she can do it 'later', 'tomorrow' or 'next week', be as good as your word! It's true that if you don't remind your toddler of your promise to let him finger-paint later in the afternoon, he may forget. Toddlers have short-term memories and a poor concept of time, so it's easy to trick them. But trusting that when the parent says 'later', that time will actually arrive makes waiting more tolerable.
- Get your child to manage the time spent waiting. When children are excitedly anticipating something, their play may become unfocused and their concentration may deteriorate. Suggest another activity.

Explaining 'why' may be one way to give toddlers the tools they need to work out conflicts without resorting to blowing up. One study found that 75 per cent of toddlers aged 21 to 24 months tried to negotiate to get parents to alter their demands. By the age of 30 months this figure increased to 93 per cent.

If children are admonished when they have difficulty waiting and hear nothing when they do wait patiently, they won't recognize that they are capable of delaying gratification of their wants and desires. When your toddler finally calms down after a scene over wanting something *now*, remember to point out her accomplishment. An hour after calm is restored, say, 'I'm proud you were able to stop crying when I told you that you couldn't paint until after lunch. I'll make sure you get to do it after we have eaten.'

Maybe your child's tantrum was so violent you were still trembling an hour later. Maybe complimenting your toddler for waiting seems like complimenting Dracula for having such a charming effect on women. But toddlers need to know they are in fact capable of waiting. They prove it every time their wish isn't gratified, and they live to tell the tale.

When pointing out a child's success at delaying gratification, focus on his achievement. Save the 'thank yous' for when your child has done *you* a favour. Children aren't doing their parents a favour by developing patience. This is a hard-won gift they are giving to themselves.

Building Frustration Tolerance

When a toddler learns that if at first he doesn't succeed he can try, try, try again and eventually get it right, he has accomplished another important emotional victory.

Temperament has a hand in dictating how toddlers react to frustration. Some concentrate long and hard on that tiny button as they struggle to fit it into the little buttonhole on their shirt, watching carefully to move all those little fingers just so to get the button lined up and in. Others have far less patience with these nerve-racking situations. Their feelings of frustration overwhelm them, and when they are upset, they can't think clearly enough to work effectively. Work with your toddler to break the cycle of difficulty, frustration, upset and giving up.

To help a toddler learn to tolerate frustration, keep the following tips in mind:

· Don't over-praise a job well done. It doesn't take toddlers long to decide that the opposite of all those 'Good job!' comments is 'Bad job!'
· Give lots of encouragement and moral support: 'You're getting it... almost... you're close... yes, I think she's about to get it!'

- Express your feelings aloud so your child can hear you actively dealing with a difficult task: 'This seat belt is stuck again! I've tried it a dozen times and I still can't get it to extend properly. If I pull hard, the belt comes out too far. If I don't pull hard, it's too short to buckle. I need to calm down. I know I can do this, but it's tricky. There! I've finally got it! Hurray!'
- Always respectfully *ask* whether your toddler wants help before leaping in. Otherwise, you may inadvertently communicate, 'You're obviously too incompetent to handle this yourself'.
- Teach your toddler to break large and/or difficult tasks into a series of small steps. Complex tasks viewed in their entirety become overwhelming. Help your child tackle one small piece of a task at a time, and pause to help him appreciate his accomplishment before he moves on to the next step.

The Road to Independence

While some toddlers never go through the 'terrible twos' stage of headstrong negativity, most pass through a period during which they become determined about handling their personal affairs themselves and making their own decisions. As independence struggles intensify, it may become readily apparent that a toddler doesn't care what she does, as long as it is the opposite of what her parent wants.

What seems to be mindless toddler negativity is actually the innate impetus to become independent working within them. Without a strong inner force to propel toddlers to pit their will against their environment, why would they tackle the challenges of walking and feeding and bathing and dressing themselves? Certainly it's much easier to sit back and let older, more experienced people carry them around and do everything for them.

'Me Do It'

The inner force that compels toddlers to do things for themselves is often a hardship for parents. The drive for independence can create a crisis when parents are in a rush to be out of the door while their youngster is doggedly engaged in the laborious project of eating his cornflakes one flake at a time as he learns to manage his cutlery by himself. The hectic schedules of modern life, to which we are all subject, certainly weren't designed with toddlers in mind.

If coping with the 'me do it' drive is hard for parents, remember that it's even harder for toddlers. Mother Nature can be capricious. She pushes youngsters to be independent, even when they lack the skills needed to do things by themselves. The same child who is determined to put a puzzle together by himself may lack the fine motor coordination needed to do it. One minute he is raging at the parent who dares to try to help; the next minute he recognizes his inadequacy and rages at the parent for *not* helping. Then, when the parent once again tries to show the toddler how to do it, Mother Nature whispers in the toddler's ear that he must do it himself, and he is again raging at the parent for having touched her puzzle. Now that the parent has defiled it, the youngster wants nothing to do with it.

Allow more time for getting ready in the morning and before going out in case your toddler suddenly decides she must handle some of the preparations herself, but don't allow your child to become a little dictator. Seize control when your child's attempts to be independent are inappropriate.

Children in the throes of an independence struggle put their parents in no-win situations because toddlers are caught in a series of no-win situations themselves. Their emotions vacillate wildly and their behaviour becomes erratic as they insist on being independent one minute and regress to helpless dependency the next.

Toddlers in this stage may revert to the familiar comforts of thumb-sucking and demand their long-discarded baby bottles back, but then treat parents' attempts to help them cut their meat as a major affront to their dignity. Long-resolved issues, such as the need to wear a seat belt and to hold Mummy's hand while crossing the street, may become battlegrounds once again. At such moments, toddlers are too immersed in their own turmoil to consider others' feelings. If youngsters at this stage demand everything and give nothing, it's because they are in such emotional turmoil they have nothing to give. When deciding how to handle independence struggles, remember that just as toddlers must be allowed to try to do more for themselves, having too much power frightens them. They are not ready to be independent, and they know it.

The Pot of Gold

Independence struggles can be expected to resolve themselves in a matter of months. At that point, youngsters will be comfortable practising independence when they can and accepting help when they need it. Then the clouds that cast such deep shadows over the household will part and the sunshine will return once again.

If parents feel as though they have survived a hurricane when the toddler years draw to a close, it's because they have. However, if they look to the distant horizon, they will see that the end result of this stormy period holds promise. It is so far off that parents may have to squint to see the glow. Still, the rainbow is there.

The beauty of the rainbow, the promise, will become apparent during adolescence, when children's hard-won victory of balancing autonomy and dependence during the toddler years finally yields its pot of gold. As teenagers, they will be able to be close to others without sacrificing personal independence. They'll be capable of forming intimate relationships without relinquishing control of their own life. That's when parents will know the struggles during the tumultuous toddler years were worth every tear.

CHAPTER 6

Potty Proud

Today's toddlers tend to complete potty training much later than earlier generations. Twenty-five years ago, 90 per cent of toddlers were trained by 30 months. Now, a third of children are still in nappies after their third birthday. Parents who wish to pursue a more lenient approach should prepare themselves for later completion of toilet training, as well as questions and an occasional raised eyebrow from older friends and relatives.

Early Learning

By providing a potty before 18 months, noting children's schedule of bowel movements and getting them to sit on it several times a day (perhaps while you read a story to encourage them to stay put), toddlers may accept the potty as a part of life. With lots of praise for an occasional success and compensation for the loss of the pleasurable time having their nappies changed, some youngsters can be trained very young – *if* they are physically capable of stopping and starting the flow of urine.

Few children have this ability before 18 months, however. In some cases, parents who claim their youngsters were trained at a very young age may in fact have trained *themselves* to predict their toddler's need to use the potty and get them there at the right time. Most children will be in nappies throughout most or all of their toddler years, so parents should consider all the options.

Environmentally Friendly Nappies

Today's toddlers will call the earth their home for many decades to come, and the only way to protect it is for each family to do its part. When the environmental toll of disposable nappies is considered, the cost is much greater than even their price tags suggest. With 432,000 new babies added each *day* to the six billion people who inhabit the world, more than a million nappies a day will be added to the landfills if just a quarter of them wear disposables. The UK produces about 600,000 tonnes of nappy waste each year. The use of washable nappies can be a step towards reducing this waste – even if you only use washable nappies part of the time, you will still help the environment.

The Cotton Advantage

Cotton nappies can aid potty training by making it easier for youngsters to feel wetness, which enhances awareness. If toddlers dislike the sensation of a cold wet nappy, cloth can increase their motivation to use the potty. Cloth nappies and plastic pants won't leak if they're 100 per cent cotton.

Cotton nappies can end up costing you less than half the price of disposable ones. Over the 'nappy life' of your baby you could spend around £700 on premium-quality disposables. The start-out cost for premium washable nappies is about £300 – but if you are planning to have more than one child, you'll use them all again. Then there's the cost of home laundering. Washing nappies for some two-and-a-half years has been costed at about £130. Wash nappies at 60°C; dry them on the washing line in good weather or, when it's wet, use a tumble drier or clothes horse.

With modern cotton nappies, you don't even need to master the art of the nappy pin. Many cotton nappies come with adjustable waistbands and easy velcro-style closures. Most also have a waterproof layer and elasticated legs for minimum leakage and snug fit. They are all machine-washable and can be tumble-dried.

Nappy Laundering Services

You can save yourself all that laundry by registering with a nappy service. Such services may provide a nappy bin and bin liners, an initial supply of cotton nappies and biodegradable liners. You start with a supply of, say, 70 nappies a week, which you can adjust as requirements change. After your baby's nappy change, all you do is flush any solids and the liner down the loo and put the nappy in the nappy bin. The full bag of used nappies is collected once a week, and the following week's supply is dropped off.

Down With Changing!

If changing time is turning into a battle of wills, check for nappy rash. If you discover a chronic or acute rash, check with your doctor. If nothing is physically wrong, it's probably just toddler independence asserting itself. Here are some tips to ease changing struggles:

· Let your toddler be the official helper, handing you each item as you ask for it.
· Change the location. Spread a towel on the floor or on a bed instead of using the changing table – which may also be safer if your child is thrashing about.

- Have everything ready and laid out so you can finish fast.
- Choose easy-to-put-on nappies – either cotton with Velcro tabs, or disposables.
- Provide a novel toy that can only be played with during nappy changes.
- Play the 'Where is Daddy's nose?/Where is your hair?' game.
- Sing a song or recite a familiar nursery rhyme. But instead of delivering it at normal speed, vary the cadence from very fast to very slow and provide a surprise burst of tickles.
- Tell your child that when he is old enough to use the potty by himself, life will be oh so much better.

If your child hates having her nappies changed, play 'magic tickles'. Bet your child that you can make her laugh without touching her. Slowly move your hands over her bare tummy, getting as close as possible without touching her, and wiggle your fingers while telling her not to laugh. Most toddlers will soon explode into giggles!

Fearless Potty Training

It's not surprising that many parents approach potty training with such trepidation. Psychologists once thought that the methods they used had a major hand in children's personality development. Sigmund Freud went so far as to state that parents' toilet-training methods dictated a child's eventual career choice! The good doctor believed that over-lax methods would result in the kind of sloppiness that would prompt adults to enter careers like painting. Harsh training methods would lead to controlled youngsters who would enter fields emphasizing the traits of frugality, obstinacy and orderliness, which Freud considered typical of bookkeepers and accountants.

There is absolutely no evidence that a parent's approach to potty training has anything to do with forming personality, much less career choices. Yet people still refer to exacting, overcontrolling adults as having 'anal personalities', and many believe that these traits stem from their potty-training experiences. Indulge their fantasy if you wish, but know that the research suggests that they're wrong.

Who's in Charge?

When potty-training toddlers, parents can do absolutely everything 'right', but youngsters won't be successful until they are physically ready, are intellectually capable, have mastered the complex mechanics involved and decide to refrain from wetting and soiling. In many families, the last point is the tricky one. Since readiness tends to occur at the time when toddlers are entering a particularly oppositional stage, the foundation for difficulties is laid if parents are very anxious to say goodbye to nappies. Starting potty training very early can be a way to lessen conflict – assuming that the child is physically ready. The time to begin is before the actively oppositional period begins. On the other hand, starting potty training very late also lessens conflict – assuming that parents can resign themselves to dealing with nappies.

Even if parents are very strict and insistent, potty learning offers parents potent lessons in accepting their fundamental helplessness. When it comes to deciding when and where to go to the toilet, all the punishments and praise and presents you offer may not make much of a difference. For once, toddlers are in control. All parents and caregivers can do is teach children what they need to know to be able to use the potty, help them acquire the specific skills, try to increase their motivation, and remain confident that if nothing else, the social pressures of pre-school or nursery will provide an incentive powerful enough to zap even the thorniest resistance.

Physical Readiness

In order to be potty-trained, children must be physically capable of controlling bladder and bowel, which means their central nervous system must have matured to the point that they can control the sphincter muscles that stop and start the flow of urine and expulsion and retention of stool. To achieve night-time control, the child must be awakened by the sensation of a full bladder, so staying dry at night typically comes later.

It's not possible to be certain whether a youngster's muscles are still automatically giving way when the bladder fills to a certain point. A toddler may have enough physical control for successful potty training if he:

- Remains dry for three to four hours at a time.
- Awakens from a nap with a dry nappy.
- Passes a substantial quantity of urine at one time.
- Has bowel movements that occur at predictable times.
- Has well-formed stools.
- Routinely goes to a specific place to urinate or have a bowel movement (e.g. a corner of the living room).
- Is able to stop the flow after urination has begun.

There is no way to be certain that after experiencing the urge to urinate, the child has the physical control of the sphincter to stop the flow. Punitive methods can cause youngsters who cannot comply with demands to feel incompetent, ashamed and humiliated. Parental kindness and patience are in order.

The bladder is the most reactive organ when it comes to stress, and people of all ages can and do respond to emotional upset by literally 'peeing in their pants'. By applying pressure to perform, parents can cause youngsters to feel anxious. This undermines bladder control. Accidents in nursery school are common, and often happen in year one classrooms, too. Be kind! Be patient!

Cognitive Readiness

Using the potty is a complicated affair. In addition to being able to recognize and communicate the need to go to the toilet, children must be able to:

- Understand how urinating and passing stool happens (that it comes from them).
- Understand the purpose of the toilet (that they are to urinate and defecate there).

· Discern when their bladder is full (recognize the physical sensation of the urge to urinate).
· Recognize the urge to have a bowel movement (recognize the physical sensation of the urge to pass stool).
· Consciously contract the muscles of the abdomen to push out urine and stool while simultaneously relaxing the sphincter muscles.

Psychological Readiness

Youngsters must also be emotionally up to the challenge. Psychological readiness includes:

· Being proud of their accomplishments.
· Enjoying independence.
· Wanting to wear underwear.
· Disliking wet or soiled nappies.
· Being able to sit quietly for five minutes.
· *Not* being in the middle of a phase of toddler negativism.
· *Not* being distracted by other major stresses.

Learning to use the potty requires a lot of effort on the toddlers' part. Don't begin when they are coping with other major adjustments, such as the birth of a new sister, an older brother starting school, a change in a parent's work schedule or an illness.

Parent Readiness

Parent readiness matters, too. Choose a time when you aren't under a lot of stress, so you can be patient. You should feel very comfortable with your baby taking yet another giant leap towards independence, and have the time to be on call for at least two days. Children need far more than two days to learn, but working parents can at least help toddlers have some concentrated practice to get them started. Then the methods being used at home need to be discussed with nursery staff and childminders so that potty training can continue during the week.

Seeing is Believing

Before toilet training can begin, toddlers must be aware that their urine and stool come from them, and that elimination is an act on their part. If they are always in nappies, they may think all those wet and soiled clothes happen by magic. They may have better luck making the connection by:

- Having the opportunity to watch others use the toilet. Some parents aren't comfortable with this, but it can really speed things along! Sometimes an older sibling is willing to demonstrate. Many children have opportunities to witness peers using the potty at nursery.
- Being repeatedly told that they are having a bowel movement when they are grunting or straining. If you can tell when your child is going in his nappy, make sure to point it out.
- Observing themselves in the act. Letting them go around the house without clothes is messy, but toddlers simply must be able to observe that urine comes from their own body. Letting them be naked in the garden in summer is a solution for some families.
- Watching the contents of their nappy being put into the toilet. This doesn't guarantee they'll make the connection, but may help some youngsters make sense of what is supposed to happen.

Reading can facilitate potty training in several ways. Read toddlers a story to prepare them. Then, after buying a potty, read to them daily while they sit on it. Check out *On Your Potty* by Virginia Miller (Walker Books) or the *My Potty Book* series (Dorling Kindersley); a comical potty story book is *I Want My Potty* by Tony Ross (Andersen Press).

What's in a Name?

The answer to that question is: far more than some parents might anticipate. Toddlers need to learn the vocabulary of the bathroom: potty or toilet, clean and dirty, wet and dry. They need words for urine and stool, too. Older children can learn that certain words are too offensive to be used in school and other social situations, but for toddlers it's an all-or-nothing proposition.

Acceptable words are 'wee-wee' and 'poo'. Some child development professionals urge parents to avoid words like 'smelly'. They point out that negative terms can make youngsters feel ashamed of what is a normal bodily function. If they feel ashamed, they might not want to admit when they need to use the potty, which makes toilet training very difficult indeed.

On Your Marks...

Buying a potty seat can be an opportunity to begin generating enthusiasm for training, but no matter how excited toddlers seem, parents shouldn't expect miracles. Once it's out of the box, they may be more interested in wearing the seat on their heads than in sitting on it. It's better to start toilet training with a self-contained potty unit that sits on the floor. Sitting on a toilet so far from the ground can be scary for toddlers. Later, parents can provide a stepping stool and a specially designed toilet seat insert, which offers additional security by ensuring they don't fall in.

When buying inserts, parents should beware of brands that have a raised splashguard. Eventually most toddlers bump into it, and that can be painful enough to make them refuse to use the toilet again. Some potties can be moved onto the toilet when the child is ready, and the continuity can make the transition easier.

Parents will need to explain what the potty is for: 'This is where people put their poo and wee so they don't have to wear nappies. I'm going to teach you how.' Putting a teddy bear on it and discussing the bear's pride in being a big boy with a potty all of his own can give a toddler a chance to observe and become comfortable with the situation before he tries it. Overleaf are some other tips.

- Unless a child wants to remove her clothing, it's a good idea to suggest she remain dressed so the feel of the cold, hard plastic doesn't alarm her. The goal should be to get the child to sit on it every day for a week with clothes on. (But of course, if she wants to remove her pants and/or nappy, so much the better.)
- Some children are more amenable to sitting on their potty while their parent uses the toilet or while being read a story, singing songs, or reciting nursery rhymes. Forcing them to spend time sitting on the potty can lead to power struggles, so parents should decide in advance whether they're going to adopt the firm 'you need to do this now' approach or let the child proceed at his own pace, although later they may decide to switch tactics.
- Whether or not their youngster sits on it, parents should be sure their toddler understands that he can use it whenever he wants, and should ask if he wants help. Take your toddler with you to the toilet after each nappy change, and reinforce the message: 'Your wee goes here' (point out the potty). 'Your poo goes here' (scrape it into his potty so he can see it).

Put down the potty lid, but don't transfer stool to the toilet for flushing until the toddler has left the room. Children may enjoy flushing, and the chance to pull the handle on the tank may serve as a big incentive to use the potty. But unless parents are certain that their youngster isn't afraid of the sound and motion, it's better not to let them do it. Flushing can take on a whole new meaning when youngsters realize that it causes something of theirs to disappear – a fact they may not have grasped when parents cleaned or discarded their disposables.

Get Set...

After toddlers have become comfortable sitting on the potty fully clothed, the next step is for them to become accustomed to the feel on bare skin. This is a good time to introduce training pants that can be pulled on and off.

Disposable training pants may prevent children from feeling the wetness. Since they need to be able to distinguish the difference between wet and dry, cloth may be a better choice while they're awake. However, disposable training pants may be more convenient at night while children are still bed-wetting.

Parents can explain, 'Kids wear training pants when they're learning to use the potty. I'll help you pull them down, or you can do it yourself.' Being sensitive and responsive to toddlers' desires to handle all or portions of the chore themselves is important for keeping them motivated. During the week that the child practises sitting on the potty seat without clothes, continue to reinforce the idea that bowel movements are supposed to go into the potty. The toddler should accompany them into the bathroom to watch the contents of their messy nappies being emptied into the potty bowl.

Go!

Lots of concentrated practice in a few days is better than practice spread out over a period of weeks. Provide salty foods to increase thirst, and encourage youngsters to drink lots of liquids. If the toddler agrees, get her to spend the day without clothing so you can catch her in the act and take her to the potty when nature calls.

Praise for being a 'big boy' or 'big girl' can backfire when toddlers are vacillating between 'me do it' and 'Mummy do it'. Saying 'Mummy doesn't want her baby to have to wear wet nappies any more' may provide more incentive than saying 'Big kids use the potty instead of going in their nappies'. Applying some cornflour or cream after youngsters have used the potty, and exchanging tickles and kisses can reassure them that mastering this skill won't turn their world upside down.

Teaching Hygiene

Using the potty will be messy for little boys who insist on standing to urinate. Learning to aim takes practice, and splashing is inevitable. If they won't sit, get them to climb onto a stool to urinate into the toilet. Make sure the stool is stable and doesn't slide. Teach children basic rules of hygiene.

·   Show them how much toilet paper to use.
·   Teach girls to wipe from front to back so they don't introduce bacteria into the vagina.
·   Provide a stepping stool so they can reach the sink.
·   Help them turn on the cold water, apply soap, rub their hands together, rinse and dry them with a towel.
·   Explain the danger of turning on the hot water.

Many stomach and intestinal upsets are actually bacteria from poor bathroom hygiene. Toddlers spend a lot of time with their hands in their mouths; they must be taught to wash carefully every time they go to the toilet.

Rewards and Praise

Lots of parents recognize that their personal interest in potty training is much greater than their youngster's, so they happily invest in a quantity of toys, stickers, biscuits or other items to make the potty experience worthwhile. At first, rewards can be given for simply sitting on the potty for five minutes. Later, the parent can up the ante. To be effective, keep these tips in mind:

·   The child must understand exactly what to do to earn the reward, whether it is just sitting on the potty for a specified period or urinating in or having a bowel movement in the toilet.
·   Don't ask the child to go for a whole day without an accident in order to earn a prize.

· Give rewards immediately; they should *not* consist of a promise of good things to come later, unless the child is unusually good at planning ahead.
· Don't give the reward if the child doesn't complete the required task. You can, however, reassure the child that he'll have another chance to earn one later.
· Change the type of reward if the toddler loses interest.

When you give rewards for desired behaviour, accompany them with verbal praise, since the ultimate goal is for the child to progress beyond the need for tangible goodies. However, if a toddler is in an oppositional stage, it may work better to refrain from verbal praise and simply say, 'Here is your prize for having used the potty' or 'You should be proud of yourself'. Effusive comments, such as 'I am so proud of you!', can trigger the rebellious impulses that make so many two-year-olds want to do the opposite of whatever they sense their parents want. Instead, try, 'Aren't you proud of yourself?' This is a bit less confrontational.

Many toddlers are content to wet their nappies, but try to avoid peeing on the floor. Many also love to run around the house naked. Allowing them to go without clothes can serve as an incentive for them to use the toilet, but you must be willing to clean up accidents patiently.

Target Practice

When parents turn potty time into a game, most kids can't wait for the chance to play. The standard procedure is to draw a bull's eye with a magic marker on a circle of tissue paper. Drop it into the potty, and see if your toddler can take aim, fire and score a hit. Alternatively, drop a square of marked toilet paper into the potty and see if the child can hit it. (This is easier for boys, but fun for all.) Boys can also try to hit a ping-pong ball rolling around the bowl. (Disinfect both the ball and the hand that retrieves it afterwards.)

But if parents lose interest in the games before their toddler and decline to participate, the child may decide nappies are preferable. As much as toddlers are determined to prove their independence by opposing every parental suggestion, they need all the attention of a little baby. If forced to choose, most toddlers would probably decline to grow up.

Tracking Progress

With a large piece of paper and a box of stars or stickers, parents can make a chart to help their toddler track her progress. After each successful use of the potty, the child gets to add a sticker to a chart under the correct day. (Instead of a chart, one mother let the child place stickers directly on the potty. He was thrilled.)

After each wet or soiled nappy, the parent may wish to note the time and day. This information can be used to determine the times of day when the child needs more help. Sometimes toddlers consider stickers a great incentive; sometimes an additional motivator in the form of a prize after the child has earned five stickers boosts enthusiasm. So you don't start the troublesome battle of 'if I do what you want, what will you buy me?', consider bestowing the gift you can feel good about giving and the present toddlers love most of all: spending time with *you*. For instance, try an extra bedtime story, ten minutes longer in the bath, a leisurely walk around the block to study the dandelions and worms, a trip to the park or extra time to finger-paint. Just remember that rewards work best when they're immediate.

Up With Undies, Down With Nappies!

Get your child to help select underwear that can be worn as her reward for sustained continence. Let her break out her new attire when she's made it through a full day without an accident.

To increase interest in using the potty for toddlers who are intently working on independence and autonomy issues (that is, going through a very oppositional stage), parents can try making a studied show of having lost interest in it themselves. Employing a bit of reverse psychology works best if a youngster has demonstrated some enthusiasm for learning, but the pattern has been for enthusiasm to quickly fade. Some of these strategies are a bit harsh; parents need to beware, since by using them they risk creating still more control struggles:

· Suggest that your tot relinquishes pants and returns to nappies.
· Allow the youngster to experience the discomfort of wet and soiled nappies by being less responsive to changing them. (Delaying a few minutes is enough – the point isn't to torture little ones or to cause nappy rash.)
· Pick her up for a nappy check or change when she's engrossed in a fun activity.
· Eliminate the fun and games when changing him.
· Be less solicitous and more business-like.

Although the interruption of usual family routines during a trip or holiday can set potty-training back, it may be better not to worry about it until returning home. Otherwise, it's a good idea to pack up the potty, since strange toilets, which many toddlers find scary, or even friends' potties, if they are the wrong shape, can cause a setback. For a truly portable potty you can use in the car, try a plastic ice-cream bucket for girls and a plastic jar for boys. Don't forget a waterproof pad to put over the mattress.

Bed-Wetting

At the age of three, an estimated 50 per cent of three-year-olds still wet the bed. Within six months, the figure drops to 25 per cent; at four, it's down to 20 per cent. Bed-wetting is considered normal until age six, but the figures remain high for young adolescents, too: 8 per cent of boys and 4 per cent of girls. The reasons for bed-wetting are not well understood. Genetics may play a role, since studies show children who achieve night-time continence late often have a parent who had a similar problem. Sleep patterns of hyperactive and depressed children are such that they may not wake up when they need to go to the toilet.

To help eliminate bed-wetting, try the following suggestions.

- Limit fluid intake before bedtime.
- Get youngsters to use the toilet just before going to bed.
- Try to determine the time at which the bed-wetting usually occurs, set an alarm, and walk your toddler to the toilet during the night.

Children who wet the bed need to be handled with compassion. Parents need to trust that children don't like to wake up in a cold damp bed, and should avoid using shame, humiliation and punishment. Instead, parents should use a plastic sheet and involve older toddlers in the cleaning up. They should be able to help with removing the sheets and putting them into the laundry basket.

Bed-wetting problems should be discussed with the child's doctor, to rule out the possibility of a medical problem and to see about exercises to help increase bladder control. Older children can sometimes overcome the problem by using a moisture-activated device that awakens them.

Bowel Problems

Many toddlers continue to have a bowel movement everywhere and anywhere, except the potty. Some are trained for a time and then regress. Is this yet another sign of the uncanny affection toddlers have for their poo? Is it a reaction to the discomfort or embarrassment of sitting naked on a potty for an extended time? Could it be a last-ditch effort to hang onto babyhood? Or is it perhaps an assertion of toddler autonomy?

Most parents never do decipher this puzzle. One thing is certain: if it's a struggle for control, parents are probably doomed to lose. Those who become angry and punitive may find themselves dealing with chronic soiling, known as encopresis (explained later). To enhance children's motivation, here is a hotchpotch of things parents have tried, with varying degrees of success:

- Get toddlers to sit on the toilet for five minutes every day at the time they are likely to have a bowel movement. As soon as the time is up, reward their success for having remained seated.

- Immediately offer more desirable treats and toys when toddlers get their stool in the right place.
- If you've already tried the enthusiastic 'hip-hip-hurrah' approach to drumming up pride of accomplishment, switch to being matter-of-fact when toddlers get it right, as if going to the potty were nothing unusual at all.
- If your approach all along has been matter-of-fact, try staging victory celebrations.
- Put them back in nappies. However, you should know that some youngsters then regress to wetting in them, too.
- Ask your child why he doesn't like to use the potty. You probably won't get an answer. Tell him if there's anything that bothers him about it, to let you know. Maybe at some point he will. Maybe it will be a problem you can solve.
- Get your toddler to tell you when he needs to go, hand him a nappy and let him retreat to wherever to do his own thing.
- See if spending time in an environment where other children use the potty, such as a pre-school group, makes a difference.
- Wait for nursery-school peer pressure to solve the problem.

How would you feel if your insides fell out and disappeared forever? This simple misunderstanding is what causes so many toddlers to work overtime to prevent disaster by becoming constipated or secreting their stool around the house. Many potty-resistant toddlers have made a dramatic turnaround after hearing the simple explanation: 'When people eat food, their body uses what it needs. Then it gets rid of the part it doesn't need, which is the poo.'

So why do some children insist on having bowel movements anywhere *but* the toilet? In the absence of an underlying medical problem, resistance that develops into full-blown encopresis – constant soiling – often develops from a predictable chain of events:

1. The child is slightly constipated, so her stool is a bit harder than normal. Because passing hard stool is painful, she tries not to have a bowel movement, worsening the constipation and pain.

2. If she uses the toilet, the hard stool causes the cold water to splash, hitting the child's bottom.
3. The combination of pain from passing stool, and the surprise and discomfort of being splashed makes the child nervous – even a bit afraid – about pooing in the toilet again.
4. A vicious cycle is created wherein the child's reluctance to use the toilet causes her to become increasingly constipated. Bowel movements become increasingly hard and painful, which further increases reluctance.

The situation can escalate to the point that a mass too large and hard to pass through the rectum forms in the bowel. Liquid that can't be absorbed leaks around the mass. The child cannot inhibit the flow, and continuous involuntary soiling occurs.

To break the cycle, increase his intake of fruits, vegetables and fruit juice, and keep him well hydrated with water. If that doesn't help, check with the child's doctor about administering a stool softener such as mineral oil. A good stool softener will make it impossible for children to contain bowel movements once it takes effect. Since mineral oil can interfere with vitamin absorption, it may be necessary to add a multivitamin; mixing it in juice can make it more palatable.

Once the child has been having regular soft bowel movements for ten days, rectal soreness should be completely healed. At that point, it is time to work on having bowel movements on the potty. Because children in this situation have come to associate the potty with physical pain and discomfort, and the whole situation may have become traumatic, breaking the negative associations and creating new, more positive ones may take some time and a lot of patience. The goal is to help toddlers recover from trauma so they can have a fresh start.

For starters, get the child to sit on the potty or toilet for five minutes every day at the time she usually goes, wearing pull-ups while seated. Wearing pull-ups should add to her feelings of safety and ensure no splashing occurs if she is on the toilet and does have a bowel movement. If her resistance is too strong to be overcome by reassurance and pep talks alone, offer stickers, toys or special privileges. Set a timer and engage in a quiet activity she enjoys, such as reading a book, playing with a toy or reciting nursery rhymes. Reassure her that the point isn't for her to have a bowel movement; it's to learn to relax while sitting on the toilet.

Once she's sat for five minutes without a struggle for at least three days in a row, it's time to up the ante. Make rewards contingent on having a bowel movement there. Leave on her pull-ups to add to a feeling of comfort and to prevent splashing, if she's on the toilet. If she doesn't go during her daily five-minute regime of sitting on the potty, provide verbal praise and tell her she can still earn the reward if she goes while sitting on the potty later. Ask her to tell you when she needs to go.

After a week of having regular bowel movements on the potty, her memories of the trauma are fading (let's hope!). At that point, get her to remove her training pants and try having a bowel movement in the potty or toilet. Continue to set a timer to ensure that she sits for five minutes, but only provide a reward after she actually uses the potty, which may be later in the day.

Toilet Explorers

No sooner have the struggles to get toddlers into the toilet finally ended than the struggles to keep them out are likely to heat up. They want to use every toilet in every shop, petrol station, park, zoo, church and museum they enter! Since getting to a public facility takes longer, toddlers quickly learn they must announce their need to use the toilet further in advance, well before the urge becomes intense. That, combined with their keen interest in exploring the toilets of the world, makes it hard for them to decipher whether their faint urge to 'go' stems from physical need or emotional desire. In time, they'll learn to more accurately predict their needs and understand their sensations and feelings. Until then, happy exploring!

CHAPTER 7

Safety First

What can toddlers get into? The obvious answer is, everything within reach. But how far, exactly, can they reach? Much further than you might think possible! Consider everything that can be climbed on, fallen off, pulled open (or over) and used to extend their reach. The list of hazards is endless. Use common sense and watch carefully to see the kinds of danger your child might get into.

Instant Trouble

Faster than a parent can dash to the next room to answer the phone, run to the kitchen to remove burning food from the oven or hurry to open the front door, a toddler can get into serious trouble. After an accident, the common parental refrain is, 'But I only turned my back for a moment.' Parents never dream their child would eat Grandad's medication lying on the table, or that their toddler, while having a bath, would turn on the hot water.

If you think your toddler has swallowed something he shouldn't, try to stay calm and call a doctor. You will need to give as much of the following information as you can. What substance has the child eaten or drunk? Write it down. How much? One tablet or half a bottle? What does the child weigh? If you are going to Accident & Emergency, take some of the substance that your child has eaten or drunk. If the child is sick, then bring a sample of the vomit too – staff can analyze it.

DON'T make your toddler vomit. Some poisons can cause a lot of harm as they are vomited out of the stomach.

Safety at Home

Some basic safety precautions should be obvious to every parent. In fact, child welfare departments consider them so basic and obvious that if parents don't adhere to them, they could be charged with 'endangering a child' or 'failure to protect', which means that their toddler could be placed in foster care while the parents attend court-ordered counselling sessions and parenting classes. So parents simply must avoid the following:

· Driving under the influence of alcohol or any illicit drug.
· Giving alcohol to a toddler.
· Leaving drugs – prescription or otherwise – within reach of a toddler.
· Putting children in a car without a safety belt.
· Exposing children to domestic violence.

· Injuring a child in any way, including hitting hard enough to leave a
   bruise or welt.
· Shaking an infant or toddler (which can cause brain damage serious
   enough to result in death).
· Dragging a youngster by the arm (the combination of a pull and a
   twist can cause spiral fractures).

Of course you should not *deliberately* hurt your child, but there is more
to it than that. Special care needs to be taken to avoid hazardous or
unhealthy situations. The best introduction to creating a safe and
healthy environment for children throughout their lives is known as
'childproofing'.

Here are some basic ways to reduce potential danger zones in
your home:

· Cover unused electrical outlets with plastic guards or heavy furniture.
· Replace frayed electrical cables.
· Install safety latches on cupboard and appliance doors and toilets.
· Keep plastic bags out of reach. (Use cloth bags or boxes for storing
   toys; store food in waxed paper.)
· Place small items that could be swallowed out of reach, including
   buttons, coins and marbles. (Don't forget to hide the dish containing
   hard sweets, too.)
· Lock up knives and other sharp or pointed objects.
· Unplug small appliances such as hair dryers, blenders and toasters;
   and don't let the cables dangle from countertops or dressers.
· Beware of rugs that slip and uneven carpeting. (Put skidproof mats on
   tile and hardwood floors.)
· Lower the thermostat on the water heater to prevent scalding
   (49°C/122°F is the recommended maximum).
· Keep garage door openers out of reach.
· Check and clean furnaces, flues and chimneys annually.

Bath Rings

For babies who can sit up, a bath ring suction-cupped to the bottom of the bath may provide you with an extra 'hand' and makes bathtime safer and more fun for the baby, too. But a ring is no substitute for keeping your eye on your baby at all times. A toddler can still crawl out of the bath ring, slip and fall, and unattended children can drown quickly. So if you use them, keep these points in mind:

- Never put your baby into a bath when the water is still running (the water temperature could change or get too deep).
- Make the bath safe: put in a rubber bathmat and cover the taps.
- Make sure the bath water is comfortably warm (about 32–35°C/90–95°F). Babies like a much cooler bath than you do.
- Do not let your child touch the taps. Even if he can't turn them on now, he'll be strong enough to do so soon, and that could lead to serious injury.
- Never leave your child unattended. Children can drown in less than 2.5cm (1in) of water – and in less than 60 seconds.

Toy Chests

When a toddler reaches inside a toy chest and the lid falls on his hand or head, the result can be serious injury or even death. When a child climbs inside and lowers the lid, the result can be asphyxiation. In the UK, toy boxes account for nearly 4,000 accidental injuries each year. The safety standards for a toy chest include the following:

- A hinged lid that will stay open rather than falling shut.
- NO latch, so a child who has crawled inside and lowered the lid can push it open.
- Air holes for ventilation.

When shopping for a toy chest, check for all three safety features. Especially check the lid's hinge or select a box with a lightweight top. If you're using a metal trunk or another box to store toys, remove the lid.

> Toddlers love to get both feet to leave the ground at once, but find it frustrating when they can't. Your toddler can learn this skill safely by bouncing on a bed or low trampoline while you hold both his hands. If your child is confident and starting to walk, you might consider buying him a junior trampoline with an integrated padded handle. Don't let him bounce on his own, though. He could have a nasty fall.

Safe Buggies and Playpens

While in a buggy, toddlers are apt to lean out to look, rock from side to side when excited, and hurl themselves about when angry. To guard against tips and spills, choose a buggy with wheels set far enough apart to provide a wide base and with rear wheels positioned behind the weight of the toddler. Before making the purchase, check to make sure the buggy doesn't become unstable when the toddler is in a reclining position. The latches should also be secure enough not to open by accident.

When your toddler is in the buggy, keep his seat belt on, even when he is sleeping. Be careful when opening and closing buggies – this is a prime time for parents and toddlers to pinch their fingers.

When purchasing a playpen, check to be sure that the holes in the mesh are small enough so toddlers can't step into them and climb up the side. Don't leave toddlers unattended in mesh playpens with a side down. Tots can become caught and strangle in the loose mesh. The bars on wooden pens should be no more than 6.3cm (2$\frac{1}{2}$ in) apart so toddlers can't get their heads caught. For both types of playpens, avoid placing large toys inside that children could stand on to gain enough height to crawl over the top. Double-check the latches to be sure they are secure enough so the playpen doesn't collapse, and so they don't catch a toddler's fingers.

For questions about the safety of any product, check the label and contact the manufacturers, if necessary.

Be Prepared!

Modern households are filled with substances that parents may never have thought of as being particularly dangerous... but that's because they never considered eating them. In Britain, about 28,000 under-fives are taken to A&E departments each year after being poisoned accidentally.

Poisons in the home range from medicines – including contraceptive pills, iron tablets, vitamins, antidepressants and painkillers – to standard household items such as cleaning fluids, alcohol, cigarettes, crayons and, particularly lethal, 'button' batteries. The main causes of long-term poisoning are cigarette smoke (from passive smoking), and lead (from old paintwork, water pipes or, interestingly, an Indian eye make-up called surma that is sometimes used on babies).

Lead

If your house was built before the 1960s, and the paint layers on windows, doors and interior woodwork are thick, the paint may contain lead. Emulsion paints never contained lead, but distempers occasionally did. Lead primers were also used – particularly on window frames – until the 1980s. Modern household paints do not contain lead. Another source of lead pollution in the home is lead water pipes.

Poisons via the Eye

If a child gets a dangerous substance in her eye, call a doctor immediately or call 999 to see if there is a need for professional medical attention. Recommendations typically include the following:

1. Fill a pitcher with tepid (not hot) water.
2. Keep the child from rubbing her eyes by wrapping her in a blanket,

sheet, or towel that is large enough to keep her arms at her sides.
3. Do not force the eyelid open.
4. Pour the water into the eye from a distance of 5–7.5cm (2–3 in).
5. Repeat for a full 15 minutes.
6. Encourage the child to blink as much as possible.

Cosmetics

It's one thing to put dye on your hair, quite another to put it in a stomach! Products whose safety you never thought to question should be kept well out of reach of little hands:

· Creams, lotions and make-up
· Eye products
· Hair-colouring agents (dyes, bleaches, rinses)
· Hairsprays, gels and mousses
· Hair removers
· Lipsticks
· Nail varnishes and removers
· Perfumes and aftershaves
· Shampoos and conditioners
· Suntan and sunscreen products
· Toothpaste, mouthwashes and rinses.

Dangerous Plants, Stinging Insects

With a toddler around, parents should give serious thought to sacrificing their plants. Besides the safety issue that arises if little ones actually eat some, they will most probably pull off the leaves, throw out the earth and rip them to shreds. Since it's a safe bet that at least a piece or two will end up in his mouth, which may mean he swallows some, it makes sense to resign yourself to doing without much greenery for the foreseeable future.

An amazing range of flowers and plants are toxic, including common ones like foxgloves, mistletoe, poinsettia, oleander, tulips, rhubarb leaves, lily-of-the-valley, sweet pea seeds, laburnum seeds, poppies, deadly nightshade and aconitum. A particularly toxic common plant is the glossy cheese plant (split-leaf philodendron). Check with a local nursery to be sure any greenery you keep in or around your house isn't toxic to toddlers.

Exposed roots, rough stones and sharp sticks are a potential danger in their own right, but they are also perfect tools for digging, poking and exploring the great outdoors. While a toddler is outside, she can also be exposed to a variety of nasty bugs.

With bees, wasps and hornets, swelling can occur immediately but may not manifest itself for five to six hours. Either way, it can be dramatic, last for three to four days, and be accompanied by bruising and itching. Apply ice for a few seconds at a time for up to 15 minutes, but be careful not to freeze tender toddler skin.

Some people are allergic to bee or wasp stings – and the allergy can be life-threatening. See a doctor immediately or dial 999 for an ambulance if:

- Your child has been stung by many insects at the same time.
- Your child has a rash or swelling that gets worse instead of better.
- The site is red, tender and swollen.
- Your child develops a headache.
- Your child feels dizzy or sick.
- Your child has pains in the chest.
- Your child is choking or wheezing or has any difficulty breathing.

Dangerous Gases

The following gases are hazardous: carbon dioxide, carbon monoxide, chlorine, methane, natural gas and propane. In the event of an accident:

1. Avoid breathing the fumes yourself.
2. Get your toddler to fresh air fast.
3. Open doors or windows (if this can be done without spreading dangerous fumes).
4. Administer artificial respiration and chest compressions if the child isn't breathing, and call 999.

Buckle Up... Carefully

The leading cause of death in children aged from one to four is unintentional injuries, and the vast majority of those are incurred during car accidents. Don't even think of starting your car engine until your toddler is securely fastened into a car seat or, for children over 18kg (40lb), until they are buckled into a seat belt. But first, be sure to have done your homework:

· In a crash at just 48kmph (30mph), an unrestrained child would be thrown forwards with a force 30–60 times their body weight. They would be thrown about inside the vehicle, injuring themselves and quite possibly seriously injuring (or even killing) other people inside the vehicle. They are also likely to be ejected from the car through one of the windows.

· Install car seats in the back seat in accordance with the directions. Unless properly installed, car seats can't be counted on to protect your child.

· Check the fit of the seat belt. Standard seat belts can be dangerous for little people, so booster seats are recommended for youngsters weighing in at 18–36kg (40–80lb).

· Consider purchasing a clip that changes the angle of the seat belt so it runs across the shoulder instead of the neck and fits securely across the lap.

· Failing to use the shoulder strap can cause the lap belt to be pulled too tight during a deceleration accident, causing abdominal injuries.

· Tucking the shoulder strap under the arm can prevent the strap from engaging properly during a sudden stop, rendering it useless.

· It is not safe to hold a child on your lap. In a crash, the child could be crushed between your body and part of the car's interior. Even if you are using a seat belt, the child would be torn from your arms – you would not be able to hold onto them, no matter how hard you try.

· It is also dangerous to put a seat belt around yourself and a child (or around two children).

· The safest way for children to travel in cars is in a child seat that is suitable for their weight and size:

Type of child restraint	Weight range	Approx. age range
Rear-facing baby seat	Group 0 (up to 10kg/22lb)	birth to 6–9m
	Group 0+ (up to 13kg/29lb)	birth to 12–15m
Forward-facing child seat	9–18 kg (20–40lb)	9m–4 years
Booster seat	15–25kg (33–55lb)	4–6 years
Booster cushion	22–36kg (48–79lb)	6–11 years

 Beware of air bags in your car. Although they can save lives, the explosion as they inflate has resulted in massive injuries and even death for children. Many parents of young children have had them deactivated. DON'T let children sit in the front if your car has airbags.

The dangers of drinking and driving are well known. However, when a toddler is on board, even one drink is too many. Depending on an individual's tolerance for alcohol, just one or two drinks can significantly slow reflexes, and driving with an active or fretful toddler requires optimal concentration and reflexes. A common side effect of alcohol is that it convinces people they are fine when they may not be fine at all. 'Just a few beers' is not safe, either. In general, one beer = one glass of wine = one mixed drink = one shot of whisky.

Water in the Garden

Hazards lurking in our back gardens prove fatal to toddlers and young children every summer. Recent government research shows that 80 per cent of pond drownings happen not at home but in the garden of a friend, relative or neighbour. It's vital that parents check where their children are playing, and whether it is safe. Your garden might be fine, but what about Granny's, or next door's?

Drowning is the third largest cause of accidental death in the home of under-fives – with most deaths occurring during the summer.

Any parent of toddlers will tell you that their small children are fascinated by water. The advice from the Royal Society for the Prevention of Accidents (RoSPA) is unequivocal: if you have a young child and a garden pond, fill in the pond with sand until the child is older, or cover it securely with a rigid mesh or grille (chicken wire is not adequate), or fence it off with a locked gate – the fence and gate being a minimum of 1.1m (3ft 6in) high.

Potential hazards are not limited to ponds. Children often drown in just a few inches of water, so any container which may have collected rain water is a potential danger. Water butts must have secure, child-proof covers. In summer, be sure to empty paddling pools and store them out of children's reach at the end of each day.

Swimming pools are, of course, just as dangerous. Make sure your child cannot possibly access yours, or next door's pool. A pool is 14 times more likely than a motor vehicle to be involved in the unintentional death of children aged four and under, with the vast majority occurring in residential pools. To minimize the risk:

- Never leave your child alone in or around a swimming pool or a spa.
- Teach children how to swim as soon as they are ready – usually at about three – but remember that being able to swim doesn't make your child 'drown-proof'.
- Teach children water safety – not to run near water or push other children under water.
- Keep a telephone, emergency phone numbers and rescue equipment at the poolside.

Fire Safety

It doesn't take much to know that Christmas tree lights on a dry tree are a fire hazard. It should be obvious, too, that smoking in bed is a no-no. The proof lies in the telltale hole or singed spot on a duvet, blanket, pillowcase or sheet. What if you'd fallen asleep?

Matches and lighters must be kept from little fingers. Just because a parent has trouble igniting a safety match or operating a child-resistant lighter doesn't mean toddlers won't succeed on the first or second try. Also, don't run electrical cables under carpeting.

Few people consider what happens when the family cat hops onto the end table and its tail brushes a burning candle. Or when the cat spends a few minutes grooming itself with its tale draped over a pot of burning incense. Once Miss Kitty feels the heat of the flames, she races through the house, spreading the fire.

Given how inexpensive smoke detectors are, there's no excuse not to have them. Here are a few safety tips about smoke detectors:

·   Position smoke detectors on each floor of the home.
·   Make sure the smoke detector is working by pressing the test button once a month.
·   Vacuum cobwebs and dust from the alarms monthly.
·   Replace batteries at least once a year.
·   Replace the alarms every ten years.

In the kitchen, install knob covers on the cooker so toddlers can't turn the oven on. Then, when cooking, make it harder for your toddler to reach hot pans by using the back burners of the oven. Always turn the handles of pans towards the back so they are less likely to be bumped by the cook or grabbed by a little hand with a long reach.

And, since fires can and do happen, despite everyone's best efforts to prevent them:

·   Buy fire extinguishers that can be used against both electrical and liquid flames. Get the kind that shows the remaining pressure. When it shows a low reading, replace the unit.
·   Create a fire escape plan by walking into each room and working out how you could get yourself and your child to safety if you were trapped there.

Keep all matches and lighters locked away; ensure that open fires have not only a fine mesh spark guard, but also a sturdy, toddler-resistant fire guard with a 'roof' that is fixed to eyelets set into the wall or fire surround. If you enjoy barbecues in summer, NEVER leave a lighted BBQ unattended when children are in the garden. The same applies to bonfires in autumn. Children find flames, like water, quite irresistible.

Keeping Your Cool

It's one thing to be alarmed, scared or frightened. It's quite another to be panic-stricken. There's no way to predict how panicked people will react – they sometimes do and say things that are so completely out of character that they don't even recognize themselves when they later ponder their behaviour during the crisis. The adrenaline surge can strengthen parents' arms to the point that they accomplish feats they never could have accomplished under normal circumstances, such as lifting the front end of a car to extricate a trapped child from beneath a road wheel.

Some acquire a steely calm. All emotion disappears and, like a robot, they go onto automatic pilot. Later, they are astounded to realize they ended up doing exactly what needed to be done. Others are overcome by emotion. Logic and reason disappear; their minds freeze; and they cannot recall the most basic information. The sayings 'She was scared out of her wits', 'He was frightened out of his mind' and 'I was so out of it, I couldn't remember my own name' are known to us all for a very good reason. We'd like to think we'd react correctly in an emergency, but until we have actually been through one, we don't know what we would do. When tapes of parents talking to ambulance control crews and staff are replayed on TV, conversations frequently go like this:

How old is your child?
I don't know! Please hurry! He's bleeding!

Even if parents are sure their minds wouldn't fail in a crisis, a panicking childminder or babysitter could certainly experience a mental lapse. The solution is to create an emergency list, duplicate it and post a copy by each telephone in the home. Make sure you include phone numbers for:

- Your and your partner's work and mobile phone numbers.
- The numbers of two close, reliable neighbours who can cope with the other child or children.
- Your GP's phone number and the hours that the surgery is open.
- The out-of-hours number and the times this is operational (to save having to write it down from the surgery answering machine).
- And finally, in capitals, 'IN AN EMERGENCY, DON'T THINK TWICE: DIAL 999'.

Emergency telephone operators should be able to help callers focus so they can describe the crisis and the victim's current condition. But make sure to keep the following critical information by the phone so the caller can simply read it aloud: your address with detailed directions to your house, visible landmarks, and a brief description of the house (eg, brown pebbledash house with a red-tile roof and a silver Toyota parked outside).

Create a subheading for each child, and list the following information:

- Name
- Age
- Sex
- Height and weight
- Medical problems
- Allergies
- Names and doses of prescription medications
- Names and doses of over-the-counter medications.

Lifesaving Skills

Basic lifesaving skills are familiar to many people, but are used by few. This is the time to refresh those skills – with luck, they'll never be used.

CPR

The skills of emergency life support are not complicated, but you should not attempt CPR (cardio-pulmonary resuscitation) unless you have been taught how. A class will demonstrate the practical aspects and allow you to practise them. The Heartstart initiative, co-ordinated by the British Heart Foundation, suggests that children as young as 10 years old can learn CPR skills. Children as young as five can learn to dial 999 in an emergency.

For more information on local CPR courses, contact:
Heartstart UK
020 7935 0185
http://www.bhf.org.uk/hearthealth/ (see Heartstart UK link)

St John Ambulance
08700 10 49 50
http://www.sja.org.uk/training

British Red Cross
Check phone book for local branch, or visit
http://www.redcross.org.uk

Artificial Respiration

Five minutes without oxygen is enough to cause permanent brain damage; a few more minutes, and death is probable. The exception is if the body is very cold, when it needs less oxygen, sometimes enabling youngsters to survive for longer periods. If a child has stopped breathing due to swelling of the air passages caused by a medical problem such as asthma, an allergic reaction or a respiratory infection, artificial respiration should be started immediately. However, if the child has stopped breathing due to an object stuck in his windpipe, artificial respiration might force it further into the child's windpipe or even the lungs. Before attempting artificial respiration, a rescuer should follow the instructions for choking (see 'Treating a Choking Victim' below).

For artificial respiration, follow these steps:

1. Place the youngster face up on the ground, lift the chin up and tilt the head back to keep the tongue from blocking the air passages. Examine the mouth and remove any visible obstructions with a curled finger.
2. Cover the child's nose and mouth tightly with your mouth and gives two gentle breaths lasting 1–1½ seconds each. Be careful not to blow too much or too hard; this will cause the child's lungs to haemorrhage. When properly done, you should be able to see the child's chest rise. The child's head must remain tilted up throughout to keep the wind passages open.
3. If the child does not resume breathing on his own, administer additional breaths at the rate of about 20 per minute until a medical team arrives.
4. If vomiting occurs, as is often the case, turn the child's head to the side to prevent choking. Then quickly clear the mouth cavity before resuming assisted breathing.

Chest Compressions

The heart delivers oxygen-enriched blood to the brain. If the child has collapsed and is non-responsive – that is, he doesn't moan, cough or move even when his shoulder is tapped and his name is called – check for a pulse at the carotid artery. The easiest way to find the carotid artery is to place your fingertips (not the thumb, which can confuse the issue because thumbs have a pulse) in the groove of the child's neck, next to the windpipe, near the jaw.

What is the carotid artery?
The carotid artery refers to either of two large arteries on each side of the neck that carry blood to the head.

If you can't find a pulse, someone trained in CPR needs to manually pump the blood via chest compressions while you call 999. Compressions can damage the heart if it is already beating, so it's important to be sure there is no pulse before beginning. Here is the procedure for carrying out chest compressions:

1. Place a flat hand on the child's chest on the lower half of the breastbone, which is located between the nipples, and push down with the heel of your hand.
2. The child's chest should depress one-third to one-half the depth of the child's chest, far less than is needed for an adult.
3. Repeat this action at the rate of 100 compressions per minute.

When you combine mouth-to-mouth breathing and chest compressions, deliver five chest compressions for each breath until help arrives, and check occasionally to see if the heart has begun beating on its own.

Treating a Choking Victim

If a child is eating or playing with a small toy and begins to choke, his air passage may be partially or completely blocked. Signs of a partially blocked air passage include choking or coughing that starts very suddenly, gagging, or breathing that is noisy and high-pitched.

If a child can manage to breathe a little bit, call 999 or get her to Accident & Emergency immediately. Trying to dislodge the object could make matters worse by cutting off the child's air completely. If a child's ability to breathe is almost completely cut off or if breathing has stopped altogether, the situation is desperate and the child must have immediate assistance to keep her alive until an emergency medical team arrives.

Symptoms of desperate trouble include:

· The ribs and chest are sucked in when the toddler tries to breathe.
· The toddler can't get enough air to cough.
· The toddler can only wheeze softly or make soft high-pitched sounds.
· The toddler can't make any sound at all.
· The lips and skin are blueish.

If the toddler is unconscious, look in the child's throat and try to remove the blockage. If that doesn't work, administer two rescue breaths. If the child doesn't start breathing on her own, start chest compressions. Sometimes the compressions will eject the object from the windpipe.

If a toddler can't breathe but is still conscious, the goal is to force her to cough; something she can't do on her own because she is unable to take in enough air. Begin by explaining that you will help her. Quickly position her in front of you, reach around her with both arms, make a fist, and place it so that your thumb rests just above the navel and below the breastbone. Grasp your fist with your other hand. Give five quick thrusts, pressing upwards and in. The object may be expelled. If not, give five more abdominal thrusts. Keep trying until the object is ejected.

If the child loses consciousness, lay the child down, lift her chin, open her mouth to look for the object, remove it if you can and help her breathe with artificial respiration. If her heart stops, start chest compressions until medical help arrives.

Take a class to learn how to perform CPR, chest compressions and other emergency first aid procedures correctly – it is all too easy to inflict injury in the process.

Toddlers' tongues, throats and facial muscles aren't well developed. That, combined with the fact that they lack a full set of teeth, increases the risk of choking. Here are some things you can do to help prevent your child from choking:

- Peel and cut grapes lengthwise.
- Mash sausages.
- Cut meat into very small pieces, or mince it.
- Don't give peanuts or crunchy peanut butter; to lessen the risk of peanut allergies, peanut-containing foods should not be given to children under three years of age if the child has a parent or sibling with a diagnosed allergy. Whole nuts should not be given to any child under the age of five years because of the risk of choking.
- Keep boiled sweets and hard mints out of reach, and don't ever let toddlers have any.
- Avoid popcorn.

Keep small toy pieces out of reach, too, and watch out for loose buttons and poppers on clothing that could fall off and be swallowed. Coins present another hazard. Most pass through toddlers' systems without doing any harm, although some get stuck in the oesophagus (warning signs are wheezing, gagging and excessive drooling) or at the point where the small intestine connects to the bowel. Coins may sit in the stomach for days. If a coin that contains zinc (ie, £1 coins and pre-1992 1 and 2p coins) sits in the stomach for more than a day, it poses a special hazard of zinc poisoning. Stomach acid begins to dissolve the zinc within two days of ingestion. (£2 coins also contain zinc, but are a bit big to swallow.)

Lengths of ribbon, rope or string – or any other dangling material longer than 40cm (16in) – can pose a strangulation hazard. Be especially careful to keep cords of mini-blinds and curtains from dangling within a toddler's reach.

First-Aid Kit

It's important to have a first-aid kit locked up safely at home, and another, simpler version kept in the boot of the car. Ready-made kits are cheap and useful, but you will almost certainly want to add extra items. The following list may be a helpful starting point:

·   Infant/child thermometer.
·   Children's and infants' liquid pain reliever: use paracetamol or ibuprofen – do not use aspirin for any child under 16. Keep a medicine spoon or oral syringe with the medicine.
·   Calamine lotion for sunburn and rashes; sting reliever spray for insect bites.
·   Antiseptic cream for cuts and grazes.
·   Tweezers and needles for splinters and thorns.
·   Sharp scissors.
·   Plasters in several sizes and shapes.
·   Assorted bandages.
·   Micropore adhesive tape and sterile gauze pads.
·   Antibacterial wipes.
·   A first-aid manual, such as *First Aid For Children Fast* (published by the Red Cross).
·   If your child has asthma, keep his medicine with you and spare medicine in the first-aid kit.
·   If your child has a life-threatening allergy (bee stings, peanuts or shellfish, for example) keep his emergency kit with you and spare medication in the first-aid kit.

Medication Safety

While it might be tempting to refer to medicine as 'yummy' when you're trying to get some down a reluctant toddler's throat, don't! Just think what will happen if he gets into a bottle or a box when you're not around.

Many parents don't realize that overdoses of vitamins can be dangerous, too. Follow these basic safety strategies:

· Call medicine by its real name.
· Use products with child-resistant packaging.
· Don't confuse 'child-resistant' with 'childproof'. (The name changed when it was discovered how quickly toddlers could get the covers off. Very few items are toddler-proof.)
· Keep medications in their original containers to avoid confusion at a later stage.
· Install childproof locks on cabinets, drawers and cupboards where medications are stored. (Don't depend solely on locks, as little fingers can sometimes work them open.)
· Keep track of how much medicine has been used. (If you discover his hand in the bottle and pink syrup ringing his mouth, or her hand in the pills and white powder on her tongue, you'll have an idea how much has been ingested.)
· Treat vitamins containing iron like the medicine it is; an overdose can be fatal.
· Check the dosages and use a proper medicine spoon or oral syringe – these syringes are ideal for toddlers and are available cheaply at chemists' or pharmacies.
· Don't mix medications without your doctor's approval.
· If the phone rings while you're administering medication, ignore it or take it with you. (Don't leave unattended drugs around a toddler.)

Don't take your own medication around a toddler – you don't want her to mimic you. Children need to learn that when it comes to prescriptions and over-the-counter medications, they are to take *only* what a caregiver or parent administer – that includes vitamins. Even when you think a toddler understands, he probably doesn't.

Use-by dates

Parents should check the medicine cabinet from time to time and dispose of expired medications and those more than two years old. Flush them down the toilet and rinse and wash bottles before throwing them away. The chemical changes that occur over time can render some ineffective, while others can become poisonous. Always discard aspirin that smells like vinegar, as it has lost its effectiveness, and throw away any liquids that have separated or changed colours. Finally, dispose of old eyedrops and eyewashes; fungus can grow in them.

Toddlers can often open containers very quickly from as young as 18 months. By the age of three, a child may be able to get the top off a 'child-resistant' container more efficiently than you can. Medicines, alcohol and cosmetics should ideally be kept in a locked cabinet. Be extra vigilant when visiting other people – especially if they don't have children – as your toddler may be able to get access to all sorts of toxic items.

Herbal Safety

There's no guarantee that a herb is safe, and some homeopathic remedies can pack a big punch. Before administering alternative remedies to a toddler, check the following:

· That it has been tested on youngsters.
· That its effectiveness has been established.
· The kinds of side effects and adverse reactions that may occur.
· That it won't interact with other prescription and over-the-counter medications your toddler is taking.
· If in doubt, don't.

CHAPTER 8

Doling Out Discipline

Many parents believe that 'discipline' is the same thing as 'punishment', and it is unfortunate that the two concepts have become synonymous in so many people's minds. Really, the word *discipline* means 'teaching' or 'learning', and comes from the word *discipulus*, which means 'pupil'. Disciplining toddlers involves teaching young pupils. It falls to the most important teachers in their lives, their parents, to serve as their first instructors.

Little Disciples

Teaching little disciples is a long, slow process. They have little experience on which to build, and their language skills prevent them from understanding much of what is said to them. In addition, their memory skills are so poor that they forget much of what they've been taught from moment to moment and from day to day. Finally, they lack the intellectual skills to use what they learn in one situation to guide their behaviour in another.

When it comes to disciplining toddlers, patience and repetition are the teacher's most important attributes.

Teaching About No

When parents say 'no', it is clear to *them* exactly what they want the toddler to stop doing or to stay away from. But what is obvious to them may not be at all clear to the toddler. How do you teach what 'no' means? Here are a few ideas:

- Change your tone of voice when you say it.
- Accompany your words with a frown and shake of the head.
- Try to get your child to repeat your words, or at least your gestures.
- If your child mimics your words or gestures, smile and praise them: 'Well done!'

Toddlers may still not associate the phrase and gesture with expected behaviour, but at least they are being helped to focus on those two important words.

Don't Just Say No

The problem with 'just saying no' is that toddlers don't learn what they *can* do. A child may not be *trying* to create chaos and ill will as she goes from one forbidden activity to the next. She doesn't know what is off limits and what is permissible. Follow up 'no' and 'don't' with 'it's all right to' or 'you can' when appropriate.

Offering alternatives may not prevent toddlers from becoming upset if they're very taken with something. Still, offering alternatives provides an important lesson: when the road we want to go down is blocked, we need to find another one.

Too Many No's

The easiest way for parents to reduce the number of 'no's' and 'don't touches' is to childproof the home by putting away and securing as many dangerous and fragile objects as possible, and to provide lots of objects for them to manipulate.

Ultimately, the goal is for toddlers to learn to control themselves instead of relying on adults to control them. But developing self-control won't be accomplished in a matter of days, weeks or even months or years. Until then, you may be better off putting more energy into controlling the environment. That way, you can spend less time struggling to control your youngsters and more time enjoying them.

The Problem with 'No'

As anyone who has studied a foreign language knows, learning to understand and use negative words is no small task. In English, things get particularly confusing. Even adults aren't always sure what answering 'yes' to a question means; for example, 'You're not going to touch the oven, are you?' When addressing toddlers, keep things simple.

Since negatives like *don't* occur at the beginning of sentences, toddlers often miss them. They don't even realize they're being spoken to until the parent has made it halfway through the sentence. So when you say, 'Don't touch the oven', the toddler may only hear '... touch the oven' or '... the oven'. It's no wonder toddlers so often do exactly the opposite of what their parents are telling them.

Make it a habit to tell toddlers what *to do* rather than what *not* to do. Instead of 'Don't touch the oven', you might say, 'Keep your hands by your sides!'

INSTEAD OF THE NEGATIVE...	TRY THE POSITIVE...
'Don't go in the street'	'Stay on the grass'
'Stop yelling'	'Use your soft voice'
'Don't hit your sister'	'Ask her for the truck. Can you say "Truck, please"?'
'Don't touch the flowers'	'Put your hands behind your back and put your nose up close so you can sniff – like this'
'Don't bang the cup on the table'	'Put your cup down until you want a drink'

Why Not?

It's not always necessary to provide reasons for 'no'. Sometimes 'no' can simply be 'because I said so'. But as children become increasingly independent, an adult won't be present at every moment to supervise. They need to be able to assess objects – and eventually situations and people – to determine what and who is safe. For example, if youngsters understand that they can't play with the lamp because it has an electric cable and a glass bulb, by middle childhood they will better be able to protect themselves when they come upon other interesting appliances and objects containing glass.

Show-and-Tell

Often parents can satisfy toddler's curiosity about forbidden objects by taking a moment for show-and-tell. Using the example of the lamp, a parent might do the following:

- Help the child look under the shade.
- Point out the glass.
- Hold the child's finger and help her touch the glass so she can feel it.
- Explain the importance of touching glass gently.
- Explain that light bulbs get hot if the lamp is turned on.
- Point out the cable and say that it's a no, too.

Young toddlers won't understand much of what is said. Still, parents' serious tone and hands-on demonstration can help satisfy their curiosity while communicating that lamps are to be handled with care.

Distraction

To keep very young toddlers away from things they're not to touch and dissuade them from forbidden pastimes, distraction is the simplest, most straightforward, least confrontational way to achieve compliance. With this technique, simply remove the forbidden object or move the toddler away from it and say, 'No, don't play with that.' Frown and shake your head, and then offer an alternative toy or activity.

If the tears don't stop quickly, the new toy or activity probably isn't very appealing, or the upset is about something else entirely. A big reaction to a small deprivation can be a sign that the child is tired, hungry, ill or coming down with something, going through a stressful period or going through a spurt of independence.

Redirection

When toddlers have matured to the point that they can remember the item their parent took away (which they demonstrate by trying to search for an object that has been removed), a teaching device known as 'redirection' works well. Redirection simply involves the following:

- Setting a limit ('No, don't play with the lamp.')
- Giving a reason ('It's dangerous. The bulb could break. And you mustn't play with anything that has a cable.')
- Enticing toddlers into a different activity ('Let's find something else for you to play with. How about your torch?')

Like distraction, redirection is a simple, straightforward way to minimize or avoid confrontations. The challenge in redirecting a child is to find an activity as enticing as the one they've chosen. Overleaf are some common don'ts and possible alternatives.

Jumping on the furniture. Slip old cases over pillows, place them on the carpet (or on blankets folded to make a pad), clear the area of end tables and other hard objects that could hurt them, and let them jump! Or you could purchase a beanbag chair that the children can jump on.

Throwing toys. Give them a teatowel tied in string, two socks rolled together, a foam rubber ball, a sponge, and let them toss. If they need the sound of the *thunk*, consider letting them hurl a plastic bottle onto a linoleum floor or into a large metal pot.

Playing in the toilet bowl. Fill a plastic dish tub half full of water, set it on towels on the laundry room floor (or on wash day, empty the dirty clothes basket onto the floor), and let them play.

Sometimes parents come up with great alternatives, but toddlers feel compelled to say 'no' because they are practising independence. This can set the scene for many conflicts. Prime times for resistant behaviour are shortly after learning to walk and during the second year.

Offering Choices

When simple redirection fails, try a different approach. Let's say that Jenny wants to paint. Her mother declines and offers her an alternative, 'How about playing in your sandpit?' Jenny loves the sandpit, but her upset over her mother's refusal to let her paint quickly escalates into loud wails and roars. What's going on? It could be that she wants an indoor activity, so the sandpit fails to appeal. It could be that she is working on self-assertion and needs to have a hand in deciding what she does next, instead of always being told what to do.

Distraction works especially well before youngsters have achieved object constancy. Until then, they don't understand that objects still exist, even if they can't see them at the moment. To them, out of sight really does mean out of mind.

Offering choices gives toddlers an opportunity to practise making decisions and to have more control over their lives.

Jenny's mother could say, 'Painting is messy, and we have people coming over soon. You can play in your sandpit or read a book. Which would you prefer?' Jenny may need to finish wailing her disappointment over not being allowed to paint before she'll be ready to move on, in which case her mother can say, 'When you decide whether you want the sandpit or a story, let me know.'

When offering choices:

Keep them limited. Toddlers can become confused and overwhelmed when considering too many options. Until the age of three, they may have trouble with more than two.

Don't insist on an immediate decision. Crying is a toddler's way of expressing disappointment. The victory comes when they're able to recover and forge ahead.

Hold firm. This can be difficult in the face of intense toddler opposition.

Dangerous Situations

The time for parents to step out of the teaching role into that of policing is when their toddler is approaching danger. That way, they can stage an immediate rescue.

For instance, sooner or later most youngsters will want to explore electrical cables. When a young toddler reaches for one and suddenly hears his parent's loud voice, he is likely to pause, smile and reach for the cable again. The parent may believe the child's pause means he understood the 'No, don't touch!' warning. From the child's ensuing smile and renewed attempt to reach for the cable, adults may assume the kind of defiance that makes them want to tear their hair out by the roots.

However, the pause may simply be a response to the parent's voice; it doesn't mean that he understood the warning. Even if he does surmise from the parent's tone that he is being warned about *something*, he may not realize he is being warned away from the cable. How can toddlers comprehend that a cord is dangerous when they don't know about either cable or danger, and haven't even touched one yet?

When a toddler is approaching danger, follow these steps:

1. Say, 'No! Don't touch!' or 'Stop!' in a firm, authoritative tone.
2. If the child pauses, be sure to smile, nod and provide positive reinforcement by saying 'Thank you' to let him know he responded correctly: he paused.
3. Don't wait to see what will happen next; grab him fast.
4. Explain, 'That's *dangerous*. It will hurt you.'
5. Say 'No', shake your head and frown to convey your message non-verbally.
6. Try to get him to say 'no' and shake his head.
7. Move him away from the danger.

If the child toddles back to the cable, you will need to either repeat the process as often as needed, distract him by providing something different to do, or offer him choices for alternative toys or activities.

To make sure your toddler listens to you and not the voice propelling her to touch anything and everything, it is imperative to establish and maintain a good relationship. To this end, pick your battles, focusing on only one or two issues at a time; praise more often than you chastise; and spend more time enjoying each other's company than you spend praising *or* chastising.

If you physically move him away from the cable, he may conclude that you are playing a wonderful chasing game. He may head back in that direction the moment he is released, hoping for more. Once again, you may see his actions as defiant. It's important to consider that by this point the cable may be the farthest thing from his mind.

Would it be easier just to issue a warning and then slap the child to drive home the message that he must stay away from a dangerous object?

Although it might seem easier in the short run, there are a number of problems with slapping a toddler to convey the 'no' message:

· Toddlers may lose trust in the parent. Slaps that are delivered 'out of the blue' can make youngsters chronically tense and uncomfortable around anyone they have learned may hit them unexpectedly. If a child thinks he and his parent were playing a chasing game and didn't realize touching the cord was the issue, the slap will certainly take him by surprise. This can seriously undermine the parent-child relationship.
· Toddlers may learn that when their parent uses that particular tone of voice, they had better run fast to avoid being hit. This is *not* a lesson that will serve them well when the danger is approaching a busy street, hot oven, swimming pool or big dog.
· Toddlers may learn that they must not do certain things when their parent is around. The sooner children can move from needing parents to control them to controlling themselves, the better for everyone.

Even after toddlers understand that they're not supposed to touch particular items, they may still be driven to engage in forbidden activities, because they have two voices inside of them issuing very different directives. Mother Nature pushes them to explore and become independent. Their parents insist that many interesting activities and objects are off limits, and oppose their desire to make up their own minds.

The Problem With Praise

Brian was contentedly munching his cereal when his mother breezed by the table and gave him the thumbs-up sign. 'Good job', she said. Brian's smile faded as he bleakly surveyed his brimming cereal bowl. He was already full, and he'd barely dented it. He wanted to please his mother, but knew he was going to have to let her down.

Just as parents use expressions like 'No' or 'That's not OK' to mean 'Stop' or 'Don't', they use expressions like 'Good job!' or 'That's right' to mean 'Yes, that's what I want you to do'. If Brian's mother had said, 'It looks like you're enjoying that cereal', he could have said 'Yes' without feeling obliged to eat more.

Contrary to popular opinion, praising youngsters doesn't necessarily improve their self-esteem. Praise encourages them to focus on their success at pleasing adults and at measuring up to other people's expectations, rather than the achievement itself.

Children with good self-esteem feel pleased with themselves. When evaluating their own behaviour, they feel they measure up to their personal expectations. But praise can actually serve to undermine self-esteem. First-born children, whose parents are apt to applaud each small gurgle and goo and record each new accomplishment in their bulging baby book, tend to be the least emotionally secure and suffer more problems with self-esteem than the rest of the brood, whose successes receive far less attention. Meanwhile, the middle child, typically lost in a no-man's land between the accomplished older sibling and the darling baby, has a harder time finding ways to impress. Yet youngsters sandwiched in the middle of the pack tend to be more self-confident.

The following parent comments point out some of the pitfalls of praise:

· 'I like the bright colours in your drawing' suggests to the child that to please the parent he should use bright colours. Expressing interest and asking a neutral question, such as 'What did you draw?' or 'Tell me about your picture' enables the child to share his drawing and his feelings about it without having his choice of crayons judged.
· If the parent exclaims 'Good catch!' when the ball lands in their toddler's arms, it's understandable why she becomes upset when it lands on the floor on subsequent tries: the youngster assumes they are 'bad' catches.
· 'Good boy!' the parent says when the toddler uses the potty by himself. This kind of evaluation – 'You're good because you did what I wanted' – can cause toddlers who are in the throes of a struggle over independence to respond by refusing to use the potty thereafter.

Instead, try 'You should be proud of yourself'. Although that still conveys your opinion, it encourages the child to evaluate *himself* in a positive light, rather than to focus exclusively on your opinion.

 There's nothing wrong with saying 'Good' to teach a child to do things in a certain way. Certainly there are 'right' and 'wrong' ways to do many things. However, giving positive feedback in situations that are meant to be fun can cause toddlers to turn play sessions into tests of their competence.

Praising Accomplishments

After an hour or so has gone by without a repetition of a particular behaviour problem, parents should make it a point to praise their child's accomplishment. Because toddlers get into so many things and break so many rules, it's easy to spend more time focusing on what they do wrong than on what they do right.

If, when you say 'I'm so glad you've left the TV off', the child runs towards it, hurry over but try to give her the benefit of the doubt. There's a good chance she'll look at the controls without touching them and say 'No', or wait for you to frown and shake your head and discuss this no with her once again. If so, she's making fabulous progress. Give her a hug and try to let her know you share the delight in her accomplishment. It's important for toddlers to realize that they really are capable of learning self-control and pleasing their parents. And parents will feel much better knowing that the child is making strides in learning to keep herself safe.

Time-Outs

Providing time-outs is an excellent teaching device to help toddlers learn to adhere to important rules and regain control when they are unable to contain themselves – but should only be used if the child is over 18 months old. Tell your toddler to sit down until she can settle down and observe the limit you have set or behave in accordance with the rules you have established.

> Many parents send toddlers to their rooms for time-out, but this isn't an option for youngsters who need to be watched at every moment, and being sent away can make toddlers feel rejected. The point of time-out is to teach, not to punish, although until children learn the advantages of being contained, they may certainly *feel* punished.

The rule of thumb is to assign one minute of time out per year of age, so a two-year-old should be required to sit for two minutes at most. If toddlers weren't upset to begin with, they may become very angry about being prevented from engaging in the activity they have chosen. You may not wish to start the clock until the child has settled down.

When the child has regained control, discuss the event that precipitated the time-out to help him learn from the experience so he knows what to do if the same situation arises in the future. It helps to begin the discussion by praising the toddler for having regained control. Besides starting the discussion on a positive note, praise helps little ones focus on their important accomplishment, and keeps both the parent and child from being overly focused on the misdeeds.

Reviewing what transpired and figuring out what to do differently is beyond younger toddlers and will be too hard for older toddlers until they are familiar with the process. In the beginning, you may have to do most or all of the talking for your toddler:

Do you know why I sent you to time-out? *Blank stare.*

Because you turned on the TV after I told you not to. *Blank stare.*

You can't watch any more TV today. Too much TV watching isn't good for kids, remember? *Blank stare.*

The TV needs to stay off, OK? *Nods.*

There's still no guarantee that the toddler understood the question. If he turns on the TV again, the parent will need to assign another minute or two in time-out. The point of time-out is to teach several important lessons children can use throughout their lives:

1. Important rules must be followed.
2. If people disregard rules, there are consequences, which may be unpleasant for them and others.
3. If people don't control themselves, someone else will control them.
4. When people are upset and out of control, taking a brief time-out can help them calm down.

Most children learn the value of time-outs in short order. In fact, once they have become accustomed to the procedure, toddlers will begin sitting down or running off to their rooms when they are upset over a parental demand or prohibition. During their self-imposed time-out, they will finish crying and re-emerge, settled, a few minutes later.

Smacking

While smacks may more quickly control a child who is repeatedly engaging in forbidden behaviour, the fatal flaw is that the parent is controlling the child's behaviour. Children need to learn to control their own behaviour. If you do smack your child for doing something dangerous, such as running into the road, the aim is for the sound of the swat and the parent's angry voice (not pain) to evoke the correct response to danger – fear.

Parents who don't spank can usually elicit the same reaction by swooping the child away from danger while shouting, 'Stay out of the street! It's dangerous!' and then refusing to comfort the crying child for a few minutes, saying, 'No, I'm not giving you a hug right now. I'm upset. You're not supposed to run into the street!'

Time-outs aren't just for kids! When parents are upset with their toddler and sense they are losing control, they should give themselves a time-out to settle down and rethink what is happening.

Smacking and the Law

Most children's charities, including Barnardo's, the NSPCC and Save the Children, want a total ban on smacking. The European Court believes that English law doesn't properly protect children from the risk of serious criminal assault.

In England alone, about 80 children die from physical abuse each year. Many parents, MPs and children's charities feel that the law on parents smacking their children should be tightened. The current legal defence (in England and Wales) of 'reasonable chastisement' can be, and is, used as an excuse for violence against children. But, at the time of publication, the government has no plans to make it illegal for parents to smack their children, although it has now been made an offence for childminders to smack their charges.

In Scotland, however, it was decided that the Victorian concept of 'reasonable chastisement' was virtually impossible to define in the 21st century. And while smacking has not been totally banned in Scotland, it is now illegal to shake children, to hit them on the head, or to use a belt, cane, slipper, wooden spoon or other implement.

Wherever you live, and whatever the law, think about these points before you decide to smack your child:

· It can be dangerous – we can forget how delicate children are, especially when we are frustrated or angry. What you thought was a light slap could cause real harm to a small child.
· It sets the wrong example: do you want to teach your child to hit people who are doing something she doesn't like, or who won't do as she wants them to?
· The effects of smacking may last much longer than the sting of the slap: your child might become angry and resentful, as well as losing confidence and self-esteem.

Instead, try to see 'discipline' as a way of showing children how to behave properly, rather than instilling obedience or doling out physical punishment. If you praise and reward a toddler when he behaves well, you will encourage both his self-discipline and his self-esteem. To begin with, this involves lots of patience and self-control. But it will work in time, and your home will feel happier for all of you. When the going gets tough, remember that research has shown praise and reward to be far more effective in dealing with toddlers than criticism and punishment.

Handling Tantrums

Not every toddler has tantrums, but most do. They are most common between two and three, when there can be as many as one to two daily for several weeks, and others intermittently. Not all tantrums were created equal. Telling them apart can be tricky.

Stress Tantrums

The toddler is stressed (tired; hungry; ill; or fretful due to a number of small disappointments, changes and/or defeats), when some unpleasant thing happens. Perhaps he hates to have his nappy changed, and Dad insisted on it. Or Mum kept her hands on the shopping trolley when he wanted to push it himself. Or his toy broke. That one small incident becomes the straw that broke the camel's back, and suddenly the toddler loses control. The screaming and carrying on is out of proportion to the problem at hand because the upset isn't about a single event. It's the result of an accumulation of stress that has taken its toll on a child who, because of his age, doesn't have a lot of emotional control to begin with.

Trying to sidestep a stress tantrum may merely be postponing the inevitable. As things heat up, it becomes increasingly clear that the toddler is trying to provoke a struggle.

To manage stress tantrums:

1. Hold the child firmly but lovingly and provide reassurance that she'll be OK in a bit. This assumes that you *can* hold her. Children may thrash too wildly to be safely held.

2. If she's endangering himself, other people or property as she rolls about the floor, clear the area if you can. Otherwise, move her to a safe place, such as a carpeted floor.
3. Let her cry it out. Tears are a great tension-reliever.
4. Sympathize with the fact that she's having a hard day.
5. When the tantrum ends, ask if she'd like to sit on your lap and have you rock her, or lie down and have you rub her back.
6. Provide reassurance that things will get easier for her when her new tooth comes through, she's rested, she's adjusted to her new daycare centre, or the stressful situation has passed.

When it comes to stress tantrums, the best cure lies in prevention. Consider them a signal that your toddler is under more pressure than she can manage, and see if there's a way to help lessen it. Remember that toddlers are already under a lot of stress because they are struggling with their personal sense of inadequacy that comes from wanting to do things and being unable to do them, having lots to communicate and being unable to say much, and wanting to be independent while being emotionally needy.

In a stress tantrum, the child isn't trying to get something; instead, she is trying to get rid of the unpleasant feelings that have accumulated. Having a momentary whim gratified helps a stressed toddler feel better, but not for long. The next small crisis produces another upset of similar or even greater intensity, because the *real* problem — feeling generally overwhelmed — remains.

Manipulative Tantrums

Some children learn to throw a tantrum to get something. Their manipulative tantrums are their way of saying 'I want something and I want it *now*!' Once their end is achieved – freedom to run around the shop, liberation from the car seat, permission to eat the biscuit or to have a toy – they settle down. Tantrums in public are common because many children have learned that if they stage a big one, they will immediately be taken home, which is exactly what they want.

> If the tantrum is causing a public, and disruptive, scene in a shop, cinema or restaurant, remove the child if you can. You can deal with the tantrum, and the issue behind it, once you're in a calm and private area.

It can be hard to stay firm in the face of manipulative tantrums. Their fearsome intensity can quickly melt parental resolve. But of course, every time you appease the child by giving in, you drive home the lesson that screaming, hitting, kicking, thrashing, breath-holding, fainting and even head-banging and vomiting are workable ways to achieve goals.

If the behaviour during manipulative tantrums is particularly dramatic, discuss the problem with your doctor to satisfy yourself that the quickest, most effective way to end this kind of tantrum – ignoring it – is a safe option. Behaviour that warrants a professional opinion includes banging his head or other self-injurious behaviour, or holding his breath to the point of turning purple, passing out, precipitating an asthma attack or vomiting. To end manipulative tantrums:

- If she's a raging puddle on the floor, tell her you'll talk to her when she's settled down.
- Carry her to an open space where she can't harm herself or something else, preferably with carpet to soften the blows.
- Step over her and busy yourself nearby (but out of kicking range) by studiously ignoring her.

The challenge is not to take manipulative tantrums personally. See them for what they are: a child's rage at rules and limits. By failing to give in and not paying attention to her, you're showing what happens when people are assailed by crushing disappointments: life goes on. When a tantrum ends and the child has settled down:

- See it as the victory it is – the child regained control on her own.
- Don't attempt to discuss what transpired before or during the tantrum – let the subject drop.
- Be warm enough to show her you're not angry with her – respond to her desire to be held, hear a story or get you to participate in another quiet activity once she's settled down.
- Don't try to compensate for having held firm by being over-solicitous.

If throwing a tantrum has worked in the past, the predictable short-term result when parents don't give in is an *increase* in both the intensity and frequency of tantrums. It may take a number of scenes before they grasp that tantrums are no longer a useful method for getting what they want.

Communication Tantrums

Sometimes toddlers throw tantrums out of sheer frustration over their inability to communicate their needs. For instance, it's very clear that your toddler wants something. It's clear to your toddler that you have it. Try as you might, you can't figure out what your child is asking for. He tries every way he can think of to get the message across, and then dissolves.

Or it is all too clear what your toddler wants: ice-cream. He is sure it is in the freezer, because that's where it's kept. Except that there isn't any ice-cream there, or anywhere else, because you haven't got any. He's sure you're withholding it, and you can't find a way to explain it to him. The only recourse is to provide reassurance that you would give him what he wanted if you could, and let him rage at the injustice of it.

It's not easy being any age, but it can be particularly hard to be a toddler. Parents who remain sympathetic as children struggle through these trying moments may also feel helpless. Remember that by demonstrating your love for your youngster when she is at her very worst, you are in fact helping a lot.

CHAPTER 9

Food Fiesta

Filling a toddler tummy with food is easy. Filling it nutritiously to meet the needs of a growing dynamo, and instilling healthy habits that last a lifetime can pose challenges. Although this is a prime time for power struggles as parents begin begging, bribing, pressuring and punishing to get youngsters to open up and swallow, the fact is that toddlers need very few calories.

The Toddler Appetite

During the first 12 months of life, children triple their birth weight, gaining about 0.72kg (1½lb) per month. But between 12 and 24 months, toddlers typically gain only 1.82–2.2kg (4–6lb) – less than 0.27kg (8oz) per month. Between 24 and 36 months, they gain only 1.6–2.5kg (3½–5½lb) – just over 0.15kg (5oz) per month! And those are averages, so in some months they'll gain even less.

Since the beginning of the toddler years is also when parents try to get them to eat a greater variety of foods, it is easy to assume that resistance is due to being finicky. But consider the following:

· When toddlers consume very little food, it's probably because they just aren't hungry or haven't become accustomed to a new flavour.
· Unless your child's health visitor or doctor suggests a need to spur weight gain, don't focus on *how much* a child is eating, but rather ensure that the *quality* of the little food consumed is excellent.
· If your child is losing weight or you're concerned about an over-dainty appetite, discuss the matter with your doctor.

When to Wean

It is unusual to see toddlers nursing, because most parents struggle in earnest to wean them from the bottle or breast early in the second year of life. This is unfortunate. Children continue to receive protection against illness as long as they nurse. In societies where nature is allowed to take its course, self-weaning occurs between three and four; the *minimum* age is two and a half. When they are ready to stop nursing, they simply taper off and lose interest.

The Department of Health now recommends exclusive breastfeeding for the first six months (26 weeks). If you feel your baby needs to start solids before this, then talk to your health visitor. A mother is the best judge of when it's time to wean, so don't feel you have to fix a deadline. When you decide to wean, don't stop abruptly: this is very traumatic for your baby and very uncomfortable for you.

If you need to wean a toddler before he's ready, it will probably be difficult. Remember that they are severing a powerful emotional attachment. You can soften the blow by trying the following:

· Choose a time when the youngster isn't coping with other major stresses in life.
· Tell your child you are going to wean him.
· Provide milk in a cup with meals.
· Nurse after meals, when the child has less of an appetite.
· Eliminate one bottle or nursing session at a time, beginning with the one the child is least attached to – typically in the middle of the day.
· Avoid the cues that trigger the desire to be nursed by staying busy and sitting in a different chair.
· Spend the time you would have devoted to nursing reading a story, reciting nursery rhymes or playing together.
· Offer bottle-fed babies a bottle of water.
· Wait five days before eliminating a second bottle or nursing session.
· Eliminate bedtime feedings last. (Provide other kinds of comfort until the child learns to fall asleep without being nursed. If possible, get Dad to handle bedtime.)

Introducing Solids

If your child is not well into solid foods by his first birthday, keep in mind that breastmilk alone does not meet the nutritional requirements of a one-year-old. If you plan to breastfeed exclusively past six months, consult your doctor for information on how to supplement your baby's diet.

Toddlers need solid food, too. Introduce new foods gradually, at least two to three days apart, so there is time to assess food allergies. Common symptoms of food allergy include itchy, watery eyes; repeated sneezing attacks; itchy skin; clear mucus running from the nose; rash; hives; 'slapped' or very red cheeks; or behaviour changes.

Five Squares a Day

Because toddler tummies are small, offer them five small meals a day rather than three big ones. An easy way to keep youngsters nutritionally well primed is to serve between-meal snacks that emphasize finger foods. That way, toddlers can more readily manage the mechanics of eating themselves, and there's less cooking and cleaning up for the chef. (Remember not to let them wander as they munch!)

Healthy snacks and finger foods:

Cheese sandwiches (cut in quarters)

Toast

Fortified cereal such as Cheerios

Fruit wedges

Hard-boiled egg slices

Dried fruit

Mozzarella cheese sticks

Vegetable sticks

Wholewheat crackers and cheese cubes

Fussy Eaters

Toddlers are notorious for being fussy eaters, and contrary, too. The pasta they loved last week they hate this week. They seem ravenous for some meals and pick at others. Again, small meals and nutritious snacks throughout the day are the answer. Toddlers never starve themselves – they will eat when they are hungry.

Don't be too alarmed if she eats only bananas and cornflakes on one day. The next she might tackle a bowl of scrambled egg or some mashed potatoes and broccoli. The following day, breadsticks and hummus seem to be her favourite food. What you are trying to achieve with a 'balanced' diet isn't necessarily a balanced diet every single day, but rather, over the whole week or ten days. Try listing everything she eats over a week. You'll be amazed how 'balanced' it turns out to be (as long as you've offered her sufficient choice in the first place!). Another tactic that seems to work is to let your toddler join you for meals whenever possible. When she sees you relishing a stir fry or a tuna salad, she may want to taste her own. Children often like surprisingly adult foods.

Toddlers are supposed to be roly-poly. They'll lose the round belly after turning three. Until then, serve whole milk to ensure they get enough fat (after two, semi-skimmed is sufficient). Don't put them on a diet except under doctor's orders, and avoid fat-free foods.

Weight Worries

Parents often worry unnecessarily that their toddler is too fat or too thin. If you are anxious that your child is putting on too much weight, simply cut down on snacks, particularly sweets, sweet biscuits, crisps and chocolate, and give sugar-free or no-added-sugar drinks. Water and pure fruit juices are excellent drinks – but dilute apple or orange juice with equal parts water. Your health visitor or doctor can reassure you, and if necessary refer your child to a dietician.

If your child doesn't seem to be gaining weight, offer several little meals a day rather than three larger ones, and try to make them as nutritious as possible. Your doctor can check for any underlying medical reasons – a food intolerance, for example.

Good for You

When it comes to menu planning, variety is important for more than making toddler taste buds tingle. No single food is perfect, so children need to eat many different foods for optimal nutrition. For instance, oranges are rich in vitamin C but lack vitamin B_{12}. Apricots are high in beta-carotene. Scientists have only just begun to unravel the exact components of plants and animals that are good for human beings, and they continue to add to the list.

Only a few generalities are certain: fresh foods are better than processed; pesticide-free food is healthier. So take up cooking and go organic! The first thing chefs need to know is that besides supplying vitamins, minerals and other ingredients needed for good health (such as fibre), foods provide energy. Energy is measured in calories. Calories come from three sources: proteins, fats and sugars. Children need all three kinds.

The number of calories needed depends on a toddler's individual metabolism, growth rate and activity level, so the average number of calories a child needs at any particular time will vary.

Nutritional Pyramid

The following sections provide details on specific serving sizes, but the pyramid is a handy visual reference. The habits formed now will help keep your child healthy as she grows.

FIGURE 9-1:
Nutritional
Pyramid

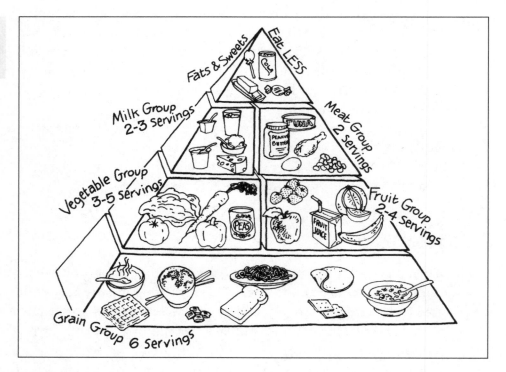

Servings of Protein

Protein, which is essential for good nutrition, comes from meats, poultry, fish, eggs, nuts and beans. It's the extras – the skin and fat or addition of oil for frying, butter for baking and cream sauces for smothering – that quickly add to the calories from fat. Milk, cheese and yoghurt are also high in protein and are rich sources of another essential nutrient, calcium. Low-fat products are preferable for children over two because they have fewer calories from fat. Provide two to four toddler servings of meat and high-protein alternatives daily, and three to four servings of milk, yoghurt and cheese. One toddler serving equals:

- 1 whole egg or 2 whites
- 150ml (6fl oz) milk
- 125ml (4fl oz) yoghurt
- 3 tablespoons cottage cheese
- 60g (2oz) baked beans
- (25g (^{3}/$_4$oz) hard cheese
- (25g (^{3}/$_4$oz) poultry, meat or fish
- 1^1/$_2$ tablespoons peanut butter

Contrary to what people often think, grains are healthy foods and are not fattening. It's when you add butter, cheese, whole milk and assorted fat-rich sauces that the calories from fat quickly add up.

Servings of Complex Carbohydrates

Bread, rice, cereal and pasta, which are made primarily or wholly from grains, provide energy from complex carbohydrates. Parents should provide six to eleven servings per day. One toddler serving equals:

- ^{1}/$_2$ slice bread (high-fibre)
- ^{1}/$_4$ English muffin
- ^{1}/$_4$ bagel
- 2–3 wholewheat crackers
- 30g (1oz) breakfast cereal
- 45g (1^1/$_2$oz) cooked pasta or rice
- 25g (^{3}/$_4$oz) cooked porridge

Servings of Fat

When it comes to calories from fat, the problem is usually keeping children from getting too much, especially after the age of two – processed foods tend to be loaded with it. But don't let round tummies and folds of baby fat fool you – toddlers don't need low-fat diets unless there's a special reason. Parents should provide five to eight servings per day from 12 to 24 months, and add a half serving to each end of the range from 24 to 36 months. One toddler serving equals:

- 180ml (6fl oz) whole milk or yoghurt
- 9 French fries

- 375ml (12fl oz) semi-skimmed milk
- 1 tablespoon peanut butter
- l egg
- ½ tablespoon oil, butter, margarine or mayonnaise

- 2 chicken nuggets
- 45g (1½oz, lamb or pork
- 75g (2½oz) poultry
- 60g (2oz) ice-cream

The World Health Organization has recommended adding DHA (docosahexaenoic acid), an Omega 3 fatty acid found in mother's milk, to formula for bottle-fed tots. Studies show it can make a significant difference in mental and physical development. Check the label of the brand (SAMA Gold adds it, for instance).

Servings of Vegetables

Vegetables contain small amounts of protein. What makes vegetables so important are the vitamins and fibre they also contain. Most of the vitamins are lost in the tinning process. The recommended daily allowance (RDA) charts on packaged foods list how much of needed vitamins and other nutrients foods contain. If you're using a lot of preprocessed foods, learn to read the labels. Keep these points in mind:

1. Frozen vegetables are better than tinned, since fewer vitamins are lost in processing. Vegetables lightly steamed in cookware with a tight-fitting lid are better still. Raw vegetables are best of all.
2. Starchy vegetables like potatoes are especially rich in nutrients, but they become a less-than-great choice when fat – butter, cheese, gravy, sour cream or oil – is added.
3. Beans, which are rich in vitamins and fibre as well as protein, can meet vegetable or protein requirements.

Servings of Fruit

Fruit – including fresh, dried, frozen and home-squeezed into juice – is rich in vitamins, especially vitamin C. Beware of fruit tinned in sugary syrup,and juices that contain mostly sugar and only a squirt of real fruit juice. A few drops can result in a label that proclaims in large letters,

'Contains real juice!' The question is *how much* juice, and you must read the label to find out.

Offer two or more servings of fruit per day. One serving equals approximately 1 tablespoon per year of life, so two-year-olds need at least 4 tablespoons per day. The equivalent is:

· 125ml (4fl oz) juice   · 3–4 tablespoons fruit

Don't Forget Fibre

Fibre is important for proper functioning of the bowels. Hefty portions serve as an antidote for chronic constipation. Offer three or more servings of vegetables per day. One serving equals approximately 1 tablespoon per year of life, so two-year-olds can have 6 tablespoons per day. Besides raw vegetables, other high-fibre foods include wholegrain breads and cereals, beans and peas, and fruit.

Calcium Counts

Calcium is required for bone growth, so to ensure your child gets enough calcium, you will need to provide daily doses from another source. Good choices include broccoli, calcium-fortified orange juice, calcium-fortified soya milk, tinned sardines or salmon (*with* the bones), goat's milk, kale, tofu and spring greens.

Serving Liquids

Toddlers need about 1l (32fl oz) of liquids daily under normal circumstances – more in hot weather or if they are ill with fever, vomiting, or diarrhoea. Besides water (from the tap or bottled, plain or carbonated), good sources of liquids include soup, fruit or vegetable juices (diluted with water) and milk. But note that milk provides only two-thirds of liquid per serving; the rest is solids.

Children need lots of iron, and one of the best sources is iron-fortified breakfast cereal. Other iron-rich foods include beef, liver, dried peas and beans, dried fruit, black treacle and wheatgerm. To help with iron absorption, serve a food rich in vitamin C at the same meal, especially oily fish such as sardines or mackerel.

Good Vitamins

It's important to try and include at least one vitamin A-rich and one vitamin C-rich food in children's diets each day.

Foods rich in vitamin A are often orange in colour and include: apricots, cantaloupe melons, carrots, mangos, papayas and sweet potatoes. Vitamin A is also found in green leafy vegetables such as broccoli and cabbage.

Foods rich in vitamin C include: peppers, broccoli, cantaloupe melons, citrus fruits, kiwi, mangos, papayas, peaches, potatoes (with their skins on), strawberries, sweet potatoes and tomatoes. As you can see, there are several foods that supply both vitamins.

Special Bodies, Special Needs

Of course, no one set diet can meet the nutritional requirements of every child. Some children's bodies are unable to absorb proper amounts of iron, so they need a supplement. In addition, many toddlers are allergic to certain foods or ingredients, and some suffer from juvenile diabetes, and must therefore avoid certain ingredients.

When playing chef for a little vegetarian, take special precautions to mix vegetables properly so kids get enough protein, iron, zinc and B vitamins. Little vegans should also get calcium supplements. Consult your health visitor for recommendations.

Chewing and Chopping

Once toddlers sprout enough teeth to chop through a carrot, hard foods become more of a choking hazard, not less. Be sure to cut crunchy foods to the size of half a grape before serving. Some squashy foods can also pose problems, given the ease with which they can become lodged in youngsters' throats. Foods like grapes should be cut in half, and sausages and other meats should be served in pieces small enough to be swallowed easily. Even very soft food can be a problem if toddlers stuff their mouths or try to talk while their mouth is full. Discourage them from doing either.

The Joy of Dipping

Some kids love sauces, salad dressings and condiments like ketchup – either because of the taste or for the sheer joy of dipping. Many go through a phase of wanting to add ketchup to everything; they think it improves the taste of everything from turkey to cereal. To date, there are no reports of children being adversely affected by this kind of strange culinary preference.

Adding sauces can encourage toddlers to do a better job on their veggies. But if they are just as happy to eat their foods *au naturel*, why encourage them to ladle on extras that are typically high in salt, chemicals and fat? Rather than passing on unhealthy family traditions to the next generation, it's better to let them die out. So, before you resort to salad dressing, try a squeeze of lemon and pinch of herbs. Don't boil rice, pasta or vegetables in salt. Add it after the food is on the toddler's plate, if at all.

Leisurely Meals

If toddlers take ages to finish a meal, why rush them? The modern trend to race through life notwithstanding, nowhere is it written that food must be consumed within 15 minutes. Toddlers need a long time to eat for several reasons. It is challenging for them to get food onto a spoon or fork and into their mouth. Furthermore, they don't have many teeth to chew with, and their poor ability to coordinate the muscles of their face and mouth makes chewing and swallowing difficult.

And of course, they must pause to enjoy the sensation of eggs sliding through their fingers and sucking spaghetti through pursed lips. Given that all that fingering and mouthing is good for their motor skills and cognitive development, they derive lots of benefit from the assorted activities they indulge in while satisfying their bird-sized appetites. Let them take their time. Otherwise, they may have difficulty consuming enough to keep them well nourished.

To end a marathon meal but still ensure they've had enough to eat, try the following tactics:

· Announce that since he's not eating, the meal is ending and you're going to take away his plate.
· If he doesn't begin aiming the food towards his mouth on cue, he may not have understood. Demonstrate by removing the plate.
· If he objects, assume he is still hungry and return his plate to him.
· If he resumes playing instead of eating, offer to feed him. (Until their fine motor skills develop, toddlers have trouble getting food into their mouths.)
· If he eats or allows himself to be fed, wait to remove the plate until the next time he begins playing. Then remove it for keeps.
· Offer water if he cries, and reassure him that he will be served again at snack time or the next meal.

Healthy Appetites

It is all too easy to interfere with youngsters' ability to interpret the physical cravings that guide them to satisfy bona fide nutritional needs. So you don't confuse them, follow these do's and don'ts:

DO	DON'T
Provide only healthy choices	Offer junk foods
Let children dawdle through their meals	Rush them
Offer to help feed them	Insist on helping
Serve previously refused foods early in a meal, when they're at their hungriest	Force them to eat things they don't like
Offer small portions, and let them know they are free to ask for more	Give large servings and coax them to eat

Make mealtimes relaxed and enjoyable	Nag them about eating
Let them eat as little or as much as they want	Play 'here comes the aeroplane' to induce them to open up and eat more
Let them eat their meals with the family if possible	

Up With Veggies

Sugar coatings work to get kids to eat cereal. Why shouldn't it work to get kids to eat veggies, too? As it turns out, it does. If you sprinkle some sugar on broccoli, peas, lettuce – or whatever – most children will gladly gobble the greens. Once they've developed a taste for the vegetables in question, reduce the amount of sugar added to subsequent servings until it is eliminated altogether.

Cute Concoctions

Kids may resist the raw carrots, celery, alfalfa sprouts and broccoli lying on their plates in traditional arrangements, which is to say in small piles. A glob of cottage cheese and smear of peanut butter on bread may not hold much appeal for finicky eaters. But turn those same ingredients into 3-D designs, and toddlers are apt to undergo a dramatic attitude change. Who can resist a figure made of carrot legs, celery arms, cottage cheese face, raisin eyes, tomato smile and alfalfa sprout hair lounging amid broccoli trees growing in peanut butter sand anchored in cement – er, crackers? To entice kids to eat good foods, be creative. Here are a few other ideas you can try:

- Cut bread with pastry cutters to create interesting shapes before topping with cheese or vegetables. The leftover bread can be frozen and eventually used to stuff chicken or turkey.
- Slice a banana lengthwise to make a boat; stand a piece of sliced cheese inside to make a sail; and float it in a pool of blueberry yoghurt. You can even infest the water with shark fins made from salami slices. (If that combination doesn't sound appealing to you, remember that your child probably won't mind, and it all ends up in the same place, anyway.)

· Spread strips of toast with cream cheese or peanut butter and top with a row of raisins for an enticing dish of 'ants on a log'.

Broadening Culinary Horizons

The first and second times tots taste peas, broccoli and any number of other foods parents consider healthy, it is common for toddlers to turn up their noses at them. After trying again and again, the best recourse, nutritionists say, is for parents to try yet again and again. It can take eight to ten exposures before a youngster develops a taste for a new food.

Offering new foods and encouraging their toddler to take a taste is one kind of 'exposure' most parents have used successfully. Heavy-handed tactics like force-feeding are more likely to harden resistance than induce acceptance... and may propel a child toward lifelong eating problems.

However, most tots are destined to dislike certain foods. Just as many adults never develop a taste for liver or cringe at the sight of salad cream, little ones have definite preferences. Other things being equal, one way to tell that a child is in a growth spurt is an increase in appetite. While her appetite is big, she may be more receptive to new and previously rejected foods. Offer them early in the meal, when she is hungry and less finicky.

Little Farmers

There is one (almost) guaranteed cure for kids who spurn leafy greens and assorted vegetables that parents consider healthy. When toddlers participate in growing them, their negative attitude is apt to undergo a dramatic transformation once it's time to eat the fruits (er, vegetables) of their labours. Homegrown tomatoes, carrots and lettuce are much more tasty, so it's much easier to get kids hooked on the taste.

Families don't need a garden; many vegetables have been developed that do well in patio pots. Herbs, of course, can be grown at any time of year; all they require is a sunny window. Help little ones pinch off chives, basil, parsley, oregano or other favourites to sprinkle on their salad or cooked vegetables.

Little Chefs

Involving little ones in food preparation creates the kind of pride of accomplishment that can bring about a willingness to eat their creations. Toddlers are good at shredding important papers, so put that talent to work tearing the washed lettuce leaves into pieces and dropping them into the salad bowls. Pull up a chair or step stool so youngsters can join you at the worktop. Enlist their help with a variety of food preparation chores by giving very young toddlers directions for one simple task at a time and giving a hands-on demonstration.

Until youngsters master a task and are old enough to remember how things were done in the past, they will need lots of feedback and repetition: 'Put this roll on this plate', 'Yes, that's right', 'No, like this. Put the roll on the plate'. Older toddlers should be able to handle more general single-step directions: 'Put the rolls on the plates', although they may also need a demonstration. As they approach three, they may be able to handle two-step directions: 'Get the rolls out of the bread bin and put them on the plates'.

Toddlers as young as 15 months should be able to help with a number of chores such as:

Scrubbing fruits and vegetables. Since a brief rinse in water is all that's required, this is an easy one for toddlers.

Pouring water. Let them pour water a cup at a time into the pot that will be used for boiling pasta, rice, eggs, vegetables or cooked cereal. Keep them away from the stove, and let them work with cold to lukewarm water only.

Spreading. Let them use a plastic knife to spread peanut butter or cream cheese on celery sticks.

Making omelettes. Let them sprinkle grated cheese onto the eggs; the eggs and pan must be cool.

Cutting biscuits. Put each ingredient for the biscuit recipe into a separate bowl. Help toddlers pour them all into one bowl, stir, roll out the dough, and cut it with biscuit or pastry cutters.

Cleaning the worktop. Toddlers can wipe down the worktop with a damp dishrag or sponge. (Not that you'll end up with a clean counter for the first year or two, or even three. Focus on the participation, not the result.)

Setting the table. Keep the directions simple. First instruct them to put a fork by each plate. When they have finished, they can do the spoons and then the bread knives. They can also put out the butter, ketchup, salt and pepper, napkins, too, if they're given one item to do at a time.

Include toddlers in the decision-making, too – for instance, 'Do you want to put baby tomatoes or sliced peppers on the salads?' and let them add some to the plates. At mealtime, be sure you give your compliments to the chef! It may take an 18-month-old ten minutes to extricate a slice of cheese from its cellophane wrapper, and it may be pretty mangled by that point. Still, the parent can place a piece of bread on the child's plate, hand him the remaining cheese, and tell him to put it on his bread to finish making his sandwich.

It only takes a few minutes spent together in the kitchen each day – by the time youngsters are three, they will be able to make a substantial contribution. In the long run, parents will be paid back with interest for the time and extra work kiddie 'help' costs them now. In the short term, the benefits include:

· The entertainment value of a fun activity.
· The boosts to self-esteem that come from actively participating in family life.
· The time spent interacting with parents and other family members.
· Increased interest in eating what they've prepared.
· A sense of accomplishment.

· Increased autonomy.
· A recognition of their worth as a contributing family member.

Food Struggles

It's easy for mealtimes to degenerate into food struggles when parents become obsessed about each pea on their child's plate, so it's not a good policy to spend mealtimes counting them. If you pay too much attention to exactly what children consume, it's easy for food struggles to develop – and they are notoriously difficult to win. Parents can lead toddlers to vegetables, but even if they try to force them down their throats, they can't keep them in their stomachs. Overall, the biggest impediment to a well-balanced diet is that bane of modern households: snacking.

'I'm Hungry'

It's not time for dinner, but your toddler is hungry. Should she have to wait? If the answer is 'yes', you risk sending her the message that the clock is more important in determining her need to eat than the signals her tummy is sending. The goal, some nutritionists suggest, should be for toddlers to learn to tune in to their internal hunger cues, not ignore them.

Offer part of the normal meal in advance, like the salad or vegetables, so the child gets a nutritious snack and a head start on dinner. A child may turn up his nose at the chance to start on his soup before the rest of the family. But if he's hungry, he'll eat it. The trouble begins when the cook prepares special between-meal snacks to satisfy kiddie culinary whims.

Eating Jags

The predictability of an unvarying menu can help anxious youngsters feel more secure. Refusing to eat anything except a few special dishes can also be a way of establishing personal control. There are two distinctly opposite, but equally valid, ways of approaching this problem.

Lots of books for toddlers deal with the issue of food. *The Very Hungry Caterpillar* by Eric Carle (Putnam, 1984) is an award-winning book they'll love learning from. *Cloudy with a Chance of Meatballs* by Judi Barrett (Aladdin Paperbacks, 1982, available from Amazon.co.uk) will tickle their funny bones.

The first way is to eliminate all food struggles by serving what your child wants. If a war for control is driving the resistance, catering to toddler demands eliminates the toddler's need to battle over food. Supplement his diet with vitamin tablets, milk and fruit juice to maintain nutrition. Continue to make other foods available by placing them on his plate if he'll allow them to be there, or place them on a separate plate nearby. If both of those create upset, simply follow your normal serving procedures for the rest of the family. If your toddler does request something additional, dish out a serving. Studiously avoid questions about whether he likes it and comments about being glad that he's eaten something besides the usual. The goal is to not draw attention to his eating or make an issue of it, thereby preventing a basis for renewed resistance.

The second way is to ignore the child's demands, serve what you will and wait until hunger motivates her to eat. The refusal to eat a well-balanced meal often stems from snacking. Some toddlers constrict their diets to the point that it seems that if it were up to them, they'd only eat one or two things – such as toasted cheese sandwiches, hamburgers or a particular type of cereal – three meals a day, every day. 'If I don't get what she wants, she wouldn't eat anything', the parents claim.

But how true is that, really? The bottom line is that many youngsters consume far more between meals than during them, so when breakfast, lunch and dinner arrive, they can afford to be choosy. The sure way to end eating jags and get the vast majority of toddlers to eat what they're served at meals is to stop fulfilling their desire for off-the-menu items and junk-food snacks.

Test of Wills

Many parents find that eliminating unscheduled snacking is easier said than done, however. Children's refusal to eat dinner means that they will be hungry soon after. If parents hold firm on their nothing-until-the-next-regularly-scheduled-meal-or-snack policy, they soon have a very cross youngster on their hands. If they hold firm through the trouble, they have a truly hungry child on their hands, and the 'I hungry' wails can be wrenching enough to thaw the firmest parental resolve.

Children will not die of hunger from being put to bed without their dinner. Unless they are suffering from diabetes or another disorder, they won't end up nutritionally deficient, either. So if parents don't back down, the problem will be solved when the child sits down to breakfast with bona fide hunger pangs.

Autistic children often have very persistent food obsessions, but although this is rare, it is possible for any exceptionally strong-willed toddler to dig in her heels and reject food despite intense hunger. More often, it is the parents' fear that the child will die of malnutrition before deigning to eat a well-balanced meal that drives them to allow continuing between-meal snacks.

Passing on the Problems

Toddlers must be simultaneously nurtured (by being fed) and given firm limits (by restraining them in a high chair and keeping them from throwing food). Balancing the two is a heady emotional experience, and research shows that parents who had highly conflicted relationships with their own parents have a harder time filling both roles.

Toddlers, like adults, will eat out of boredom. If the parent responds to requests for a snack by offering a drink or several healthy alternatives but the child refuses anything but a biscuit, she's probably not hungry. An appealing activity or nap may do a better job of eliminating the crankiness.

All the emphasis on food can make the toddler years particularly trying for adults with eating disorders. This is a good time to enter counselling, therapy, or join an eating disorders support group to get some real culinary help. The Eating Disorders Association has information and help on all aspects of eating disorders, including Anorexia Nervosa, Bulimia Nervosa, Binge Eating Disorder and related eating disorders. To find your nearest Self Help Group, visit *www.edauk.com* or telephone their helpline on 0845 634 1414.

No Sweets!

Some parents are determined never to allow sweets to pass their children's lips so they won't develop a taste for them. Unfortunately, this strategy can backfire by imbuing creamy, crunchy, gooey, sugary foods with the heady mystique of the forbidden.

Although palates differ, anthropologists believe that the human love of sweets is inborn. Apparently our taste buds were designed to guide primitive humans towards edible, calorie-rich plants (typically sweet) and away from poisonous ones (generally bitter). Unless children are being raised on a desert island, sooner or later they will discover the wonders of sweets, biscuits and chocolate. And if they have a normal set of taste buds, they will probably love them.

If a bank assistant or doctor's receptionist offers your toddler a lollipop, jumping in to forbid the gift in the absence of a compelling reason may be exerting the kind of control that causes youngsters to work overtime to satisfy their inborn sweet tooth. (A compelling reason to step in would be if the child has a medical problem, such as diabetes or an allergy.) Certainly it is reasonable to insist that toddlers wait to consume their gift until after lunch or tea. In doing so, parents may teach the most important lesson: it's OK to eat sweets at certain times. It's when they're consumed just 'whenever' that they become a problem.

Strange Cravings

Rather than satisfying the normal toddler urge to explore anything and everything with their mouths, some youngsters actually consume materials not meant to be ingested. Pica is a craving for unnatural foods or items such as soil, paint, string, cloth, hair – even faeces and animal droppings. It is a desire for items that aren't food at all and have no nutritional value. Pica does not usually signal a deficiency of vitamins and minerals. It is most prevalent among mentally retarded children, but can develop among otherwise normal youngsters, too. It typically occurs in children from 18 months to two years, and parents must monitor these children carefully to prevent them from satisfying their cravings. Pica usually lasts only a few months before disappearing on its own.

Children with rumination disorder vomit their food into their mouths without signs of nausea or retching or stomach upset. They may eject it from their mouths, or proceed to chew it again and swallow it without signs of disgust. It occurs most commonly among children with Sandifer's syndrome, oesophageal reflux and mental retardation, typically beginning between three months and a year. Consult your doctor if your child shows signs of these disorders.

High Chairs and Booster Seats

When purchasing high chairs, choose one with a wide base, since that adds stability. To keep toddlers safe:

- Position high chairs away from hazards, such as ovens, windows and curtain or blind pulls.
- Don't allow the child to stand in the chair unsupervised. (If the chair tips or the child loses her balance and falls, it's a long way to the ground head first.)
- Use the safety harness, rather than relying on the tray to hold the child in.
- Make sure that the tray is properly latched on both sides, as babies tend to push against the tray when seated.
- Regularly check for loose screws and a wobbly base.

Stewed apple, milk and tomatoes dribbling down your toddler's legs will eventually land on your floor. Until her aim improves to the point where most of the food ends up in her mouth, spread a few newspapers or a plastic mat under her high chair to cut down on cleaning up.

For some parents, the ideal solution is to buy a foldaway highchair with integral tray for the early months of weaning, and then a wooden 'Tripp Trapp' highchair (made by Stokke). Although it doesn't have a tray, the chair has an adjustable seat and footrest so it grows with your child. It's sturdy, looks good and gives customized support whatever your child's height, and means that the child sits up to the table with the family.

Buying a booster seat for everyday use so that older toddlers can sit at the table has some advantages. Tending to toddlers can be easier when they are sitting at the same level, so adults can eat with fewer distractions. Putting the child's plate and cup on a tray can help contain the mess, and being on the same level with everyone else makes her feel more like part of the family. As she mimics those around her, her behaviour, manners and even food choices may improve.

Restaurant Survival

Toddlers can make very unpleasant dining companions in restaurants because dining out requires two skills they haven't yet mastered: sitting and waiting. Taking them to places designed for adults is apt to be a miserable experience for the parents, the child and other patrons as well. The rule of thumb is not to look to restaurants as a place to relax and enjoy yourself.

You can minimize upsets, however, by arriving prepared. In general, the fancier the restaurant, the longer the wait; so if you haven't brought any breadsticks, don't even wait – as you're being seated, ask the waiter to bring bread or crackers posthaste. It's a good idea to arrive with entertainment, too. Try to bring something new and different, otherwise the novelty of items on the table will hold much more appeal. Rather than beginning the litany of 'no's' the minute a small hand gravitates towards a coffee cup, scan the table for items your toddler can safely play with. Trying to prevent youngsters from touching anything guarantees a series of noisy scenes. Toddlers simply must have something to do, so be realistic. Allow them to bang a spoon if there's a tablecloth to dampen the sound, or to shred a paper napkin.

Be careful to keep your voice down when chastising your toddler. Parental nagging is often louder and more incessant than an occasional whine from a toddler, and hence more disruptive to other diners.

Given the challenge of coping with toddlers in standard establishments, it's better to stick to kid-friendly restaurants. Many places have been specially designed for families with tots. Unfortunately, they often come up short in the nutrition department, but areas for climbing and crawling offer some compensation by offering opportunities to practise their physical skills. Parents shouldn't expect to relax while toddlers entertain themselves, however. Most structures are too challenging for tots, and if bigger kids are playing roughly, play areas can be plain dangerous. Close monitoring is imperative – if a sign forbids children under a certain height from entering an area, believe it. On the other hand, ignore the signs prohibiting big people from entering if your toddler is in a potentially dangerous situation. Climb in and stage a rescue!

CHAPTER 10
Sleepy Time

Minding a toddler is an every-waking-moment job. It's no wonder that caregivers look forward to toddlers' sleep time like thirsty desert wanderers crawling towards an oasis. Many parents can recover and regroup, work on a personal project for more than ten minutes, or have an adult conversation only when their youngster's eyelids gently close.

Counting the ZZZs

Like everything else about the nappy-and-training-pants crowd, the need for sleep varies dramatically from child to child. Survey any group of toddler caregivers, and they report tremendous variations. Some 12-month-olds subsist on only nine hours of sleep in any 24-hour period, rarely napping for more than an hour. Meanwhile, some three-year-olds are still getting enough sleep each night to rival Sleeping Beauty and supplement their night-time slumber with a long afternoon snooze, too, for a total daily sleep time of 13 hours or more.

SHUT-EYE AVERAGES				
AGE	TOTAL SLEEP	NIGHT-TIME SLEEP	NAPPING SLEEP	NUMBER OF NAPS
12 months	13³/₄ hours	11¹/₄ hours	2¹/₂ hours	2
18 months	13¹/₂ hours	11¹/₄ hours	2¹/₄ hours	1
24 months	13 hours	11 hours	2 hours	1
36 months	12 hours	10¹/₂ hours	1¹/₂ hours	1

The journal *Sleep* reported that nine- to 12-month-olds averaged two naps per day. At 15 to 25 months, the average dropped to one afternoon nap. Most children continue afternoon naps until the age of four.

How are parents to decide how much sleep their toddler needs? If a child is relaxed and content, it's doubtful that he's sleep-deprived, even though his parents have deep circles under their eyes from entertaining him eight hours a day. But since fussier toddlers tend to have more difficulties sleeping, it can be hard to sort out whether the fussiness is caused by a lack of sleep or if their high-strung personalities keep them from getting concentrated, restful shut-eye.

Your toddler may be sleep-deprived if he or she is:

·   Routinely falling asleep in the car.
·   Hard to wake in the morning and from naps.

· Fretful and irritable during the day.
· Hyperactive before bedtime.
· Likely to fall asleep before bedtime.

Sleepy Face

As any adult insomniac knows, being sleepy and being tired are very different. Being overtired makes falling asleep difficult because, in response to the achiness that often accompanies being overtired, the muscles tense. It's impossible to relax mentally to the point of drifting off when the body is physically primed for action. It is much easier to get sleepy children to close their eyes than it is tired ones.

Parents should make an effort to notice the subtle changes in their toddler's appearance so they can more readily discern whether she's rested, sleepy or tired. When toddlers are very sleepy:

· Their faces look softer, even puffy.
· The muscles around the lips and chin may droop.
· Their movements slow down.
· They become less animated.
· They may yawn.

If they are tired, on the other hand, they are apt to show signs of tension and increased physical strain:

· Their faces show signs of strain.
· The muscles around the eyes tense.
· The eyes may appear sunken.
· Activity level may increase.
· Play becomes less focused.
· Fretfulness is common.

To facilitate getting a toddler to sleep, try getting her into bed when she's sleepy. This means she's physically more relaxed. It's harder when she's physically and emotionally tense from being tired.

Reading the Signals

A common reason that children of all ages don't want to sleep is because life is so grand. They want to live every moment to the fullest. They don't want to be shut up alone in a room while other family members are out in the living room having fun. Even if everyone else is in bed, some youngsters would rather be out in the living room having fun all by themselves than lying awake in a darkened room.

Toddlers don't connect crossness to a need for sleep. They have to be taught to recognize these bodily sensations and emotional reactions. Then they will eventually recognize the signals. If they actively fight going to bed, they may become upset by the mere comment, 'You look sleepy now' or 'I think you're unhappy because you're tired' because they suspect those fateful words 'Time for bed' will soon follow. Nevertheless, parents should continue to share their observations.

Just as toddlers need to tune into the internal signals that let them know when and how much they need to eat, it is essential that toddlers learn to interpret the internal cues that indicate a need for sleep so that one day they can take care of themselves.

Routines Are Vital

Whether parents put tired toddlers down for the night and let the tantrums run their course or let them stay up until they collapse from exhaustion in the wee hours, conduct 'rise and shine' at the same time each morning and prevent longer-than-usual naps that compensate for missed sleep. Studies on insomnia demonstrate that establishing a routine is crucial. Being extra-tired ups the odds that children will be ready to sleep at the next nap or bedtime.

The invariable routine of rigid bedtime and nap time can go a long way towards regulating toddlers' sleep patterns. The human body operates in circadian rhythms – a predictable cycle that causes people to fall asleep at night and awaken in the morning at about the same time each day. These rhythms change over the life span. If left to their own devices, teenagers would stay up half the night and sleep half the day; on the other hand, senior citizens naturally fall asleep early and wake shortly after dawn.

A sudden increase in need to sleep in the absence of extra exercise or stress is often a signal that a virus or another illness is brewing. Keep your eyes open for the signs.

Not all toddlers run to the same clock, however, and it is difficult when their routine doesn't adhere to the rest of the family's. Some night owls have a hard time sleeping at night, no matter how early they get up; early birds may wake long before the rest of the family, despite having gone to bed late the night before. Instead of their biological clocks being reset by a consistent schedule that conforms to the rest of the family, they lie awake in bed and are chronically sleep-deprived.

Resetting the Alarm

There are no guarantees, but many parents can sometimes reset their toddlers' internal clocks by following a rigid routine that will bring them more in line with the rest of the family. To do this:

· Wake young toddlers at the same time each morning.
· Put them down for naps at the same time each day.
· Wake them from naps at the same time.
· Wake them from afternoon naps by 4pm to ensure sleepiness at bedtime.
· Keep bedtimes consistent.
· Coordinate with other caregivers to make sure that the daily routines are the same.

The Battle of the Bed

So many parents struggle with getting children to take naps and go to bed at night that, when surveyed, sleep problems routinely appear near the top of the list of child-rearing problems. The bedtime battles being waged across the UK are by no means universal. In cultures where families bed down together – and that includes most of the world – sleep problems are virtually unheard of.

When non-Western parents hear about the accepted British practice of isolating little children in darkened rooms and placing them in beds that have bars like cages, they are shocked. To them, this sounds unspeakably cruel. 'Put children to bed by themselves?' they exclaim. 'But aren't they frightened and lonely?'

Certainly the continuing after-lights-out attention-seeking from toddlers, and the ongoing worries about monsters and burglars among older children suggest that fear and loneliness are exactly what they experience. In many cultures, parents get toddlers ready for bed, then allow them to rejoin the family until they express an interest in sleeping. If they don't ask to go to bed, parents wait until they fall asleep on the couch or wherever, then carry them into a shared sleep area.

When British parents wait for youngsters to conk out on their own before carrying them to bed, some find the problems persist. That's because they are taken to their own bedroom. So as not to end up alone, toddlers may fight their feelings of sleepiness and become overtired. That can end up with them being chronically sleep-deprived.

The Family Bed

Older taboos are quickly falling by the wayside as more parents find that the age-old solution of letting toddlers sleep with them virtually eliminates bedtime scenes and helps everyone get better rest. But although this practice appears more kid-friendly on the surface, there's no guarantee that it will enhance a toddler's life. The loss of the parent's alone time can make it harder for them to remain patient with their youngster during the day, which is clearly not in a toddler's best interests. Additionally, the loss of private time with their partner can jeopardize marital relationships, which, given the stress of rearing a toddler, may already be strained.

Big Bed Safety

Toddlers are probably in greater jeopardy from sleeping alone in cribs than from sharing with their parents, given the risk that they'll climb over the bars and fall to the floor, become trapped between the mattress and the bars, or that another emergency will arise that a parent asleep in another room won't hear. Still, accidents in big beds do occur, and there are some precautions that parents should take before deciding to sleep with their little one.

Each week in the UK, seven babies die as a result of cot death. Most are over one month and under 12 months old. The Foundation for the Study of Infant Deaths says 'It's lovely to have your baby in your bed with you for a cuddle or a feed, but put them back in their cot before you go to sleep if you or your partner smoke, have recently drunk alcohol, take drugs or are extremely tired. If you plan to sleep with your baby, don't let his head get covered by the pillow, do use lightweight blankets not duvets, and do place your baby in a position where he cannot fall out of bed.' No single cause of cot death has yet been identified, but overheating, when covers rise up over baby's head, is one of several factors likely to be involved.

· If you push your toddler's bed up against yours, check to make sure he can't become wedged between the mattresses of the two beds, or between his mattress and the wall.
· Don't use a slatted headboard, foot railing or side railing that could trap a child's head.
· Don't sleep together on a waterbed.
· Keep your child's bed away from dangling cords from curtains or blinds; they are strangling hazards.
· Do not sleep together if you are under the influence of drugs or alcohol, which might keep you from being aware of having rolled on top of your child.

Co-Sleeping

In a co-sleeping arrangement, the cot or toddler bed is pushed up against the parent's bed, or a specially designed co-sleeper is attached. The bars can be lowered as needed for breastfeeding and hands-on comfort, and raised to keep her within her space. When the youngster graduates to a twin bed, her sheets can be tucked in around her so she doesn't gravitate towards her parents.

To enhance the decor of co-sleepers, buy a duvet or bedspread one size larger than your bed and use it to cover both. A double bed next to a single one will look like a queen-size; a queen will look like a king.

Bad Bedfellows

Many parents find that having the family snuggled up together in the same bed produces some of their warmest moments. Others find it far from pleasant. Some toddlers thrash, toss, elbow, wiggle, wet and are generally difficult sleeping companions. Early risers may chatter, hum, poke and play.

If parents don't want to share their bed, moving the cot or toddler bed into the parent's bedroom can eliminate the loneliness and enhance children's sense of safety and security. This usually translates into less resistance at bedtime. Some children can tolerate being on the opposite side of the room with a curtain or room divider to provide some privacy for the parents.

Experimenting to see whether sleeping together at night is a workable arrangement can prove costly. Once children have discovered the security, warmth and comfort of sleeping with a human teddy bear, they are likely to be more resistant than ever to going back to a darkened bedroom with the stuffed variety. Of course every child is different, and after spending a few months in a parent's bed, some may feel sufficiently secure so that sleeping alone becomes much easier. Some toddlers relish the privilege of being 'big enough' to have their very own bed and are delighted to make the switch to sleeping in their very own room.

If parents decide to oust a small bedfellow, the best time to initiate the project is when separation and attachment issues are less of a factor – typically around the age of three. Otherwise, aim for a period when the child isn't going through a lot of other difficult adjustments, separation anxiety isn't a major issue, the child wants to grow up rather than regress to baby days, and independence conflicts aren't paramount.

Little ones love how their parents smell. Assuming that a youngster won't fall off a bed that lacks bars, tucking him between the parent's sheets at naptime, if not at bedtime, can increase his sense of safety and feeling of well-being. To make sure you can tolerate his smell when you tumble into bed at night, spread out a waterproof pad before you tuck him in.

From Cot to Toddler Bed

Cots are recalled due to safety defects and hazards from time to time, so check with the manufacturer before making your purchase. When conducting your own inspection, watch for the two common problems. First, the slats shouldn't be more than 6cm (2 ³/₈in) apart so children can't get their heads caught between them. Second, make sure older models weren't painted with a lead-based paint.

Cots are not for climbers. Be careful about putting toys into a toddler's cot; if she steps on top of them, it may give her just the boost she needs to make it up the side and over the bars. It is dangerous for toddlers to climb over the bars of the cot because a fall from such a great height poses the risk of injury. Some little monkeys surprise their parents by managing to climb out not long after their first birthday. Put some padding on the floor beneath the cot to soften it in the event of a fall. As soon as your little one begins scaling the bars, it's time to move up to a toddler bed.

Toddler beds are a great next step because they have rails to keep youngsters from falling out – and from feeling afraid they might fall out.

They are also lower to the ground and pose less danger to climbers; although if a child is routinely crawling out, it may be better to keep the bars down to reduce the risk of a fall.

Many children are in love with their toddler beds initially because they're so easy to climb out of. Parents must decide whether it's better to lower the bars, which makes climbing less dangerous, or to keep the bars up to prevent a fall while sleeping. Another option is to have the child sleep on the mattress on the floor.

Since many toddler beds use the same size mattress as a cot, it's best to stick with the old one if at all possible. The familiar feel and smell of the old mattress can help smooth the transition from the cot. The quality of toddler bed frames varies dramatically from brand to brand. If you plan to lie down with your child to read stories or sleep, make sure you get a model sturdy enough to support both of you.

Making the Transition

How will your toddler handle the transition from cot to toddler bed? There's simply no way to predict it. It's as smooth as silk for some, decidedly difficult for others. If a child is very resistant to change, slow to adapt to new situations or a sentimentalist, leaving the safety and security of the cot can be trying. Given a toddler's love of predictability and routine, it's a bad idea to let him step into his room to find his beloved cot gone. He may not find his parent's idea of a great surprise to be so wonderful. Perhaps he didn't like his cot at all. Nevertheless, it was the steady friend that kept him safe night after night for as long as he can remember. If possible, provide a gradual transition.

The secret to getting youngsters to give up their cot more willingly, many parents say, is to have them participate in the process from the very beginning. If parents assume the role of enthusiastic cheerleaders trying to whip up excitement about the change, it will be infectious. Try these ideas:

· Get toddlers to help pick out their very own 'big boy' or 'big girl' bed, or at least the sheets.
· Get them to help as you haul the bed into the room and set it up.
· Ask if they want their cot toys moved. If so, hand over the toys one by one and let them do the arranging.
· Let a doll try it out for size, or ask if you can lie on it.
· Play a pretend game of 'night-night' so the youngster can try it out long before naptime or bedtime, when they're likely to be less frazzled and fretful.

No matter how well toddlers seem to be handling the switch up to this point, it's anybody's guess how they will react when it's time to bed down for the night. Many toddlers find the change upsetting. Here are a few more ideas to help ease this transition:

· Let your youngster choose which bed to sleep in if possible. Some youngsters take to it instantly, but months may go by before they suddenly decide they're ready.
· Raise the bars on the toddler bed so they feel more secure and aren't afraid of falling out.
· Consider leaving the bedroom door open or a night light on to lessen fearfulness.
· Put a gate across the doorway to discourage roaming.
· Avoid making the change when other major upheavals are occurring, such as a house move, change in daycare arrangements or the birth of a sibling.
· Provide some extra bedtime TLC to help your toddler calm down so she can drift off.
· If you must remove the cot, it may help to let an upset child sleep on the mattress on the floor next to the toddler bed.

Some toddlers gladly make the move and never again express an interest in their cot. However, for many the excitement and enthusiasm about being a 'big boy' suddenly disappears at naptime, or a youngster may be happy to nap in his new bed during the day, only to appear shocked and appalled when it's suggested that he sleep there at night. Many children like to take naps on it for a few days before tackling it at night.

Toddlers who are initially very resistant may continue to want their cot for a few days or weeks, then spontaneously opt for the toddler bed. Some continue to ignore it for months before deciding they're ready. Many parents find it's best not to apply any pressure, since toddlers can be so quick to dig in their heels and do the opposite of whatever their parents want. They suggest leaving the cot up and remaining indifferent as to where the child sleeps.

Sometimes a toddler can't have a choice. A new baby is coming, so parents need her to relinquish her cot and move on. Parents in this situation may worry that being ousted because of a sibling will be yet another terrible blow that adds to the toddler's feeling of being displaced.

If the transition turns out to be very hard, sometimes the only consolation is that in a matter of hours, days or weeks, the new bed will become sufficiently familiar and the toddler will adjust. Sometimes it turns out to be surprisingly easy. The youngster is delighted to participate in the preparations for the new baby, is thrilled because the move makes the coming sibling seem more real, and enjoys her lofty status of being big sister. There's no second-guessing a toddler.

Staying Put

The toddler who won't stay put in a toddler bed poses a real dilemma for parents: what to do with a little one who scurries out of bed the minute parents have finished tucking him in? What to do with the little insomniac who rises in the middle of the night when everyone is asleep and forays into the house? The first step to getting a child to stay in bed is to discuss it.

Explain that it is dangerous for him to be up by himself, that he must stay in bed unless it's an emergency, and that he is to call Mummy or Daddy from his bedroom if he needs something. After that explanation, which a child may or may not understand, make it a policy to studiously avoid further conversation. Limit verbal exchanges to repeating in a firm tone of voice, 'You're supposed to stay in bed unless it's an emergency. Go back to bed and call if you need something.' (This assumes that the parent has a baby monitor or is close enough to his room to hear him call.)

> As with anything you are trying to teach your toddler, bedtime procedures are established with baby steps. Be patient and consistent as you train your child to stay in bed for the night.

Walk him back to his room, help him into bed, issue another reminder to call if he needs something, and leave. Toddlers in this situation are apt to cry or call before you make it through the bedroom door. If that happens, turn around and go back to his bedside to check on him, just as you promised you would.

In getting across any new idea to a toddler, you need to go one step at a time and show him how things are supposed to go. Stepping out of the room and turning right back around to go back in demonstrates what is to happen: he calls; you respond. That can provide reassurance that having to be a big boy sleeping in a big bed doesn't mean he is expected to be independent. If a toddler doesn't start climbing out of bed the moment the parent turns to leave, that should be considered a victory.

Remain calm and matter-of-fact as you approach your child's bed, and say, 'I heard you calling/crying. Is everything all right? What do you want?' Provide a drink of water if a child says he's thirsty, do the monster check if he's scared; then give him a pat and tell him he's doing fine, that it will take a while to get used to the new bed. Repeat the procedure several times, avoiding all conversation except:

> *I heard you call. What do you want?*
> *No. You're fine now. It's time to get some sleep.*
> *Goodnight.*

Begin extending the time between visits to the child's room. Difficulty with the transition to a strange bed is understandable, too. Many adults have a hard time sleeping when they're away from home – for the very same reason.

It may seem unfair to install a door protector and close the door to contain a toddler who keeps popping out of a toddler bed after everyone else is asleep. But given the danger youngsters can get into roaming the house, it may be the only recourse. Be sure to completely safety-proof the bedroom first!

Bedrooms As Prisons?

Many parents work hard to make their youngsters' bedrooms more appealing in the hope that toddlers will be less resistant to bedtime and naps, only to find that although they love the Snoopy sheets and Little Mermaid wallpaper, they continue to act as though they're being sent to the torture chamber when carried there at night. In many cases, the reason for the resistance is clear: if children are sent to the bedroom for time-outs to contain problem behaviour during the day, they may come to associate the bedroom with being punished, which worsens bedtime struggles.

Time-out is a positive teaching device. Most youngsters eventually retreat to the comforting solitude of their bedroom without being instructed because they recognize their need to separate themselves from the family and calm down. But as long as they resist being exiled, they can develop negative associations to the area in which they are confined.

The logical solution is to use an alternative location for time-out. Unfortunately, what is logical may not be practical. In general, it is recommended that children sit on the floor in the same room as the parent during time-outs so they're not left unattended, but sometimes a parent needs a physical separation at these stressful moments. A playpen in another room can work for children who won't try to climb out.

Winding Down

Insisting that toddlers nap or go to bed if they aren't sleepy can provoke power struggles. Instead, have them observe quiet time. A noisy environment can certainly interfere with a child's ability to fall asleep.

After entering dreamland, some can tolerate a lot of hullabaloo; others remain susceptible to being woken by sounds, especially during lighter phases of sleep. If you can't produce a quiet environment on cue, classical music can help to mask tell-tale sounds that suggest interesting happenings are going on elsewhere in the house.

To create a quiet and relaxing transition, help them unwind by providing soothing entertainment, such as listening to music or looking at books. Bathtime routines help, too. Discourage continued requests to get up by putting a kitchen timer in their bedroom. Tell them that, unless it's an emergency, they must wait until the alarm sounds before getting up or calling to you.

Once they do relax, sleep may not be far behind. Even if sleep doesn't follow immediately, children need to learn to relax and spend time entertaining themselves. Common strategies parents use to help their toddler fall asleep include rocking them to sleep, singing lullabies, telling stories, giving back rubs, holding their hand and taking the child into their bed.

Nursing and giving children a bottle to help them fall asleep is *not* a good idea, dentists say, because the milk pools in their mouth, rotting their teeth. The same problem applies to juice and other sweet beverages. Remember: only water.

Meanwhile, some desperate parents have gone so far as to childproof their little night owl's bedroom, leaving no outlet uncovered, no hard edge exposed. They empty it of all toys except board books, stuffed animals and other toys that can be safely enjoyed without supervision, and remove all furniture but the bed. They install a gate across the doorway to contain their darling, and allow them to play until they're ready to sleep, instructing them to call Mummy and Daddy if they need anything. Then they head off to dreamland, and let their night owl entertain himself.

Stress and Exercise

Little insomniacs may not lie awake pondering their worries like their adult counterparts do, but stress definitely makes it harder for them to unwind at sleep times, or fall back asleep if they awaken. The birth of a new baby, a change in childcare staff, weaning, cross parents – anything that produces stress – can complicate sleep and result in sudden difficulties at bedtime.

Exercise relieves pent-up energy born of stress, tension and the basic need to be on the go. Make sure your child gets lots of chances to run and jump and engage in active physical play during the day. A kiddie music and movement or exercise class may encourage more sedentary types to move more and sit less. Then, spend more time engaging in quiet, pleasurable activities before naps and bedtime to soothe frazzled nerves. Try an extra-long bath, a second storybook or a third chorus of a lullaby. Remember, however, that although stress can make it harder to relax enough to sleep, this too is something children need to learn to do. Any time they are able to recover from an upset during the day, point it out. This skill will serve them well at night.

Rituals

Rituals that induce relaxation can help toddlers make the transition from a busy, active day to sleep. Going through an invariable progression from taking a bath to hearing a story, listening to a lullaby and saying prayers helps toddler insomniacs, just like their adult counterparts. As toddlers come to associate the night-time ritual with sleep, their bodies automatically begin to relax.

Many parents don't consider instituting naptime rituals, but they can make a real difference. It's good to communicate with your babysitters or childminders, if possible, so that the routine never varies. Rituals should be designed to soothe, so avoid stimulating activities like rough play, tickling, and exciting or scary stories.

Some children engage in troublesome rituals, such as repetitive rocking, which can escalate into head banging, as a way to soothe themselves. This usually stops by 18 months. You can help by not over-reacting, by padding the sides of the cot and by boosting other bedtime rituals to provide a more gradual transition.

Sleep Skills

The downside of all that rocking and singing and back-rubbing and music-playing to quieten fretful children and help them fall asleep is that they come to depend on someone or something outside themselves – a real problem if they wake up in the middle of the night. Children need to learn eventually to handle the task of falling asleep – and of going back to sleep – unassisted.

Many parents dedicate themselves to learning how to put their child to sleep, when the goal should be for *toddlers* to learn to put *themselves* to sleep and to put themselves back to sleep after waking. Sleep experts point out that children need to acquire a specific set of sleep skills – but they don't come naturally to many. Children must learn how to fall asleep, go back to sleep, and sleep through the night.

To help toddlers wind down at bedtime, check out books like *Goodnight Moon* by Margaret Wise Brown (Campbell Books, 1991), *Dr. Seuss's Sleep Book* (Picture Lions) and *Can't You Sleep, Little Bear?* by Martin Waddell and Barbara Firth (Walker Books).

The first step is for toddlers to learn to spend time alone. Being comfortable spending time alone in a cot or toddler bed is a prerequisite for falling asleep and for going back to sleep. By handing toddlers a stuffed animal after they wake in the morning or from a nap, leaving the room, and waiting up to 15 minutes to rescue them, parents can give them time to practice being by themselves in their cots. Some experts say this can serve them well at night.

Sleep Cycles

Children drift in and out of different sleep phases throughout the night, entering a light sleep phase six to eight times. It is during these light sleep periods they are most likely to waken. Adults typically wake three to four times per night, although they may not be alert enough to remember. If toddlers wake fully during each and every cycle, and have to depend on a parent's help to get back to sleep... well, there's no real need to finish that sentence.

Sometimes parents can alter the sleep cycles by breaking into them. Try waking the toddler just before you go to bed. Spend a few minutes smiling and chatting, then help her go back to sleep.

Many parents assume that hunger pangs are causing her to wake at 10pm, at 2am and again at 5am. More likely, she's going through sleep stages. If you suspect hunger is an issue, serve a big before-bedtime snack then set an alarm so you can awaken her at midnight for another. Scheduling a regular midnight feeding helps toddlers develop a schedule, and effectively separates food from sleep issues.

Aromatherapy can produce short-term relief from anxiety and induce sleep. In a study of geriatric patients, lavender oil dispersed in the air enabled them to sleep as well as they did on prescription medication. The patients were less restless, and their rooms smelled better. Manufacturers are now concocting lavender-laced lotions and sleeping aids for toddlers. Consult your doctor or health visitor.

Bear in mind, however, that popping a bottle into a child's mouth each time he cries at night encourages him to use food as an emotional crutch, and that the point of a bottle should be to satisfy a nutritional need. If you do decide to use bottles as soothing devices, stick to serving water to prevent the major cause of childhood cavities: sugary liquids sitting in the mouth.

Night-Time Rituals

When parents go out of the bedroom and leave a little one screaming, they don't have to feel like meanies who are abandoning helpless babes to a dangerous world. They could think of themselves as teachers who are confident that their child is safe, and that with time and practice, he can discover the state of relaxation needed to fall asleep.

The problem with continued quick responses to soothe crying tots is that it perpetuates their dependency and helps them avoid the task at hand: learning to fall asleep on their own. As the sleep-teacher, the parents need to:

- Set up the conditions that are conducive for sleep.
- Check from time to time to be sure a wailing toddler is safe.
- Provide frightened youngsters with a comforting pat and reassurance that 'you're OK'.
- Remain confident that the child can learn.

Holding Firm

In two-parent homes, it may be best to get the adult who is less intensely connected to the child to be the one to manage bedtime complaints and middle-of-the-night pleas for attention. Since bedtime brings up separation issues for adults as well as for children, the more connected parent may experience some anxiety on which the child picks up. This can intensify the distress and separation anxiety of both. The parent in charge of putting the child to bed should follow this approach:

1. Say 'Goodnight', tell the toddler she'll be fine, give her a comforting pat and leave.
2. If crying persists, return after two to three minutes to see that she's OK.
3. Give her another pat, tell her she's fine and leave.
4. Return after five minutes for another quick check to make sure the screaming doesn't mean she's ill or injured.

5. Provide another comforting pat, calm reassurance that she's OK and leave.
6. Continue checking and providing this reassurance at up to ten-minute intervals.
7. Avoid checking if the intensity of the crying is abating (so as not to disturb her if she is beginning to relax or fall asleep).

The advantage to this approach is that children learn to fall asleep and to go back to sleep by themselves. By continuing to show up at the cot at regular intervals, the parent makes sure that the child is all right and provides reassurance that she has not been abandoned. Try to provide reassurance without reconnecting – keep talking to a minimum; don't pick your child up. Many parents are amazed at how quickly the youngster they thought would never settle down proceeds to do just that.

Meanwhile, others are amazed that two weeks later the child still manages to scream for an hour. With toddlers, there's no way to predict what will happen. Sometimes the parent's attitude plays a role: if the parent is distressed about the child's intense crying, the youngster will sense it, and the timed parental visits to the nursery, meant to reassure, may have the opposite effect.

Handling Hysteria

What happens when parents refrain from running into their wailing toddler's bedroom to help him fall asleep, and he is so upset he vomits? Or he cries so hard he can't catch his breath and begins gasping for air? This is the point at which many parents decide that the 'give him time to learn to settle himself down' approach is doing more harm than good. Check with your doctor to see whether it's OK to stand firm under these circumstances. If so, be as sympathetic as you would towards any little person who is having such a hard time mastering something difficult. Then change the sheets, clean him up, tuck him in, give him a pat and tell him he'll be all right. Tell him it's time to sleep, wish him sweet dreams and leave. Return a few minutes later to check on him to be sure he's not ill.

Sleep Strategies

If a child wakes up crying and her parents determine that she isn't ill, they can verbally reassure her that she is fine or offer a stuffed animal or other favourite toy for comfort. What happens next is up to each family. Philosophies of what's best for toddlers differ. Sleep problems are among the toughest, and what is acceptable to parents in one household is definitely not workable in another. You can:

· Leave and stay away no matter how hard the child cries, so that he can eventually learn to fall asleep by himself. (Make sure that hard crying doesn't signal illness or injury.)
· Remain physically present to provide some reassurance and moral support, moving a chair a few centimetres further from the crib each night until you are out the door, thereby helping the child to feel more secure while he learns to fall asleep on his own.
· Hold, rock, sing, carry and otherwise soothe the child to help him fall asleep.
· Invite the child into your bed.

Whether you sleep together or apart, or respond to each call from the bedroom, only go in when your child is hysterical, or resolutely stay away, don't judge others negatively for doing it their way – and don't let them judge you.

Toddlers are spiritual beings, too. Like adults, they can derive comfort from prayer and from having religious objects in their rooms. Knowing that God is watching over them can help put their minds at ease.

Parental Paranoia

It's certainly normal for parents to get tired and cross when dealing with a difficult toddler. It's understandable that parents might take it personally when a youngster is so exhausted that his eyes are closing, yet can rise to battle when parents try to get him into bed. But it is dangerous to cross the thin but all-important line from irritation to paranoia, where parents conclude 'My child is refusing to go to bed in order to upset me'. Thoughts like that make them question their child's love and undermine their own self-confidence. Some then feel justified about evening the score with the youngster who is 'trying' to get to them.

It is a serious distortion of reality to think that a child doesn't want to sleep just because he's angry with his parent, when the truth lies elsewhere: toddlers don't want to go to bed because they don't like to go to bed. Full stop. And that often makes parents angry.

Independent Types

When the terrible twos' negativity sets in and toddlers feel driven to disagree with every other thing the parent does or says, they may resist going to bed just because they've been told that's what they must do. Again, parents need to resist taking this personally and remain focused on the child's innate struggle for autonomy and independence.

Letting toddlers be in charge of some bedtime decisions can help satisfy their need to be in control. Let them pick which story is read, which pyjamas are worn, which stuffed animals go into the crib, whether the night-light is on or off and which music you play.

Bored to Sleep

When older toddlers refuse to stay in bed, some parents have successfully bored them to sleep. They refuse to provide any attention, announce that they themselves are going to bed, proceed with their normal bedtime preparations and climb into bed, feigning sleep.

Ideally, children become bored enough from the lack of attention and ask to be taken to bed, or they wind down and fall asleep on their own. Then parents can climb out from under the covers, carry the youngster to his bed and enjoy the rest of their evening undisturbed. Obviously this trick is only workable if it is safe for the toddler to be up and about the house by herself.

Monster Control

If fears of the dark are keeping your toddler awake, try catching monsters and assorted goblins in beams from a night-light. It can stop them in their tracks. Often a fear of a night-time visit from a wild animal or cartoon character can be overcome by outfitting the child with a special repellant guaranteed to render a beastie harmless. The repellant can be anything from a torch to a small magic stone (make sure it's too big to fit in the mouth) to a designated stick they can wave like a magic wand. Since sound can banish monsters, keeping a rattle under their pillow to shake at the shadows in their closet and the branches outside their window can also hold imaginary beasts at bay. Placing a protective object in the room, such as an oversized teddy bear to stand on protecting watch, can be reassuring.

Nightmares

The brain waves of tiny babies suggest that even the youngest members of our species dream. Similarly, many toddlers have nightmares. Because children in this age group have such a poor ability to distinguish reality from fantasy, it can be impossible to convince them that the monsters and big bad bears weren't real. Nevertheless, provide lots of reassurance that 'it was just a dream'. When they're old enough, they'll understand the difference.

There are no proven ways to eliminate nightmares, but the following techniques can help:

· Reduce your child's overall stress level.
· Avoid scary bedtime stories.
· Keep bedtime rituals soothing and relaxing.
· Avoid rough play before bedtime.
· Avoid mentioning scary things.

Encourage your child to share the bad dreams, since this helps many toddlers feel better. If his vocabulary is limited, try to help him tell it. If he says 'Bear', ask 'Was it a scary bear?' Avoid questions such as 'Was the bear trying to eat somebody?' so as not to implant more fear.

'Goodnight, sleep tight, don't let the bed bugs bite' can conjure up frightening images that are later replayed in dreams. Instead, try the far gentler Spanish saying: *'Duérmate con los angelitos'* (pronounced *d'where-mah-tay cone lows ahn-hay-lee-toes*) or the English equivalent: may you sleep with the little angels.

Sleep Terrors

These sudden, unexplained bouts of screaming and wild thrashing within the first few hours of going to sleep can be terrifying to parents who find themselves unable to comfort their youngster. Although children appear to be awake, they are actually asleep during these episodes and have no memory of them on waking. Sleep terrors are believed to occur at the transition from one phase of sleep to another. The only reported dangers are sleep walking, which can lead to injury and some very upset parents. If sleep terrors are occurring regularly, some experts recommend re-setting the sleep cycle:

1. Rouse the toddler from sleep about 15 minutes before the episodes typically occur.
2. Keep him fully awake for five minutes.
3. Continue nightly until the episodes stop – usually in about a week.

Recipes for Insomnia

Almost everyone knows that coffee and tea deliver a hefty dose of caffeine, the ingredient of choice for increasing the heart and respiration rate and keeping people awake. But some people don't realize that:

· Most brown-coloured fizzy drinks, such as cola, contain this self-same stimulant.

- Some light-coloured fizzy drinks now contain caffeine, too.
- Some cold and headache remedies also contain caffeine.
- Black and green teas contain caffeine; herbal kinds do not.
- Caffeine can pass through breastmilk, although the quantities are small.
- Chocolate contains a caffeine-like substance called theobromine, a weaker stimulant than caffeine.
- To determine whether a manufactured product contains caffeine, read the label.

Some toddlers are affected more than others, but anything containing caffeine is on the list of before bedtime no-no's – exactly *how long* before depends on the toddler. Some adults complain that drinking a cup of coffee at 3pm keeps them from falling asleep when they turn in at 10. Similarly, it's a good idea to keep anything with caffeine off the list of toddler foods and beverages if getting them down for naps is a problem.

Cane sugar and artificial colourings have also been known to turn some youngsters into whirling dervishes. So do some food allergies. Exercise greater-than-normal caution about bedtime snacks for toddlers who have a hard time winding down and dozing off. Having the child undergo allergy testing may be a good idea.

Just as there are foods that keep people awake, there are foods that promote sleep. All those feelings of heavy-lidded peace and contentment after a Christmas dinner aren't just from the warmth of an extended family meal. Turkey, which is rich in tryptophan, induces sleep. Stuffing, a complex carbohydrate, facilitates the absorption of tryptophan. A snack that combines a food high in tryptophan with a complex carbohydrate can help induce feelings of well-being and slow brain activity. If you're not up to roasting a bird with homemade stuffing for a toddler bedtime snack, try these ideas:

- A chicken or turkey sandwich.
- An egg with cheese and toast.
- Pasta with cheese.
- Tuna with wholewheat crackers.
- Chicken and rice.

Exhausting Work

It's not surprising that so many toddlers resist bedtime. Having to make their sleep/wake cycles conform to those of other family members isn't easy when your body is running on a different biological clock. The bad news is that lots of youngsters continue to resist bedtimes throughout their childhoods, and getting teenagers to cooperate with lights out can be even more difficult since their biological clocks begin to change, turning them into night owls.

The good news is that it's far easier to deal with the fretfulness of a sleep-avoiding older child than with a sleep-deprived toddler. Parents can anticipate that even if they're not getting much rest now, once children have mastered basic sleep skills, things will get better.

CHAPTER 11

Fun and Games

Toys designed especially for kids are a relatively new invention. Just a few generations ago, toddlers spent their time with everyday household objects. Getting modern youngsters to confine themselves to items that have been specially purchased for them can be difficult. Their favourites will probably turn out to be very different from what toy manufacturers would like them to choose!

The Best Toys

Perhaps children are programmed to master the world they will one day inherit, and that is why they automatically gravitate towards the everyday household objects their parents use. In any event, until TV ads and trips to the shop change their minds, it won't matter to youngsters that the house doesn't contain a single bought toy. Toddlers' attention spans are short, but they are easy to entertain. Since everything is new to them, every room is filled with objects they find fascinating. (That, of course, is both a blessing and a curse!)

Parents already have all they need on hand to keep their child busy for the next two years. As every toddler knows, the pots that parents only consider useful for cooking make wonderful drums, hats, dolls' houses and containers for filling and emptying. The plastic lids from juice tins are fun to stack, and the sound they make when smacked together is music to little people's ears. Before you buy lots of manufactured toys and trail your toddler around the house with long litanies of 'don'ts', ask yourself if the household object she's chosen to investigate must really be off-limits:

·   Could she actually ruin it?
·   Would it be dangerous if she mouthed or chewed it?
·   Does it have sharp edges or rough surfaces that could cause abrasions or cuts?
·   Does it have dangling cords or cables that could strangle her?
·   Could small parts be bitten off, swallowed or cause choking?
·   Could moving parts or hinges catch a hand, pinch a finger or smash a foot?

If not, maybe it's all right for your toddler to play with it. Try not to inhibit learning – with supervised independence, your toddler will find plenty of safe items in your kitchen or bathroom to keep her entertained for hours.

Is the toy small enough to fit through the middle of a toilet paper roll? Then it's small enough to fit into a toddler's throat... meaning that it's *not* a safe toy.

Plastic Containers

Many foods come in plastic containers and the casings make great toys. Just wash them and hand them over. Save the containers from cottage cheese, whipped topping, soft-spread margarine and yoghurt. The colourful plastic tops from cans of cooking spray, and other non-toxic aerosol products, also make pretty toys.

Kitchen Utensils

Take a quick look around the kitchen and you'll see lots of items a toddler would be delighted to manipulate, bang, stack and, inevitably, taste:

· Beaters from electric mixers (kids love the shape).
· Ladles (show them how to use one to scoop up a ball).
· Tongs (useful for picking up small objects).
· Spatulas (show them how to slide them under a small object; see if they can move from squatting to standing without dropping it).
· Pie and cake tins (for filling, emptying, banging and clanging).
· Wooden spoons and saucepan lids (great drums).

Nesters and Stackers

It's not easy to stack a few metal spoons, but toddlers are practising visual/motor skills when they try. They also learn important information about shape, size and volume by fitting items inside one another. Try nesting plastic bowls, measuring cups, measuring spoons, and nesting plastic funnels.

First, give a nesting demonstration. Next, turn the cups upside down and give a stacking demonstration. Then let them do their own thing. Just don't hover and try to dictate how toddlers play. Stacking three objects is a challenge for an 18-month-old. It may take days, weeks or months to figure out how to fit nesting objects one inside the other or how to stack a group from biggest to smallest. While they might be able to create an organized pile or tidy arrangement much sooner if a parent were to guide and coach every step of the way, learning to solve problems on their own spurs intellectual development.

Little Drummers

Toddlers love to drum, and, for many, their high chair tray is their favourite instrument. For safety's sake, you must draw the line if they begin beating on something breakable. Drumming can also become dangerous if they create enough vibration to cause hot liquid to slosh or spill, or a bowl to topple over. Say 'Don't bang the plate. It might break!' while removing it, but don't expect young toddlers to understand. If you prefer the serenade of toddler banging to toddler wailing, swap a breakable plate for a sturdier item.

Boxes

Cardboard boxes are great for kids of all ages, providing entertainment that can last for hours. Keep a supply of various sizes and shapes on hand, including empty shoe boxes, Elastoplast boxes, tea boxes, tissue boxes, gift boxes, packing boxes and breakfast cereal boxes.

The most wondrous of all, of course, is an appliance box. If you haven't bought a refrigerator or wide-screen TV lately, you're bound to find a giant box at your local recycling centre or at shops that sell large appliances. Cut a door, windows, even a small escape hatch, and your toddler has a castle, fort, spaceship, cave or anything else she can imagine.

You can go all out with paint on the exterior, wallpaper and fabric scrap curtains. Kit out the playhouse with a small pillow and blanket to make a little bed. Better yet, let your child decide how he wants it decorated. But don't go too far. Even the best packing boxes don't last forever.

Use boxes to make a toy kitchen scaled to your child's size. Cut a square in the side of a box for an oven door and draw or paint burners for a oven top, a refrigerator and a freezer door so they'll open, just like on your kitchen appliance. Cut a small hole in the top of a box and insert a plastic ice-cream for a sink; then cut cabinet doors in the front. Stock the kitchenette with cottage-cheese-container bowls, pots, yoghurt-container cups and a few plastic spoons. Show toddlers how plastic coffee-can lids can be platters and plates.

At-Home Favourites

Looking for ideas that will keep your kids entertained for hours? Try these time-proven favourites. You can create many of these toys using materials you already have around the house, and you'll probably have as much fun as your child does. In addition, the assembly process is a great bonding experience for parent and child – something you can't say about many shop-bought toys.

Shakes, Rattles and Rings

Sew dried beans, rice or peas into a sock or a piece of stocking; and put some sand or pasta into a plastic bottle (topped with a lid that stays put despite prying fingers) – your toddler has a start on a percussion band. Stitch jingle bells onto a cloth (sew them well – if the bells come off, they're small enough to swallow), and let the tambourine music begin. What about cymbals? Why, pie tins, of course!

Pull Toys

Tie a short cord to a box or stuffed animal to make a pull toy, or tie several boxes together with string for a train. But beware – 40cm (16in) is the maximum length for cord; this reduces the chance that it will create a strangling hazard. A toddler's ability to get entangled in seconds is quite amazing.

Homemade Blocks

Use shoe boxes or cereal packets cut in half crosswise and pushed together to make blocks. To jazz the blocks up, cover them with plain paper or fabric and colour the sides with different shapes (triangles, circles and squares), lowercase letters or numbers. Or glue on pictures of animals cut from magazines.

Who says blocks have to be square? Show your toddler how to build a giant tower from a variety of household items, including pots, pans, books, cardboard boxes or cardboard tubes.

Puzzles

To make a beginner's puzzle, cut a hole in the top of a cereal box 12mm (^{1}/2in) larger than some puzzle pieces so toddlers can drop wooden blocks, measuring spoons or juice-tin lids through the hole. Or cut several holes of different sizes into the top and sides of a shoebox so your toddler can fit small cars and other toys inside.

To make an intermediate board puzzle, cut a large circle from the centre of a heavy-duty cardboard box with a craft knife (using every precaution around both young fingers, and your own). Glue the piece of cardboard from which the hole was cut onto another square of cardboard, which will create the backing. Show your child how to fit the circle into the puzzle. Using other pieces of cardboard, make more puzzles in the shape of a square, a diamond, an arrow and a cone. Paint them in bright colours to add to their eye-catching appeal.

To make more advanced puzzles, cut the front of a cereal box into three pieces and show your toddler how to put them together. Or glue a colourful picture from a magazine onto a piece of cardboard. Cut it into three to five pieces.

Sock Puppets and Dolls

To make a puppet, slip an old sock onto your hand to work out where the eyes should be, and sew on buttons (sew them well – buttons are choking hazards) or round pieces of felt. If you want to be really creative, make a whole family of puppets and add wool for hair, felt ears, red felt tongues, bow ties or lace collars.

To make a doll, use one stuffed sock to make the head and torso, another to make the arms, and a third to make the legs. Then add felt eyes, nose and mouth; wool hair; and clothes; or leave her as she is.

Bubbles

Make them yourself by mixing 125ml (4fl oz) cup water, 125ml (4fl oz) cup liquid soap and 1 tablespoon cooking oil. To add to the fun, stir in some food colouring. A straw, an egg holder from an Easter egg dye kit (for those really big bubbles), or a wire or pipe cleaner bent into the shape of a *P* make good bubble-blowers.

Play Dough

It takes a few litres to get modern kids through primary school, so why not learn how to make your own? In a saucepan, combine 60g (2oz) salt, 125ml (4fl oz) flour and 2 tablespoons cream of tartar. Then add 250ml (8fl oz) cold water, a few drops of food colouring and 1 tablespoon of vegetable oil. Mix until smooth, and cook over medium heat, stirring frequently. When the mixture sticks to the pan, sticks together firmly and is no longer slimy to the touch, it's finished. Turn it out onto greased paper, knead it a dozen times, and let it sit. When the dough is cool, store it in a container with a tight-fitting lid or sealed plastic bags to prevent drying.

Now comes the fun. Sit down with you child and show him how to:

· Roll bits of play dough into a worm or snake.
· Roll a bigger piece into a ball.
· Flatten the ball into a biscuit or pancake.
· Pinch off little bits to make peas and put them onto a tiny play-dough plate.
· Prick it with a pen or pencil.
· Slice it with a cheese slicer.

- Cut it with a plastic knife.
- Cut it with pastry cutters.

Supervise carefully to be sure your toddler doesn't try to make a 'meal' of the biscuits and pancakes. Remember that the fun and learning come from the doing, not the final product.

Potty Putty

Pour 1 tablespoon of liquid starch into a bowl. In a separate bowl, mix 2 tablespoons of PVA (white) glue and 2–3 drops of food colouring. Pour the glue onto the starch and allow it to stand for five minutes, or until the glue absorbs the starch. Remove the mixture from the bowl and knead it until it reaches the desired consistency; more kneading improves the consistency. Store the mixture in a sealed plastic bag.

Finger Paints

Pour 60g (2oz) cornflour into a large bowl. Blend in 250ml (8fl oz) of cold water; then add a further 500ml (16fl oz). Microwave the liquid for eight or nine minutes, stirring every two minutes until thickened. Pour it into six separate bowls and stir in food colouring. Let it cool. Then roll up your child's sleeves, give her some paper and let your little Picasso begin. Demonstrate how to smear a layer of a single colour over a multicoloured drawing, and then use a fingernail or plastic spoon to scrape through the top layer to expose the colours beneath.

tips

For easy cleaning up, put paper, finger paints and your naked toddler in an empty bathtub. Toddlers can do their Picasso number without constantly being reminded to not make a mess. You need to remain close at hand to enforce a few important rules: don't turn on the water, don't throw out all the paint, and don't eat your masterpieces. Leave a few paintings in the tub to dry; then hang them on the fridge.

Science Fun

Simply stirring water into sugar or salt and watching it dissolve counts as a bona fide scientific experience for a toddler. So does seeing skin turn wrinkly during an extra-long bath, hearing a kettle sing, feeling the cool air inside a refrigerator or smelling the aroma of cooking food.

Watching a tomato fall to the floor and roll until it bumps into the table teaches cause/effect, inertia versus motion. With so many fascinating things everywhere tots look, they don't need such a thing as specific science training.

To really impress a youngster with science magic, though, get her to put a teaspoon of bicarbonate of soda in a small bowl. Then put some vinegar in a child-size pitcher and let her pour it slowly into the bowl. If you don't know what happens when you mix these two ingredients, you're in for a surprise, too. Of course, since you *do* know what happens when toddlers are given powder and liquid to pour, you need to conduct this experiment when you can tolerate a bit of a mess.

Whether parents keep their households free of toy guns and rifles is a decision for each family. But if reducing violence is the goal, the best way is to curtail yelling and hitting among family members. If parents want to discourage children from re-enacting violent scenes, eliminate the one object that is clearly associated with an increased preoccupation with blood, gore and violence: the TV.

Art Box

Decorate a box and fill it with an assortment of non-toxic supplies:

· Bows and pieces of ribbon
· Colouring book
· Construction paper
· Cotton balls
· Crayons or markers (washable)
· Envelopes

- Glue sticks
- Paper or old newspaper
- Paper bags, cups and plates
- Pictures from magazines, greeting cards and postcards
- Pipe cleaners
- Stickers
- Watercolour kit
- Wrapping paper odds and ends
- Wool and string (40cm/16in or shorter)

Pull out the art box when you can enjoy it with your toddler. The possibilities are limited only by your imaginations. Younger toddlers can put stickers on paper plates and cups and dab markers onto newspaper. You can cut out the centre of a paper plate to make a crown tots can decorate. Help older toddlers fold construction paper and glue on pictures or stickers to make greeting cards. Then drop them into an envelope and mail them to Nanny and Grandad, who will cherish them more than shop-bought cards. Here are some other crafty ideas:

- Punch small holes on each side of an upside-down cup and insert pipe cleaner arms. Do what you will to create a face. Glue on cotton for hair and beards.
- Glue magazine pictures onto paper plates to display on the refrigerator.
- Lunch bags make great hand puppets.

Remember that toddlers don't care what they make as long as they get to roll, rub, pat, dab and draw while they're making it. Adults might care about the finished product; little ones prefer just to potter about.

Personalized Puppets

Cut out a picture of your child. Glue it onto a lolly stick, leaving room so the toddler can hold onto the bottom half. Voilà! Your child has a puppet of her favourite person! Create a family of dolls using pictures of other family members.

Dress Up

With so many garage and car boot sales around these days, it's easy to stockpile an array of wardrobe items befitting a queen, princess, mermaid, superhero, pirate, cowboy or anything else your child likes. Keep your eyes open for cloth remnants, costume jewellery, hats, handbags, scarves (pin them to shoulders; don't tie them around little necks) and shoes.

Kids will also appreciate things to put in the handbag, such as an old comb or wallet. Applying a bit of colour from half-used tubes of lipstick, eyeliner and face powder is a great accent for any outfit. (Make sure you supervise this part.) Turn your child into a superhero by pinning a pillow-case cape to your child's shirt, bestowing a pizza pan shield, fashioning a tinfoil hat and wrist bands, providing a pair of gloves and adding a plastic spatula to fend off the baddies.

Water Fun

Kids love to play with water as much as parents dislike the mess. So open the dishwasher and place a pan filled with water on the open door. A lot of the splashes will run inside. Then bring out the margarine- or yoghurt-container boats, and add a cup of rice or dried beans (supervising to be sure she doesn't swallow them) so she can scoop them into the cups. Add a touch of food colouring to the water – blue for a lake or green for the sea. When cleaning up, let the overflow drain into the dishwasher, but empty the pan into the sink.

An empty plastic dish soap or shampoo bottle makes a great water pistol. Travel-size bottles are easier for little hands to squeeze. (Water pistols are great bath fun, too!)

For fun in the bath, toss in plastic water bottles, clean plastic fizzy-drink bottles or hand-lotion bottles. Punch holes in the bottoms of some of the bottles to create a tot-sized shower (or give them a plastic colander to play with). Cut a large plastic lemonade bottle in half, smooth the cut edges with sandpaper and show your child how to use the top half for a funnel and the bottom half for a cup. After he's finished straining water in the colander, store his bath toys in it so they'll drain and dry.

Down and Dirty

Toddlers *know* they've landed in heaven when they're given a garden spade or some plastic kitchen utensils, a bucket or a few plastic whipped-topping or soft-spread margarine containers, and a chance to play in the mud. Add to that a bucket of water, and they'll probably be more contented than with any other toy. It's a given that they'll end up with some around their mouths; the challenge is to keep younger ones from getting too much in their mouths.

Of course they'll get dirty – make that filthy – but it's got to be better for kids to wallow in nature than to stare passively at yet another video. Certainly it's easier to clean up their bodies than their minds.

If you prefer a down-and-far-less-dirty experience, sand is cleaner and can be more fun for toddlers to play in than dirt. If a traditional sandpit is too expensive, try these alternatives:

- Dig a 15cm (6in) hole, and line it with plastic. Punch holes in the plastic for the water to drain through, and fill the hole with sand until it's level with the ground. Cover it with another sheet of plastic weighed down with rocks to help keep out the rain and the cats.
- If the home-made kind is too much work, look for a rectangular plastic storage bin at a discount store, pour 15cm (6in) of sand in the bottom, and pop your toddler inside – leaving the lid off, of course!
- Fill an inexpensive plastic paddling pool with sand.

Some shop-bought, time-tested toys help toddlers develop everything from visual/motor skills to imagination. Duplo and Brio train sets will provide hours of fun for years to come. (Keep any pieces small enough to be swallowed out of reach until your child is older.) With classics, more is better, so add them to your child's birthday wish list, next to the other tried-and-true favourites: books.

Forbidden Toys

Some seemingly harmless objects that toddlers love are too dangerous to allow. Don't try to teach them that these are forbidden; to do so would be to risk an accident. Instead, keep the following items carefully out of reach:

- Any toy marked 'not suitable for children under 36 months'.
- Glitter, which has edges sharp enough to damage eyes when they're rubbed with glitter-speckled hands.
- Clingfilm and bags.
- Small toys and objects that could be swallowed, such as buttons, marbles, Lego bricks and deflated balloons.
- String, wool, cords and long thin objects, such as necklaces and bracelets, which can choke or strangle children.
- Styrofoam products (cups, plates, bowls and packing materials) that could be eaten.
- Anything powered by 'button' batteries, which can be lethal if they are swallowed.

Outdoor Play

Playing outside is essential for children and parents. Fresh air and sunshine; room to run, yell and tumble; and all sorts of things to explore make the outdoors a whole new world. Playing outside is also an opportunity to teach garden and road safety, and boundaries. The games overleaf can be modified for city or suburban play as needed.

- Get your toddler to lie down on the pavement. Trace his outline with non-toxic chalk. Then ask him to draw in the eyes, ears, nose and mouth (you can use different colours of chalk).
- Place a series of parallel sticks on the ground spaced 20–30cm (8–12in) apart. See if your toddler can walk through them without stepping on any.
- Play follow-the-leader: walk with one or both hands on your hips, above your head, while swinging your arms.
- Blow tufts off the head of a dandelion.
- Collect leaves and line them up on the pavement in a long chain.

Use the money you saved from making indoor toys on kiddie transportation that your toddler can play with outside. Invest in a small shopping trolley or toy buggy that your child can push. She'd love to pedal a tricycle. Finally, don't underestimate the hours of fun she can have with a traditional wooden push-along baby walker.

Check It Out!

When buying toys, always check the targeted ages noted on the box. That should help ensure that they are developmentally appropriate and safe. Also consider whether the toy needs batteries. If so, are they included? So many toys require them that investing in a battery charger can save not only money but also the headache of making frequent runs to the shop.

The British Standards Institute (BSI), which promotes safety and uses the 'Kitemark' symbol on approved products, says:

- New toys must satisfy essential safety requirements. Toys must not have sharp points or edges, or pieces that can be easily pulled off (such as eyes or noses).
- Toys cannot be made of cellulose nitrate, be painted with lead, cadmium, chromium or other toxic paint, or operate at more than 24 volts.
- Plastic bags holding toys must be smaller than a child's head or made from very thick plastic.

- Small objects that look, smell or taste like food, are scented, or are of the size that could choke a baby, are banned.
- Toys must have the CE marking, which shows that the requirements of the regulations have been met (note that the CE marking is not a safety marking).
- Toys must come with necessary safety warnings.
- Toys must have the name and address of the person or organization responsible for the safety of the toy.

You can subscribe to the consumer magazine, *Which?*, online at *www.which.net*. This reviews toys (and most other consumer products)

Toys sold in Early Learning Centre shops (*www.elc.co.uk*) have all been carefully selected for play value and safety.

Toys, Toys Everywhere

There are a number of compelling reasons why toddlers need to learn to pick up their toys – and not just to fulfil your desire for a neat house. Not only will toddlers break the toys by walking on them, but also possibly hurt themselves tripping or stumbling amid the rubble. In the process of learning to care for their possessions, toddlers learn to sort and organize. Little ones won't know how to do that, so plan on doing most of the work for quite some time.

Because toddlers slow things down to a snail's pace, it's often easier for parents to pick up everything. But when parents look ahead and consider that playthings will need to be picked up every day for the next 18 years, they'll realize how important it is to work actively on teaching this skill in the early years.

Toddlers do like to go back and forth between toys, playing with one for a while, moving on to another one, then returning to the first, so the strategy of insisting that one toy be put up before the next is taken out is too rigid. But to hold the chaos in check (which makes many toddlers, like many adults, feel scattered), to keep toys from becoming trampled on and broken, and to teach organizational skills, consider these guidelines:

- Only allow two or three different toys out at once, not counting that special truck, doll or ball he wants to keep close at hand at all times.
- Keep the quantity down to items that can be carried to his room or piled into a container that he can drag to the toy storage area in a single trip.
- Store toys that aren't being used much in a cupboard. Bring them out for a rainy-day surprise.

'Tidy Up Time'

When your toddler is looking for something new to play with, say, 'Let's pick these up and find you a new toy.' Then make the picking up of toys into a game. Ask 'How many of these can you carry?' Place one toy in her right hand, one in her left, tuck one under her arm, and another under her neck if she's a practised walker. Keep up the fun by giving a quick tummy tickle and seeing if she can manage not to drop any or all of them.

If you're putting away toys in a carrier that a toddler can drag from room to room, toss a toy inside and then hand her one to toss inside and continue taking turns. Count aloud as you alternate placing toys in her box. Have a race and see who can pick up toys the fastest. Make the trek to her room pleasurable – this is a great time for a hiking song or a chorus of *Ten Green Bottles* – although you might want to hold it to four bottles for such a short trip.

A Place for Everything...

Designate a special spot in the toddler's bedroom or toy storage area for each toy. Show young toddlers where to put each item, handing him one item at a time, while giving verbal instructions. 'The clown goes on your bed.' 'The ball goes in this box.' 'The bricks go in this basket.' When the toys are put away, congratulate him ('You did it!') and help him select a new toy or activity.

When a child is old enough to want to have a say in the matter (ie, when he's going through the stage in which when you say, 'Let's pick up the toys', he refuses, and if you say, '*Don't* pick up the toys', he proceeds to pick them up), defer to his need to make some decisions by asking him what goes where: 'Where should I put the bricks?' 'Where does your clown go?' If he's being 'terribly two' and refuses to put away his toys, don't argue. But stand firm that no other toys can be played with until all the other ones have been picked up.

Toy Storage

Now that traditional toy chests have fallen from grace (see Chapter 7), you can be more creative about designing toy storage that solves some of the problems big chests posed. For instance, consider these solutions to typical problems:

PROBLEM	SOLUTION
Small toys slip to the bottom of deep chests, where they are lost or broken.	Use a shallow storage box.
Everything gets mixed together so toddlers can't find the toys they want.	Use a number of smaller containers rather than a few large ones to keep toys separated and organized. Remove the lids so toddlers can see inside. Place toys on open shelves low on the wall so toddlers can easily see and reach their toys.
Toys have to be carried to the chest a few at a time, requiring many trips back and forth when putting toys away.	Use small- to medium-size cardboard boxes, lightweight laundry baskets or pillowcases that children can drag. They'll enjoy playing in them, too. Use gym bags or small suitcases with handles.

Store toys low to the ground so children can reach them, rather than on high shelves (which beg to be climbed), and beware of brick-and-board shelves that can topple. Try these other storage solutions:

· Make a stuffed animal holder from a fishing net or see-through beach bag and hang it on a low hook or hooks.

- Attach Velcro dots to the wall and to toys so your child can pull them down and stick them up.
- Store books in a plastic dish drainer.
- Attach wicker baskets to the wall (low enough for children to reach them) and drop toys inside.

Birthday Parties

At two, children are old enough to be excited about the prospect of having relatives and/or friends over... of receiving presents... of eating cake and ice-cream... of 'Me birthday party!' To make sure your child's party is a success, keep these tips in mind:

1. Include your youngster in the planning, getting her to help select the refreshments and the theme.
2. Beware of guest appearances by a face-painted clown or mask-wearing magician; they tend to provoke more terror than mirth.
3. Remember that the Number One Rule is to keep it short, around two hours. The anticipation beforehand and the excitement of the party itself are apt to fray your child's nerves – not to mention yours.
4. Ask other parents to stay for the duration. It's hard for one parent to supervise a group and keep everyone safe.
5. Consider getting your child to open presents after the guests leave, so they don't get upset about wanting presents, too.
6. Provide party bags to help everyone feel included.
7. Consider limiting the number of guests to the age of your child – a three-year-old party with four tots plus three sets of parents can work brilliantly.

CHAPTER 12

Parenting Tricks
and Tactics

The easy definition of parenting is 'raising a child'. The complicated reality, however, involves providing a safe, loving, structured and consistent environment in which your child can grow to be well-adjusted, disciplined, sociable, confident and happy. It requires as much hard work and discipline from you as it does from your child.

Misbehaviour Management

The dictionary definition of *misbehaviour* is 'to manage one's actions wrongly or badly'. Most of toddlers' 'wrong' and 'bad' actions stem from their ignorance or lack of physical skill. It doesn't mean they are bad. Concepts like the proper timing for eating cake (after lunch or dinner but not before, and not before *or* after breakfast) are very complex for a toddler. In addition, getting that cake from the plate to the tummy requires coordinating hundreds of muscles. Learning to do life isn't easy.

The following sections are a sampling of behaviour (not misbehaviour) that, with supervision and patience on your part, can be modified for your child to preserve her safety and your sanity.

Hitting Henry

Say, 'Let me show you how to pet the dog.' Clasp your child's wrist and make stroking motions while saying, 'Be gentle with the dog, and pet him this way. Say, "Good Henry." Yes, that's right. See? He likes to be petted like this.' Supervise toddlers carefully until they learn. Be firm in correcting older toddler misbehaviour too, so the child isn't bitten or scratched.

Pounding the Piano

Sit your toddler in your lap on the piano stool. Help her make fists and stretch out her index fingers. Clasp a fist in each of your hands. Help her strike the keys with her index fingers. Help her raise her hands high and drop them hard so she can get enough leverage to make a sound. If the pounding resumes when you remove your hands, say, 'No, that hurts Mummy's ears.'

Rocking Chair Wildness

Say, 'No. You might fall over backwards. Let me show you how.' Place your hands on his shoulders and teach the correct motion by controlling the rocking. Hold the chair back and say, 'Now you try.' Stop the chair if he rocks too hard and explain, 'That's too hard. Let me show you again.' Give positive feedback: 'Yes! You've got it! Now I'll let go, and you try it by yourself.' Jazz up the practice session with a stuffed animal that needs to be rocked *gently*.

Controlled rocking requires subtle flexing movements that are hard for toddlers. Practice sessions are good physical therapy, which help develop coordination and motor control. But if rowdiness persists, make the rocker off-limits and substitute an active game to burn off some high-octane toddler energy.

Emptying Drawers

You need to explain, 'That drawer has to stay closed. The clothes will get dirty and wrinkled if you take them out.' Let her open the drawer for a look inside. Then say, 'Yes, see all your pretty shirts? Can you say "shirts"?' Let her touch the shirts. Say, 'No, don't pick them up.' Put her hand in her lap if she grabs them. Say, 'Now see if you can close the drawer gently. No, that's too hard. Try again, like this.' Place your hand over hers to help close the drawer. Let her try by herself. Give positive feedback for successes: 'Yes! That's the way to close a drawer!'

Younger toddlers won't understand much of what you're saying, so remember to say 'yes' while smiling to signal permissible behaviour, and 'no' when they're doing it wrong.

Grabbing in the Shop

Remove his hand and say, 'Ask if you can touch that first. Can you say "Touch, please"?' If it's too fragile, say, 'No, that might break.' Find something else to practise on. Extend his index finger and guide it over the object, 'Yes, use one finger so you don't break it.'

Saying 'No!'

Maybe tots can't yet say what they do want, but by saying 'No!' they can at least exercise a veto. Reverse psychology can sometimes induce them to comply: 'I changed my mind', a mother said in the midst of one losing battle to get her toddler into his coat and out the door. 'Forget it. We'll just stay at home.' 'No!' he screamed, trying to put on the coat he had thrown onto the floor a moment before. His mother replied, 'Take your coat off!' as she helped him into it and added, 'Whatever you do, do not put on your hat!'

You guessed the rest. He had his hat on and was out of the front door.

Always in Trouble

There is a saying among psychologists that 'negative attention is better than no attention'. This is a hard concept for parents to grasp. 'What child in her right mind would want to be yelled at?' they ask. The answer is 'A child who isn't getting enough attention'. How much is 'enough' depends on the child. Humans are social animals. Extroverted types with outgoing dispositions desire constant interaction. They find having to spend time alone stressful. Meanwhile, introverts can happily entertain themselves for extended periods, and too much social stimulation makes them irritable.

If pleas for parents to play pat-a-cake, read a story or sing are ignored, it doesn't take toddlers long to fathom that one guaranteed way to get attention is to stir matters up a bit. When toddlers engage their parents by getting mischievous, they are not conscious of what they are doing. They don't harbour thoughts like, 'Dad will pay attention to me if I hit the baby'. Research shows that when adults are rewarded for picking the 'right' answers, they soon begin answering correctly – even if no one tells them what the problem is! Their intuition guides them long before they understand the rules of the game. Similarly, intuition guides toddlers towards rewards. If the choice is being ignored or being yelled at, they're likely to opt for the latter. In saying 'Chantal is only doing that to get attention', her father is acknowledging his daughter's need for attention. The trick is to give it for the right behaviour.

Parents may feel too tired to keep little ones entertained. Yet when misbehaviour develops, most summon the wherewithal to respond. If they had responded before problems developed, they could have expended less energy. It's hard to offer praise when a child is playing nicely by herself, for fear she'll want you to play with her. But by ignoring children when they're entertaining themselves, parents discourage them from engaging in this important parental sanity-saving skill. So, when toddlers are playing quietly, lavish them with praise.

Hyperactivity

Attention deficit hyperactivity disorder (ADHD) and attention deficit disorder (ADD) refer to a range of problem behaviours associated with poor attention span. These may include impulsiveness, restlessness and hyperactivity, as well as inattentiveness. These 'symptoms' could all be ascribed to pretty much any toddler. In the USA, many children, some as young as two years old, are being prescribed mind-altering psychiatric drugs for hyperactivity.

In Britain, psychiatric drugs such as Ritalin and Prozac are, by and large, only given to children of school age. Doctors very rarely prescribe such drugs to toddlers or young children.

- If your child is running circles though the house, open the door so he can run circles in the garden. Don't say it's too cold out. What do you think kids do in Russia? They wear heavy coats!
- If she's climbing the walls, take her to the park so she can climb the climbing frame.
- If he breaks everything he touches, put the breakable stuff away and teach him how to handle objects gently.

If she doesn't nap and hardly sleeps at night, she's probably not getting enough exercise. If more vigorous play doesn't help, cut out junk food and try to eliminate stress, since kids get 'hyper' when they're nervous – just like adults. If that doesn't work, be happy for her – she'll have extra time every day for the rest of her life to work and play, while the rest of the world is snoozing.

Approaches to Discipline

Some simple parenting tactics can solve a wide range of behaviour problems. The following methods come highly recommended by a variety of psychologists, teachers, doctors and parents.

Hear No Evil, See No Evil

A tried-and-trusted disciplinary technique psychologists recommend is to ignore problem behaviour. In reality, it's hard to turn a blind eye to the mud pies being constructed from the soil of your potted plants, or to turn a deaf ear to the drum of a high chair tray being pounded with a spoon. Although you may be compelled to swoop in to rescue the plants to stop the destruction, there may be an advantage to ignoring the clanging kitchen band – assuming that your strained nerves can last through the serenade.

At some point children must learn that spoons aren't drumsticks and loud noise at the dinner table is unacceptable, but some lessons are better postponed. It would be easy to spend all day, every day chastising more active, inquisitive, inventive toddlers, but it isn't good for them to have their failings and inadequacies constantly spotlighted. Since feistier personalities will learn to either tune out the never-ending litany of nagging harangues, or enjoy this proven way to get attention, reprimands may not serve much purpose, either.

When parents ignore problem behaviour that they have attended to in the past, children escalate it. Parents may have to react, despite their determination to turn a blind eye and deaf ear to small crimes. In this case, they need to teach the child more acceptable ways to get attention. This may require parents to notice and respond when their child begins to act bored or restless, suggest activities that they can do together, and comment on behaviour that pleases them.

Warm Comments

If the loving, helpful things toddlers do are ignored, youngsters may give up trying to please. Further, negative parental comments teach children to attend to flaws, so toddlers learn to pay attention to things parents don't do for them and ignore the loving, helpful things that parents do.

To keep from focusing on the bad at the expense of the good, set a kitchen timer to remind you to make a positive comment at least once every ten minutes:

- 'Thanks for holding still while I change your nappy.' (Even if the wiggling only stops for ten seconds.)
- 'I'm glad to see you eating your peas.' (Even if she's only swallowed one so far.)
- 'I'm glad you told me you need to use the potty.' (Even if this is the only time he's told you this week – and it was *after* he wet his pants.)
- 'I appreciate your sitting still in the shopping trolley.' (Even if it's been briefly enough to classify as a pause.)
- 'Thanks for helping to put away the toys.' (Even if she only got one brick into the basket and you did all the rest.)
- 'I appreciate your waiting while I talked on the phone.' (Even if it was only for the minute he ran into the other room to look for the cat.)

Bribes

It can be so easy to offer a biscuit, treat or toy to soothe tears, head off tantrums and garner cooperation. And bribes often work – at least temporarily. But it's important to consider what children learn in the long run from this behaviour management short cut:

- 'When I'm upset, eating is the route to feeling better.' This is the stuff of which modern eating disorders are made, not to mention plain, old-fashioned obesity.
- 'When I'm upset, being given a toy or special activity cheers me up.' Materialists are made, not born. If you want to set children on a course of seeking hugs from a human instead of items from a department store, the time to help set the pattern is now.
- 'If Dad wants me to do something, he should make it worth my while.' If you believe that family cooperation is its own reward and your child should do the right thing whether or not she's paid, avoid bribes, which will jeopardize your child's values.

· 'If the reward isn't good enough, I won't cooperate.' The problem with having to buy good behaviour is that it can be very expensive.

When toddlers are developing a sense of themselves as people in their own right, the attractiveness of bribes may fall by the wayside. No reward is good enough, and *not* doing what a parent wants actually becomes more desirable than any reward.

Contracts

Although bribes ultimately reward bad behaviour, contracts are arrangements between the toddler and parent to reinforce the 'first things first' principle, as in '*If* you pick up the blocks, *then* you can play with your dolls.' The dolls aren't a reward; they're a privilege that can be exercised once business has been taken care of.

Decide in advance whether the toddler can in fact make a choice. Don't say, 'If you'll put on your shoes, we can go out for pizza' if the toddler *must* get dressed because it is time to run errands. The toddler might decide the pizza isn't worth it.

Logical Consequences

One approach to discipline is to provide 'logical consequences'. This strategy requires parents to work out what the consequences of misbehaviour would be if committed by an adult, and to design similar consequences for the toddler. The goal is to teach responsible behaviour and prepare little ones to deal with the realities of life. For example:

· In the 'real world', adults must clean up their messes. So, instead of yelling at a toddler over spilled milk, getting him to fetch the cloth and help clean up teaches a basic skill.
· If cleaning up is so much fun that the toddler spills the milk on purpose, say 'I suppose you're not thirsty', and take the milk away. A logical consequence of wasting food is having none.

- Adults can't eat according to their whims, and must control their diets. So, instead of sending a toddler to her room for having dipped into the sugar bowl, the logical consequence might be that the youngster gets no dessert because she already ate her allotment of sweet things.

- Adults are sent to prison to be contained if they're out of control. Send the toddler into time-out.

- Since mistreated possessions get broken and people lose the use of them, remove the toy a toddler is mistreating so he can experience what it's like to be without it.

Sometimes, parents try to impose logical consequences, but they often fail for the following reasons:

- The consequence has nothing to do with the crime. 'If you eat that, no TV for you for the rest of the day!'

- The consequence accomplishes exactly what the child would like to have happen. 'If you don't behave in the shop, we're going home.'

- The parent backs down rather than allowing the child to suffer the consequence. The child isn't supposed to get to hear a story because he was tearing up the books, but the parent reads one anyway.

- The parent sets consequences that can't be carried out. 'If you take your coat off again, we're not going out.' But the parent has to run errands and must take the child.

'The Big Cahoona'

Charlie was angry because his grandmother wouldn't take him outside to play. 'Shut up, stupid!' he exclaimed.

'Charlie', she said gravely. 'Have you forgotten? I am the Big Cahoona. You must never say "shut up" or "stupid" to the Big Cahoona.'

'What Big C'oona?' Charlie asked nervously.

'That is me. *I* am the Big Cahoona.'

'Why?' he asked.

'Because that's what I am', she answered. Charlie nodded gravely. 'Why don't you play in the other room until it's time to go outside?'

Later, when Charlie began asking to go outside again, he was irritated and impatient but not disrespectful. At lunch, when Charlie's grandmother told him not to pour milk onto his plate, he persisted.

'What did I tell you?' she asked.

He smiled. 'Big C'oona', he said. He stopped pouring the milk.

Every toddler needs a Big Cahoona – a caregiver who is authoritative, firm and in charge.

Don't resort to hitting an unruly child. Instead, try phoning a helpline, which can be a vital safety valve and stop a difficult situation from getting out of control. The NSPCC's Child Protection Helpline is run by trained child protection officers who don't just deal with calls about child abuse, but can help with a range of childcare problems. Tel: 0808 800 5000, or visit the website at *www.nspcc.org.uk*.

Or try Parentline, a confidential service for anyone in a parenting role. The helpline workers are all parents who have undergone training to help callers deal with a whole range of parenting issues. Tel: 0808 800 2222.

Street Brawlers

Some children escalate to the point that even time-out doesn't settle them down. They leave the time-out area or destroy property. Parents must not allow destructive behaviour. If children are out of control, parents need to control them. Biting cannot be allowed. The easiest cure is to give your little Jaws something she can safely sink her teeth into, like a sock or a thick rubbery something she can't shred or bite through.

Children must not hit parents, either! Sometimes it helps to ground their energy to place your hand firmly on their forehead to hold them away from you. With your feet, and their feet, planted firmly on the ground, let them flail away. Don't smile at the 'cuteness' of their impotent rage or otherwise reinforce this forbidden behaviour.

If they persist:

1. Firmly say, 'No! Biting/hitting me is not allowed!'
2. Send them straight to time-out.
3. Do not give them any additional attention; some children thrive on being yelled at, so don't waste your breath.
4. Do not comfort them when you release them from time-out.

Other Problems

Beyond the motor development and social skills that need constant encouragement are the emotional skills and traits that are unique to your child. Whether they are nervous and easily frightened, sensitive and easily upset, or impatient and easily frustrated, toddlers will need your patience and guidance as you both learn how to communicate what the problem is and find an effective solution for it.

Cry Babies

Toddlers are still babies, and some are more sensitive than others. Lots of crying is to be expected. Here are a few tips to help a little one whose taps are constantly dripping:

· Encourage them to use words to express their feelings.
· Recognize that crying doesn't always signal sadness. Many children cry when they are angry. Model how to express frustration and irritation by using words when you are upset and by helping them say the magic words, 'I'm *angry!*'
· Just let them cry. Tears can relieve tension. They're only a problem when parents work overtime to make them go away.

Whining

Whining drives parents crazy. So why do youngsters do it? Because parents who have ignored requests and demands suddenly respond when the plaintive pleas begin. To cure kids of whining, respond before they switch into their high-pitched, plaintive voice, if only to ask for a minute to think about it. Insist that the child ask again without whining. Say

'Ask me nicely' or 'Use your normal voice'. Then try to comply with the request to reinforce your child's polite request.

Fears

Typical terrors that make young toddlers tremble are loud noises, large objects and buildings, something that has startled them and strangers. Fear is instinctive – a response to a perceived threat that sends adrenaline surging through the body and mobilizes the muscles for flight. It is an inborn survival mechanism. Difficulty distinguishing reality from fantasy sets the stage for many toddlers' fears. If there's a monster in the toilet bowl on TV, what's to keep it out of the toilet bowl at home? (The possibility of your child seeing that advertisement is reason enough to pull the TV plug or keep it tuned to Ceebeebies.) Standing in line for 30 minutes while other kids have their pictures taken with Santa is one thing, but you want her to sit in that hairy stranger's lap? Go back when she's three, and she might consider it.

To help toddlers overcome fears, try the following:

· Confidently approach the frightening object yourself to show that it is safe.
· Let them cling, cry and hide their faces.
· Say, 'You're OK. You're safe' in soothing tones to desensitize them.
· Ask, 'Are you afraid of that dog?' Toddlers must know that you have identified the correct danger to feel reassured.
· Do not urge or force toddlers to touch something that frightens them. Let them continue to trust their instincts rather than trying to teach them not to.
· Later, continue desensitizing them by encouraging them to talk about the scary situation. They should appear less traumatized each time.

Do not ridicule, shame or tease frightened toddlers. If you do, they learn to hide their fears, not overcome them. Fears may also be relayed in nightmares, or the child may lose the ability to sense danger. The goal should be to develop courage, not to create a daredevil.

Bathtub Woes

Help a toddler overcome a fear of the tub by taking her into the shower with you or by joining you in the bath. Or consider this desensitization method (but note that it's dangerous because of the risk of falling!): Put her on the edge of the dry bath, keeping one hand on her at all times, with her legs dangling inside. Give sponge baths from a pail of water sitting in the bath. Sponge the hair, too, using very little shampoo. Put toys in the bath in the hope that she'll reach for them. (Put a non-slip mat in the bath, as wet feet make it easy to slip and fall.) If she does reach for a toy, see if she wants to sit in the dry bath for her sponge bath.

Then follow a routine something like this:

Days 1–2:　Keep the bath dry.
Days 3–4:　Put a splash of water in the bath before the child enters the bathroom.
Days 5–6:　Add a few more splashes to the bath.
Days 7–11: Put a few centimetres of water in the bath.
Day 12:　Put a few more centimetres of water in the bath. Alternate between sponging water from the pail and from the bath.
Days 13–?: Add more water to the bath each day.

Self-Soothing

Children who have a hard time accepting physical comfort get upset more often and stay upset longer than children who readily accept it. Some youngsters may try to soothe themselves by rocking or clinging to a soft object. Others employ destructive strategies, such as head-banging.

Physical pain can be soothing in that it distracts toddlers from their emotional pain.

If your child bangs her head, bites or claws herself, or inflicts other kinds of self-injury when she's upset, do the following:

· Hold her in your lap, rock her and speak to her in a soothing tone.
· Tell her that you love her and don't want her to hurt herself.
· Tell her that when she feels like hurting herself she should come to you for hugs.
· Teach her other strategies for releasing intense emotions, such as hitting pillows.

Talking on the Telephone

It's totally predictable. The minute you pick up the telephone, your tyke suddenly appears at your elbow and tries to distract you. 'She just wants my attention', irritated parents say. In a way, that's true, but the struggle for attention isn't as calculated as it seems. It is a toddler's attempt to restore a sense of connection to his beloved lifeline. Contact with a parent is so vital to a youngster's survival that he can become anxious when it disappears, however briefly.

There don't seem to be any good solutions for this age-old problem. You can try stroking the toddler's hair while chatting on the phone. The physical contact may quieten her down for a minute. Another idea is to set limits for the caller and the toddler. 'I'll set the timer and when it rings, I promise...' The tot will know that the psychological absence will end soon. Finally, try offering your tot the chance-of-a-lifetime opportunity to jump on the beds, play in the dishwater or tear up the plants while you talk.

Even that might not keep them content for more than two minutes. Threats and anger might be moderately effective, at which point your phone call has been derailed beyond recovery. The best solution may be to let Father Time usher the toddler to an age where he or she can tolerate not being at the centre of your universe. Typically, that's the stage also known as 'adolescence', and by then the phone will always be busy and you still won't get to talk on it!

Attachment Issues

Children who have difficulty bonding fly into rages readily, and are notoriously difficult to soothe because of their inability to trust others. Try the following strategy to promote bonding. When a toddler is spent and exhausted from a tantrum, follow this procedure:

1. Carry the toddler to a rocking chair and hold him as if nursing, maintaining eye contact if the child is willing.
2. Rock the toddler lovingly but avoid speaking, so the youngster can focus on the physical and emotional warmth and closeness.
3. Use your intuition to determine when the toddler is ready to re-engage with the world, or carry him to bed if he falls asleep.
4. Do not discuss what transpired before or during the tantrum unless the toddler brings it up.

Once toddlers are familiar with the procedure, parents can ask, 'Do you want me to rock you like a baby?' when a stressed tot is losing control. Often the tantrum suddenly ends and the child hurries to the rocking chair. (See Chapter 8 for more on handling tantrums.)

Breaking the Soother/Dummy Habit

If going cold turkey is too tough, some children have found it less traumatic to lose their soother a piece at a time. The parent pokes a small hole in the tip on day one. The next day, the hole is enlarged. On subsequent days, tiny pieces are cut from the tip to gradually shorten it. Children receive less pleasure from sucking as it disappears. After it has been reduced to a fragment, some parents report that their children lose interest and simply toss it aside.

Thumb-Sucking

Infants suck their thumbs in the womb. Toddlers suck their thumbs or fingers to soothe themselves. If a child is turning to his thumb for comfort, should parents worry? It depends on which expert you ask.

- Some experts say it is a harmless activity that usually disappears on its own.
- Some recommend trying to get toddlers to swap the thumb for a soother, blanket, stuffed animal or doll for reasons of hygiene.
- Some warn that the seeds of addiction are sown when toddlers use oral stimulation to comfort themselves. The desire to suck should be the parent's cue to nurse, hug, rock or cuddle.
- Some say that thumb-sucking is positive in that toddlers comfort themselves rather than using something artificial, such as a soother.
- Some say that since the thumb is so readily available, it's hard to give it up, so plastic is preferable.

Most experts agree that parental nurturing is a healthier way to soothe. Try to increase toddlers' feelings of well-being by criticizing less, praising more, and resolving family and personal problems to reduce the household tensions that can make toddlers feel tense and insecure. (See also Chapter 5 for details on a child's attachment to 'comfort objects'.)

Use of thumbs, soothers and bottles usually ends between three and four. If not, the social pressure of nursery school is a powerful deterrent. Talk to your dentist to be sure that no damage is being done. There's not usually a threat until the permanent teeth start to come in.

Spoiling

Is Grandma spoiling her grandson by thinking he's the most wonderful child in the world? By providing unconditional love and acceptance? By showering him with sugary treats and expensive toys? By letting him jump on the sofa and generally get away with murder? Probably not, as long as when she does occasionally say 'No', she holds firm.

Maybe she keeps him safe when he jumps on the sofa by standing at his side so she can catch him if he falls. Of course, that means he'll want his parents to provide the same personalized service. Maybe she does allow foods you'd prefer him not to eat, but only if he does a good job on his veggies first. Maybe she rarely says 'No' because she works overtime to make most things permissible.

Will a toddler wish his parent would say 'Yes' to him as often as Grandma, buy him treats 'just because', and let him jump on the beds at home? Of course. But that doesn't mean he's spoiled or that he loves her more.

That will make it harder for the parents, who fear they will be seen as the baddies for holding to stricter rules at home. Indeed, toddlers may test limits when they return home, to see if the rules have magically changed. And, given that toddlers only express their frustrations and irritability when they're with people they really trust, they may be a handful after spending time with a doting relative, just as they save up their less savoury emotions at daycare and explode when they get home or the parent appears.

Rather than attempting to control your child's relationships with others, try to let them work things out between themselves. Instead of controlling gift-giving, respond to inappropriate gifts as you would to a neighbour. Thank the sender, and then put the gift away until the child is older, or give the gift away, or suggest that the gift remain at Grandma's house so that the child can play with it there (if that wouldn't hurt Granny's feelings).

The Waiting Room Blues

If you use car keys to entertain your toddler whenever you're in a waiting room or office trying to conduct a bit of business, boredom will set in fast. All that naughtiness and grabbing items from peoples' desks isn't because she's naughty. She's not misbehaving, either. Her goal is to relieve boredom, so her behaviour is appropriate, if decidedly inconvenient. Before heading out on errands, drop some brightly coloured plastic lids in your purse or pocket to entertain a young tot; for older toddlers, buy some small toys that can only be played with during errands.

The solution to many problems becomes obvious once parents understand what is driving toddlers to act as they do. Don't assume that troublesome behaviour stems from naughtiness, contrariness or mindless negativity. Look at what toddlers are trying to achieve. Be flexible as you help them achieve their goals in an acceptable manner.

Dealing With Death

Toddlers can't comprehend that death means forever. They may appear unmoved when a beloved person or pet passes away. They may continue to anticipate that the person or pet will return, ask again and again when he or she is coming back, and require repeated explanations. Whereas talking is adults' primary vehicle for expression for coming to terms with difficult emotional issues, toddlers re-enact their confusion and upset in their play. Following a death, it is not unusual for them to replay any rituals to which they have been exposed, holding funerals for a stuffed animal, digging graves in the sandpit or sending a doll off to heaven.

Many parents try to shield toddlers from the reality of death. This can backfire, precipitating more confusion and insecurity. The fact that no one seems to notice or care that someone special has disappeared may cause toddlers to worry about who might disappear next. Seeing adults cry and grieve helps make death more real to them, communicates that feeling sad is an appropriate response to loss, and enables toddlers to grieve, too.

If it is decided that attending a funeral might be too difficult or traumatic for a toddler, holding some sort of ceremony at home can help make the death more real and enable tots to say goodbye. It is hard to provide little ones with information that is accurate yet simple enough for them to understand, but that is what they need. However, some common ways to communicate may prove more upsetting than helpful:

· 'He went bye-bye.' Can trigger fears that parents won't return when they go bye-bye, too.
· 'Henry went to sleep' or 'We put Henry to sleep.' Can instil fear of going to sleep.

- · 'God took him.' Can instil fears that they or a loved will be taken next.
- · 'She was ill so she died.' Can make toddlers worry that they'll die when they get ill.

Instead, try, 'Grandma got so *very* ill that her body couldn't heal. She died, so no one can see her any more. I'm sad, because I will miss her.' Toddlers need to hear explanations many times before they comprehend.

A good book is *Little Bear's Grandad* (£4.99) by Nigel Gray and Vanessa Cabban (Little Tiger Press). Little Bear visits his Grandad every week for tea and Grandad tells him stories. One day, Grandad falls ill. Little Bear's mum takes him to see Grandad in hospital where they share one last story together, but this time Little Bear tells the story. Then Grandad falls into the very deepest sleep. But one day Little Bear will be a lovely Grandad too.

More Quality Time?

Forget it, because some experts are now saying that *quantity* is more important for toddlers. Fortunately, it can be easier to share more moments than parents may think:

Turn off the phone. At meals, try turning the answering machine on and the mobile phone off. Ensure that you have uninterrupted time to interact each day. Turn off the TV, too, especially if no one is watching it. By hitting the off switch, parents eliminate the wall of noise separating toddlers from other family members. In fact, turn off the TV even if someone is watching. It's better to sacrifice shows than your toddler. It's better to be behind on the news than behind on your toddler's development. Be a good role model and find another way to relax, such as reading.

Sleep together. Sharing the family bed helps strengthen attachment and eliminates negative bedtime struggles that can eat up so much time (see Chapter 10 for more on sharing beds).

Cook together. Inviting toddlers to play on the kitchen floor while parents are preparing the meals, instead of sending them to another room to play, puts youngsters where they belong: in the heart of the family. If parents can talk to their youngster while waiting for the water to boil and pause occasionally while stirring the eggs to look at those blocks she's stacking, that's about as engaged as toddlers need parents to be during play. Just learn to walk carefully as you make your way from counter to table so as not to trip over a toy or (heaven forbid!) your child.

Clean the house and do gardening work together. Give your toddler a few drops of water in his pail and a sponge to use when you're washing the floor. Attach a broom handle to a cardboard or plastic box to make a kiddie broom or lawnmower.

Run errands together. Accept that a toddler shopping companion will slow you down. Interact amiably while cruising the supermarket aisles. Notice that while most of the parents are tangling with their troublesome two-year-old, some are getting along well – because they're talking nonstop and enlisting the toddler's help at every turn.

Turn off the car radio. Little wigglers tolerate the confinement better and benefit from the time to and from day care if parents talk and sing to them in the car. Outings to the zoo and funfair are great, but it's more important to relate well to each other on an everyday basis. Alternatively, put on a children's song tape or CD, and sing together as you drive

If you can't expand the quantity of time you spend with your child, improve the quality by carving out a 20-minute slot to spend with your little one, during which you studiously avoid any kind of teaching, disciplining, reprimanding and controlling. Stick to singing, reading, tickling and laughing.

And Toddler Makes Three

Caring for a toddler is so draining that it is easy for spouses to neglect each other. Marital satisfaction typically decreases during the toddler years. Worse, it continues to decrease until the children leave home. The risk of divorce is all too real. Children of all ages need their parents to live together, love each other, express genuine affection towards each other and resolve any differences they might have.

Your toddler can unite rather than divide you and your spouse by your sharing your toddler, working together to solve problems, supporting each other's disciplinary measures if you can or taking a hands-off approach if you can't, going on family outings, and becoming members of family-centred groups or parenting classes.

Friends and Lovers

Keep the friendship alive between you and your partner by expressing appreciation more, criticizing less, conversing on subjects besides your child, not taking out frustration on each other (and apologizing if you do), holding a weekly family meeting to discuss issues and seeing a counsellor for help resolving differences you can't work out yourself.

Keep the romance alive by getting a babysitter and going on weekly outings, taking turns getting up early to make breakfast to serve each other in bed, finding out what pleases your partner and doing it more often, and finding out what displeases your partner and doing it less.

Divorce

Although divorce may be better for toddlers than living in an environment fraught with tension and anger, the loss is hard on them. Being shuttled back and forth between households is taxing given their need for predictable routines. At a time when youngsters are struggling to learn so many household rules, having to learn two sets is especially difficult. You can make the situation a little easier by doing the following:

· Coordinate schedules to create as much continuity as possible.
· Provide a comfort object that toddlers can take back and forth.
· Don't grill toddlers about what goes on in the other home.
· Respect their love for their other parent.
· See a counsellor to work out issues that affect the toddler.

- Communicate with your ex-spouse about what is happening in your toddler's life, including everyday events and special problems, so each of you can make sense of toddler conversation and behaviour.

Parenting Styles

Different people have different styles of dealing with children. Work on learning to appreciate yours as well as your spouse's, and discuss ways to help each other by minimizing the inherent drawbacks.

Permissive Pals

Give some youngsters a lenient, laid-back, anything-goes parent, and they flourish. Parents who adopt a hands-off approach to child-rearing may operate more like friends than authority figures. Their strength is their ability to enjoy tots as people in their own right, which can lead to exceptionally warm, joyful relationships. For some youngsters, a bit of parental advice now and then is enough to help them find the right path and stick to it.

However, most children need more solid guidance. When given a lot of freedom, instead of rising to the challenge, they falter. Open classrooms, all the rage in the early 1970s, were built on the philosophy that children would do well if given learning materials and the freedom to do their own thing. The results were mixed. Many students used the time to good advantage; some were lost in the shuffle and wandered aimlessly for years.

On the home front, too much autonomy and independence can translate into a very insecure, spoiled, out-of-control youngster who begins looking to siblings, friends, teachers and eventually police officers and judges to set limits and contain her. Whether or not you adopt a firmer approach, don't undermine teachers and other adults who impose rules and limits, especially your partner. If people complain about your child's behaviour, believe them.

Soldier Strict

Very strict parents believe that teaching the difference between right and wrong and obedience are the top child-rearing priorities. They are conscientious about communicating expectations, providing structure, setting limits and following through with consequences if youngsters fail to toe the line. Their children may not like many of their rules and regulations, but they have the security of knowing what is expected and the consequences for failing to comply.

Whatever your parenting style, if you need to expand your parenting skills, there's help available in the form of numerous books, workshops, classes or even counselling. A good place to start is by talking with your child's doctor, doing a search on the Internet, or looking in the Yellow Pages under 'childcare'.

Strict parents' emphasis on respecting authority may make it difficult for them to step out of the parenting role long enough to engage in light-hearted play, which can turn child-rearing into an 18-year chore. They may also over-invest time in work, where they feel more at ease because of the clarity of rules and roles.

Although strict parents have a sense of what they want their youngsters to accomplish, many are at a loss as to how to get them there. Being more comfortable in the role of police officer than teacher, the parent may assume children break rules and do things improperly because they are wilful or lazy, and may fail to see that little ones need to be taught. This can lead them to punish children to try to combat misbehaviour when teaching is called for. Fearful children may develop an exaggerated sense of their own inadequacy as they fail in their efforts to please, while bolder types become increasingly defiant.

Authoritative Adults

Authoritative parents believe in taking children's individual needs into account when making child-rearing decisions. They include youngsters' opinions when making decisions, but believe that adults must have the final say. They are flexible in the parent role, being strict or lenient as the situation dictates. Thus they can engage in playful silliness one minute and quickly call a halt to the shenanigans if a little one is getting out of hand. They see themselves as teachers. They break goals into a series of manageable tasks to help little ones get where they need to go, one step at a time.

Authoritative parents' willingness to consider many factors when making decisions can backfire as little ones learn to use logic and advanced negotiating strategies. It may be in each child's interest to have a separate food menu each day, to get their parent to help them paint, take them for a walk and read their favourite books to them. It's also unrealistic. Unless such accommodating parents give sufficient consideration to their own needs, they run the risk of becoming drained and suffering from burnout.

CHAPTER 13

Super Toddlers

Some experts think that extra educational stimulation during the toddler years can boost youngsters' intelligence: if brain development depends on interaction with the environment, a richer range of activities can translate into higher IQ. Other experts say that although a deprived early environment slows development, an exceptionally stimulating one can't necessarily do much to expand intellectual powers: potential is dictated by genetics.

The Magic of Books

Your toddler is nagging you to buy her something at the shop. You're tempted to get her a book. After all, a book is better than sweets, right? Perhaps... but good books nourish the mind just as good food nourishes the body. To decide what to serve your child, read the labels – look for stickers on covers (and on the boxes of videos and CDs).

There are various awards for children's books to look out for, including the Carnegie Medal (awarded for an outstanding book by children's librarians); and the Kate Greenaway Medal (also awarded by children's librarians, but specifically for a children's book with outstanding illustrations). The highly regarded Nestlé Smarties book awards have gold, silver and bronze medal categories in various age groups, including under-fives.

Booktrust (45 East Hill, London SW18 2QZ) is a charity that helps people find out about books. Its website – *www.booktrust.org.uk* – has excellent advice on books for children. This organization initiated Bookstart – the national books for babies programme – in 1992.

To find quality books for your child, you need to do your homework:

· Read the book reviews in quality daily or weekend newspapers.
· Check editorial and customer reviews at *www.amazon.co.uk*.
· Ask children's librarians for recommendations – they're experts!
· See if your bookshop has a section for award-winning or quality children's literature.

Research shows that reading to toddlers translates into better reading ability in elementary school; reading ability in elementary school is a prime predictor of school success; and school success is a predictor of lifelong achievement, occupational success, and overall life satisfaction.

Building Kiddie Libraries

Reading to tots provides great intellectual stimulation and teaches vocabulary. However, what matters most at this age is instilling a love of reading. To choose books:

- Identify your child's special interests, be they dogs, dinosaurs, doctors or dust.
- Get books with sturdy cardboard or plastic pages so young toddlers can 'read' without damaging the pages and older children can tote them about without destroying their tomes.
- Look for books with exceptionally large print; although toddler vision is about the same as adults', some studies suggest bigger is better for learning to read at an early age.

Between 12 and 18 months, tots begin to enjoy simple stories (though they don't often want to hear them from front to back; they spend most of the time studying the pictures), so get a mixture of board and standard books. For holiday gift-giving, ask relatives to add a good volume of nursery rhymes, an alphabet book and a counting book to add to your child's permanent collection.

Budding Bibliophiles

The secret to reading lots to tots is to keep it fun. The secret to keeping it fun is to keep it interactive. Don't expect toddlers to sit still or listen quietly. Follow their lead. If they want to start in the middle and look at two pictures before moving to another activity, let them. Let toddlers turn the pages. Teach them how to grasp a corner, pull it gently towards them and lay it down. This requires a well-developed pincer grasp and fine motor coordination. Until they've developed the physical ability and have practised, they use their entire hand, which means some wrinkling and ripping. Board books are better.

As you read to your child, keep the humour going. Tell older toddlers that the picture of a cat is a horse. So as not to confuse things, be sure your youngster gets the joke.

Give vocabulary 'lessons' by pointing to the pictures and talking about them, so youngsters associate the object with the word: 'See, this is a dog. This is a cat.' Ask questions to keep them engaged: 'Can you find the daddy duck?' Avoid drilling and grilling. If your child doesn't answer the question, answer it for him: 'Here's the daddy duck!'

Teach your child to point by making a fist and extending an index finger. If a toddler points to a picture with a finger or hand, he is expressing interest and a desire to discuss it. The parent can say, 'That's an elephant. He's eating peanuts. I wonder if he'd like a peanut butter sandwich? I would!'

As you and your child look at pictures in books, round out her education by pointing out:

Colours. 'Look, here's a red hen. I think there's something else "red" on the next page, too. Oh, here it is. The cat has a red bow.'

Sounds. 'The chicken says, "Cluck, cluck". The cow goes "Moo".'

Categories of objects, such as clothes, foods, vehicles and animals. 'The dog is an animal. Can you find another animal?' 'Yes, the cat is an animal. And look, here's another one. A horse.'

Numbers. Extend your child's index finger and help her count the bunnies, stars, tomatoes or anything else.

Location. Point out the house, the barn, the haystack, the pond and buildings or areas (such as the top, bottom, front or back).

The Book Nook

To instil a love of reading in children, don't just read to them – cuddle up with your books, too. If that sounds like a pipe dream amidst the chaos of toddler-rearing, make it a habit to curl up with your own book as your child's nap time approaches. Refrain from all conversation except to state (again and again), 'Sorry, I can't talk to you now. I'm reading. We'll talk in a little while.'

When the terrible vision of you paying attention to something besides them compels youngsters to protest, clamour for a video, hurl a toy across the room and otherwise let it be known that they need attention *now*, you can take the bait and lecture about the inappropriateness of throwing toys and the ill effects of video-watching. Or, you can avoid the call to battle by suggesting that the toddler looks at a book, too. Then keep your eyes glued to your book to drive the message home: 'I'm busy. I'm doing something important! I'm reading.'

Some children will escalate until parents are forced to close their book to tend to their toddler. But just as little ones hold tea parties because Mum cooks and push toy brooms because Dad sweeps the garage, if they see parents reach for a book when it's time to relax, they will begin to do the same.

Television Time

Reading to a toddler for just 15–20 minutes per day adds up to 165–224 hours from ages one to three. On the other hand, watching just one hour of TV per day adds up to 730–1,460 hours from ages one to three! Parents read an average of 8.9 books per week to toddlers, according to a 1994 study. Considering that toddler attention spans are under ten minutes, that probably means the average child spent less than 90 minutes per week with books – the equivalent of only three cartoons.

All parents use television or a video as a babysitter from time to time – but consider this. One study looked at three groups: children who could watch as much television as they liked; children whose access was limited but who watched on their own; and children whose access was limited AND who watched with a parent. The last group did much better academically than the other groups.

Try to keep your toddler's viewing time under control. Children under two get little benefit from watching television, so don't bother with it, or, if you do, then limit it to a couple of ten-minute sessions a day (the length of a toddler's attention span). Ideally, two-to-three-year-olds should not watch more than an hour a day. Don't put a telly in your toddler's bedroom, and please switch it off at mealtimes.

Try structuring viewing – check the listings; circle what is worth watching and either watch it when it's on, or tape it and watch it when you feel the time is right. Tell your toddler in advance that the TV will go off when *Tweenies* (or whatever) ends, to lessen the risk of tears or tantrums. Research has shown that action-type cartoons are confusing for toddlers, and if the cartoons are violent, your child is more likely to exhibit aggressive behaviour. It is far better to watch programmes that emphasize interactivity – *Balamory* or *Teletubbies*, for example. Anything that gets your child moving, dancing or copying sounds is good for her.

The Road to Reading

Toddlers can readily learn the rudiments of reading. Buy blocks in the shapes of letters and numbers. Turn on *Sesame Street* or another informational children's programme. Then, when you play with your tot, focus on the *Sesame Street* letter of the day: 'I'm giving *T* a ride in this car. Look out! Here comes *T!*' Buy or make a poster showing the letters of the alphabet. Position the poster so your child can see it when lying in bed. As part of your bedtime ritual, pick a letter and practise saying words that start with it: 'Tuh-tuh-tuh-table! Tuh-tuh-tuh-turtle!'

Help your tot add a *T* page to his homemade alphabet book. Here's how to make the alphabet book:

1. Put 26 pieces of notebook paper in a loose-leaf notebook.
2. Print a different letter of the alphabet on each page.
3. Find a picture that starts with each letter, cut it out and get your toddler to paste it onto the correct page.
4. Slip each page into a plastic protector.

5. Glue a picture of your child on the front of the notebook and include your child's name in the title: *George's Alphabet Book.*

P Is for Phonics

Teach children to recognize letters by pointing them out in books and teaching the sounds they make the same way you teach about animals and the sounds they make. It doesn't matter if a toddler isn't yet talking. All that matters is that youngsters listen and look.

Here's how one mum taught her four children their letter sounds and animals before they reached age four.

PARENTS' READING GAME

	ANIMAL RECOGNITION GAME	LETTER RECOGNITION GAME
Parent	'This is a duck. Can you say "duck"?'	'This is an *m*. Can you say "em"?'
Child	'Duck.'	'Em.'
Parent	'The duck says "Quack" Can you say "Quack"?'	'The *m* says "mmmm". Can you say "mmmm"?'
Child	'Quack, quack!'	'Mmmm!'
Parent	'Where is a duck?'	'Where is the *m*?'
Child	(Points)	(Points)
Parent	'That's right. Can you find another duck?'	'That's right. Can you find another *m*?'
Child	(Points) 'Duck!'	(Points) 'Em!'
Parent	'And what does it say?'	'And what does it say?'
Child	'Quack, quack!'	'Mmmm!'
Parent	'Look, the daddy duck is big. The baby duck is small. What do they say?'	'See? This is the big *M*. This is the little *m*. What do they say?'
Child	'Quack! Quack! Quack!'	'Mmmm!'
Parent	'And here's what I do when you say "Quack, quack, quack" – tickle, tickle, tickle.'	'And here's what I do when you say "Mmmmmm" – I tickle, tickle, tickle.'

Sight-Reading

To help a child progress from prereading to sight-reading when reading stories, point to each printed word as you say it, taking care not to block the child's view. Occasionally the child will follow your finger and glance at the text. After two years of having words pointed out as they're read, toddlers should be able to associate some spoken words with written ones.

The Leap to Reading

Point to a word that occurs often in a story that your child is very familiar with, such as 'ham' in Dr Seuss's *Green Eggs & Ham*. After pointing and reading the same word dramatically several times, focus your child's attention by pausing before you say it. Try to get him to say it with you. The next time the word comes up, pause but don't say the word. Encourage your child to say it with you. Don't insist if your child resists. The point is to get him to notice your chosen word, not to ruin the story. If your child says the word on his own, praise lavishly: 'Wow! My baby can read! You were exactly right! It says "ham", see?' Continue reading and pausing before saying the word to see if he can 'read' it again. Write the word on a note card and get him to amaze other family members by reading it to them. On another day, add another word. Make another note card to add to his collection.

If your child insists on the same story repeatedly, remember that hearing words in context is the best way to build vocabulary. The more words kids understand at age two, the better they read in Year One. When toddlers know a story by heart, it is easier for them to match the written words to the sounds as you run your finger along the text.

Or try this sorting game: cut pieces of three different colours of cloth into triangles, squares and circles. Show children how to match by shape and by colour. As your child becomes more advanced, so can the card-sorts. Make (or buy) cards with pictures and 'bits' of information on them.

Show kids how to sort them into categories (such as house pet or farm animal), and create new categories (such as animals that give us food or animals you see at the circus).

Gifted Children

Gifted children develop skills in the same sequence as everyone else, but they do it faster. When the backgrounds of geniuses were examined, one study found that they had begun talking at an average age of nine months – and since that's an average, many began much earlier. Still, many were far less precocious, so even exceptionally late talkers aren't out of the running for a Nobel Prize.

Currently, it is not possible to assess intelligence in toddlers reliably. However, in one study on children aged from 2 to 12 years old with top IQs, parents reported the following personality characteristics:

· 90 per cent were described as 'sensitive'.
· 83 per cent liked to concentrate on one activity at a time.
· 79 per cent had high energy or activity levels.
· 50 per cent needed less sleep than other children.
· 44 per cent were sensitive to clothing labels and other tactile sensations.

Some studies have found that gifted children appear to have short attention spans because they become bored so easily. Others have found them to be overly excitable and unusually intense, with greater emotional extremes, including more compassion, sadness and depression.

More intelligent toddlers are likely to have more frustrations to contend with than other youngsters. Their minds can concoct projects, problems and solutions, but they are blocked by their physical limitations. For example, they can work out how to solve a puzzle but lack the motor coordination needed to fit it into the proper place. Or they may have complex ideas to express, but don't have the verbal skills to communicate them.

The exquisite sensitivity that enables them to note subtle differences in texture, movement, colour and shape means that what others perceive as a blank wall can appear to them as a vibrant palette. Because they are constantly bombarded with sensory stimuli, they are more stressed. The extreme interpersonal sensitivity causes some tots to tune into other people's feelings. They are aware of hints of criticism and displeasure that other toddlers don't notice. Ironically, the combination of extreme sensitivity, high energy level and reduced need for sleep are characteristics of children often diagnosed as 'hyperactive'. There may be a lot of very misunderstood toddlers out there.

Gearing Up for Greatness

In the USA and China, special programmes designed to nurture child prodigies advise the following:

- Focus on the total child, including emotional, behavioural and social development.
- Toddlers should be free to follow their own inclinations by having a range of materials available for them to explore.
- Toddlers should not be pressed to pursue structured learning activities.
- Use a loving and nurturing approach when working with toddlers.
- Participate actively; your role in learning is central.

Giving lessons is often a struggle. The time you both spend trying to get her to pay attention would be better spent if she worked on her own. Teaching children how to do puzzles and solve problems with toys actually inhibits learning, if you think about it. The ability to mimic someone else's solution to a problem doesn't require much intelligence.

In-depth, complex, high-power thinking takes place as children struggle to work things out for themselves. Anyone who says 'She's just playing' doesn't understand how toddlers learn! (For more tips on teaching toddlers, see Chapter 4.)

> Teaching strategies appropriate for older children actually inhibit toddler learning. Toddlers seem to have an innate sense of what they need to learn next; structured learning activities imposed by adults distract them from the work *they* know they need to do.

Genius Troubles

If your toddler is exceptionally difficult to manage, it could be because she's literally too clever by half! The National Association for Gifted Children has an excellent website – *www.nagcbritain.org.uk* – including a questionnaire to indicate whether your child may be gifted. An estimated 20–25 per cent of gifted children have social and emotional problems – twice the normal rate, according to Ellen Winner PhD's article, 'Uncommon Talents: Gifted Children, Prodigies and Savants' (*Scientific American*, 28 February 1999). Meanwhile, for moderately gifted children, the rates of maladjustment were the same as for average children. Similar problems with hyperactivity and attention have been found among highly gifted (IQ 140–154) and learning-disabled boys.

If your child truly is a handful, don't think Prozac. Think Oxford!

Early Achievement

In the same study, reported characteristics of genius toddlers included:

· 94 per cent were very alert as infants.
· 94 per cent had a long attention span as an infant or toddler.
· 91 per cent showed early language development.
· 60 per cent showed early motor skill development.
· 48.9 per cent were ambidextrous at some period of their development.
· 37 per cent had imaginary playmates.

It's also interesting to note that the age at which mothers of gifted children gave birth was much older than average – 30.8 years. Is that because older mums tend to be more patient and tolerant than younger ones and work with them more? No one knows.

Special Gifts

Regardless of whether parents suspect giftedness, they should provide a wide range of learning experiences to stimulate brain development. They also need to respect toddlers' choices about how to spend their time. Pushing and pressuring can propel toddlers down the path of rebellion, burnout or the trap of moulding themselves to fulfil someone else's dreams.

Children's abilities differ. Some are intellectually superior; most are average; and some are clearly slow. When intelligence is very limited, the challenge for parents may be learning to appreciate their youngster's other special gifts.

Rest assured – each child has them. For instance, the typically loving natures and sunny dispositions of children with Downs syndrome remind the rest of us about the importance of pausing in our self-absorbed, busy lives to share a heartfelt smile with a stranger, and grace an acquaintance with an affectionate hug.

Look for your child's strengths and cherish them!

APPENDIX A

At This Age: What Toddlers Are Learning

AT 12–18 MONTHS

LANGUAGE

Responds to own name

Knows the meaning of 'mama', 'dada' and 'no'

Repeats words and imitates sounds

Jabbers, hums and 'sings'

Identifies two pictures in books

Communicates needs by pointing and
  making sounds

Points to a part of the body

Responds to one-step commands (eg, 'Come here')

COGNITIVE/INTELLECTUAL

Understands that a hidden object still exists

Explores via touch and taste

Empties things out

Takes things out of a container and puts them
  back in again

Tears paper

Repeats actions to learn cause and effect

Sorts simple objects by shape

Does 3-D puzzles (eg, inserts a block into a square hole)

Remembers some things seen or heard hours or
  days ago

PHYSICAL/MOTOR

Stands alone

Lowers herself from standing to sitting

Walks alone

Walks while carrying toys

Bends over and picks something up

Claps

Points with index finger

Picks up small objects with thumb and index finger

Puts an object in a container

Scribbles

Opens drawers and cabinets

Tosses or rolls a ball

Throws a ball

Stacks two to four blocks

Stirs with a spoon

Climbs 30–60cm (1–2ft) objects

SOCIAL

Imitates demonstrations

Initiates simple games

Looks to caregiver for praise

Is proud of accomplishments

Signals a need for help

Waves 'bye-bye'

Shows affection

Smiles at favoured objects and people

SELF-CARE

Washes hands

Takes off an article of clothing

Drinks from a cup with a lid

Uses a spoon

AT 18–24 MONTHS

LANGUAGE

Understands the meaning of 'don't'

Knows names for familiar people and objects

Uses 50 words (if talking)

Makes two-word sentences ('Go bye-bye')

Listens to short books and nursery rhymes

Points to six parts of the body when asked

Speaks in gibberish that has the cadence and rhythm of speech

Identifies four pictures in a book with words (if talking)

Follows a two-step command ('Get your coat and come here')

COGNITIVE/INTELLECTUAL

Categories (eg, toys, books, foods, people)

Points to specific pictures in books when asked

Tries different ways to do something

Works out how to do things by trying different strategies

Learns from looking at books

Pretends (eg, the piece of play dough is a snake)

Focuses on an activity for five minutes

Chooses between two things

Inspects something by looking (not tasting or touching)

PHYSICAL/MOTOR

Runs

Stacks six blocks

Rides a toy by pushing on the floor with alternating feet

Walks up steps

Kicks a ball forwards

SOCIAL

Makes an impact by saying 'no' or resisting

Feels concerned when someone is crying

Tries to comfort someone who is very upset

Handles simple responsibilities

Is interested in other children

Feeds a doll

SELF-CARE

Drinks from a cup without a lid

Uses a spoon and fork (still has trouble turning the hand)

Washes and dries hands

Takes off some clothes

Puts on an article of clothing

Puts arms and legs through holes when being dressed

AT 24–30 MONTHS

LANGUAGE

Speaks in two- to three-word sentences (if talking)   Has short conversations (if talking)

COGNITIVE/INTELLECTUAL

Listens to books with simple stories   Identifies one colour

Understands the concepts 'one' and 'two'   Plays make-believe and fantasy games

PHYSICAL/MOTOR

Draws   Kicks a ball forwards

Matches objects that are the same   Throws a ball

Makes play dough or clay snakes and balls   Stands on one foot (briefly)

Stands on tiptoes   Climbs low ladders

Stacks eight blocks   Leans forwards without falling

Pedals a tricycle   Goes up and down stairs using alternate feet

Jumps forwards

SOCIAL

Plays next to other children   Participates in interactive games

Categorizes people as boy or girl   Identifies a friend

SELF-CARE

Puts on a pull-over shirt   Puts on or pulls up trousers

AT 30–36 MONTHS

LANGUAGE

Says the names of pictures in a book when asked (if talking)

Names six body parts (if talking)

Describes what two objects are used for (if talking)

Makes three- to four-word sentences (if talking)

Speaks so that others understand him most of the time (if talking)

Says 50 words (if talking)

Understands most of what is said to him

COGNITIVE/INTELLECTUAL

Follows a two-step command ('Find your hat and put it on')

Reasons through problems themselves

Counts to two

Identifies four colours

PHYSICAL/MOTOR

Copies a straight line	Balances on one foot (two seconds)
Copies a circle	Stacks eight blocks
Confines colouring to the paper	

SOCIAL

Says 'please' and 'thank you' when prompted	Negotiates and compromises
Takes turns (with guidance)	Asks for information
Asserts rights with peers	Approaches other children to play in daily care setting
Knows not to bully other children	Plays with other children
Contributes to joint activities and discussions	

SELF-CARE

Uses the potty	Dresses herself
Eats with minimal assistance	

Appendix B

Resources

Books and Magazines

For Parents

Books

Brazelton, T. Berry, *Touchpoints: Your Child's Emotional and Behavioural Development*, Perseus Publishing

Cohen, David, *How the Child's Mind Develops*, Routledge

Dorman, Helen and Clive, *The Social Toddler: Promoting Positive Behaviour*, The Children's Project

Faber, Adele, et al, *Siblings Without Rivalry*, Piccadilly Press

Faber, Adele, and Mazlish, Elaine, *Siblings Without Rivalry: How to Help Your Children Live Together So You Can Live Too*, Avon Books

Garcia, W. Joseph, *Sign with Your Baby: How to Communicate with Infants Before They Can Speak*, Northlight Communications

Iovine, Vicki, *The Best Friends' Guide to Toddlers*, Bloomsbury

Leach, Penelope, *Your Baby and Child*, Dorling Kindersley

Nathanson, Laura Walther, *The Portable Pediatrician for Parents*, HarperPerennial

Nathanson, Laura Walther, *The Portable Pediatrician's Guide to Kids*, HarperCollins

Parker, Jan, and Stimpson, Jan, *Raising Happy Children: What Every Child Needs Their Parents to Know*, Hodder Mobius

Saunders, Jacquelyn, and Espeland, Pamela, *Bringing Out the Best: A Guide for Parents of Young Gifted Children*, Free Spirit

Sign Language for Babies, Hay House

Smutny, Joan Franklin, ed., et al, *The Young Gifted Child. Potential and Promise, an Anthology*, Hampton Press

Stoppard, Miriam, *Baby and Child Healthcare: The Essential A–Z Home Reference to Children's Illnesses, Symptoms and Treatments*, Dorling Kindersley

Magazines

Mother & Baby Magazine
Published monthly

Practical Parenting
Published monthly

BBC Parenting
Published monthly

Web Sites

www.babycentre.co.uk: A brilliant site that has a clear, easy-to-use design and allows you to communicate with helpful fellow parents. Their toddler link covers the following areas:
· Caring for Your Toddler
· Feeding Your Toddler
· Health
· Multiples
· Penelope Leach on Toddlers
· Potty Training
· Safety
· Sex and Relationships
· Sleep
· Toddler Development
· Traditions and Celebrations
· Travel
· Work and Childcare

www.bbc.co.uk/health/parenting/index.shtml: Visit this excellent website for informative and helpful material on bringing up toddlers. Expert advice as well as tips from other parents. Subjects include an A–Z of children's ailments, potty training, diet and keeping them safe.

www.bbc.co.uk/cbeebies/: The CBeebies websites aim to reflect the BBC's range of television programmes for toddlers and pre-schoolers, and to take children's participation with their 'friends' a step further. There are games, stories, pictures to download and colour, and lots more. A perfect introduction to computers for little ones. The site has all the main TV characters your toddler will encounter on one site: Fireman Sam, Bob the Builder, Andy Pandy, Fimbles, Teletubbies, Tweenies, Pingu etc.

www.allkids.co.uk: Excellent online parenting magazine and directory. The site covers everything from furnishing a child's room, to great days out with toddlers, illness worries, development information, advice on childcare, food additives and fun links for kids too: Barnie, Sesame Street, Playschool, Barbie, Action Man, Bob the Builder, Noddy, Scoobie Doo, Tarzan, dinosaurs and insects, to name a few.

www.childcarelink.gov.uk: The government launched the ChildcareLink helpline (freephone 08000 96 02 96) and website in December 1999 as part of the National Childcare Strategy, which aims to help people go to work by making childcare more accessible. It is funded by the Department for Education and Skills and the Scottish Executive.

Videos for Children

Wow! That's What I Call Nursery Rhymes
Animated effects, dancing and singing. Songs include: 'The Grand Old Duke Of York', 'Polly Put The Kettle On' and 'A Sailor Went To Sea'.

Maisy (any in the series)
Colourful stories that toddlers love, narrated by Neil Morrissey.

I Want My Potty And Other Stories
Ten stories by Tony Ross and David McKee, including 'I Want My Potty' and 'Not Now Bernard'. Narrated by Victoria Wood, Steven Steen and Johnny Morris.

Thomas The Tank Engine Singalong With Thomas
Animated songs from the series.

Kipper (any in the series)
Gentle, charming and funny. Grown-ups love Kipper too. Based on the
  books by Mick Inkpen and featuring the voice of Martin Clunes.

Pingu (any in the series)
Hilarious short adventures.

Jane Hissey's Old Bear And Friends – Little Bear's Book And Other Stories
With the voice of Anton Rodgers. Three stories from the award-
  winning series.

Useful Organizations

The National Association for Gifted Children
www.nagcbritain.org.uk
Tel: 0845 450 0221

Down's Syndrome Association
www.downs-syndrome.org.uk
Tel: 0845 230 0372

The National Deaf Children's Society
www.ndcs.org.uk

Royal National Institute of the Blind
www.rnib.org.uk
RNIB helpline tel: 0845 766 9999

Scope
www.scope.org.uk
Tel: 0808 800 3333

Index